Children of Colonialism

Anglo-Indians in a Postcolonial World

Lionel Caplan

BERG

Oxford • New York

First published in 2001 by
Berg
Editorial offices:
150 Cowley Road, Oxford, OX4 1JJ, UK
838 Broadway, Third Floor, New York, NY 10003-4812, USA

Berg is an imprint of Oxford International Publishers Ltd.

Library of Congress Cataloging-in-Publication Data
A catalogue record for this book is available from the Library of Congress.

British Library Cataloguing-in-Publication Data
A catalogue record for this book is available from the British Library.

ISBN 1 85973 531 2 (Cloth)

Typeset by JS Typesetting, Wellingborough, Northants.
Printed in the United Kingdom by Antony Rowe Ltd, Chippenham, Wiltshire.

For Dorothy

Contents

Contents

Preface

This book seeks to contribute to current debates regarding the 'post-colonial condition' by considering the case of the Anglo-Indians, a 'mixed-race' and culturally composite population which emerged out of the imperial encounter and still retains a distinct identity today. It offers an ethnography of their contemporary world as this has been shaped by both colonial and postcolonial circumstances.

My first introduction to Anglo-India occurred in late 1963 when I travelled by ship between Genoa and Bombay (the first leg of a journey to fieldwork in Nepal) and shared a cabin with Mr Joe Smith of Calcutta. Then, on arrival in Bombay, I stayed for a few nights in the 'retiring rooms' of Victoria station, which were, as it happens, presided over by Messrs Kelly and Fernandes, who were also Anglo-Indians. I was beginning to wonder if they were a ubiquitous part of the Indian scene, rather than a 'microscopic' element, as those I later met were to insist. It was not until 1974, when I was in Madras engaged in research on Christians, that I encountered members of the Anglo-Indian community again, though only fleetingly, since they were not considered, nor did they consider themselves, as belonging to the Indian Christian fold.

When I began this project I spent nearly four months in Madras during the autumn and winter of 1991-2, and made further visits of two months each in 1996 and 1999. These field trips were made possible by grants from the Nuffield Foundation and the British Academy, to both of which I express my thanks.

In the course of a long research engagement with members of the Anglo-Indian community in Madras I have accumulated a considerable number of obligations. First and foremost I am deeply indebted to the many people – too numerous to mention here – who made me welcome in their homes, answered my numerous questions, related their life stories and shared their experiences. I am particularly beholden to a number of persons who not only took a special interest in this project, but gave generously of their time and patience to help me in manifold ways: Beatrix D'Souza, Geoffery Francis, Denzil D'Monte, Anne D'Monte, Irwin Passagne, Lionel Pearson-Joseph, Clive Hurley, Cynthia Ignatius, Jean

Preface

Fernandez, Cedric Windsor, Adrian Almeida, Carlton Lazaro, Douglas Gibson, Barbara Pavey, Hugh Wilkins, Fred Francis, Rachel Thurley and the late Tom Thurley.

Gerrard Lee, Errol Arnette and Alister Dubier – three young members of the Madras Anglo-Indian community – acted as my assistants at various stages of the research and earned my deepest gratitude for their invaluable help. Terence and Margaret Dubier, Dass and Saro Asirvatham, and Joe and Kalyani Nityanandan provided – each in their own way – agreeable domestic breaks from the rigours of fieldwork, and I thank them for that.

In preparing this book I have profited greatly from the interest shown by Christopher Hawes, who not only shared generously his considerable knowledge of Anglo-Indian history, but read the manuscript and offered detailed, sage advice. Finally, as always, I benefited from the constant support, encouragement and critical insights of Pat Caplan.

Lionel Caplan

-1-

Introduction

I'll tell you the facts. The Anglo-Indians were the maharajahs in India. Indians used to call us *dorai* and *missi-ama*, terms of respect. Now, it's changed. What they are telling us is that when the British were here you all came under their banner, they looked after you. But the British left us in the lurch, so we are not able to lead the lives we led then, when we were well-off. That time, everything was for the Anglo-Indians. Now we are destitute.

The community is changing. There is a definite upgrading from the Tommy [colonial] days to now. The Tommy days were the negative days of the Anglo-Indian community, not the golden days.

Of late, scholars in a range of social science and humanistic disciplines have been pondering the attributes of postcoloniality. This book engages with these debates by considering the predicament of 'hybrid', 'métis' or 'mestizo' populations, enduring legacies of the colonial encounter which fostered sexual relations between European men and local women. It considers the case of the Eurasians of India, or Anglo-Indians as they came to be designated, who are descendants of such unions, and still identified as a mixed-race and culturally composite community. Focusing on that part of the population resident in the south Indian city of Madras (recently renamed Chennai), it offers an historicized ethnography of their contemporary lives as these relate both to the colonial past and to conditions in the postcolonial present.

Colonial Sex and the Creation of a Mixed-race Population

Numerous British officers, soldiers and civilians in the service of the East India Company and later the Government of India, as well as many other men who, in the course of the colonial period, came to trade or seek employment in various subordinate sectors of the economy, established domestic relationships with Indian women. Understandably, Anglo-Indian writers have tended to stress the propriety and legitimacy of the unions: some have credited the East India Company's 'deliberate policy of avowedly encouraging inter-marriages' between their employees and local females, with 'officially [bringing] the Anglo-Indian community into existence' (Anthony 1969: 12). Others have suggested that Christian missionaries were instrumental in promoting matrimonial links. Bower (1939: 108) writes:

> Well over a century ago a paternal European ancestor of mine married a mission girl, who was a daughter of this land, and so, of almost all my community in the past, and of me it cannot be said that we are 'sprung unwarranted by priest or book or marriage line'.

While many undoubtedly did marry, the majority are reckoned by most Western historians to have entered less formal unions, especially during the eighteenth and early nineteenth centuries. This is sometimes attributed to the fact that, for much of this period, European women were denied access to the colonies and that most of these men could not in any case afford to marry the European women who did manage to reach the sub-continent (Ghosh 1970: 68–70; Stoler 1989: 139). Moreover, married men were often excluded from recruitment to positions in colonial administration and business, further contributing to the European gender imbalance and encouraging liaisons with local women (Ibid.)

Whatever the reasons, in India, as in many areas of the colonial world where European men found themselves sexually isolated, the local mistress became a 'recognised institution' (Dodwell 1926: 206–9; see also Wilkinson 1976: 118). Many of these relationships would probably be best described as 'concubinage', although it has to be said that such a term provides a Euro-American gloss on a domestic association which may very well have been regarded as in most senses legitimate by local women themselves (see MacMillan 1988: 122). Even then, as Stoler points out, the term – normally understood in the West as cohabitation – suggests a greater degree of autonomy than most such women really enjoyed (1991: 59). It inadequately conveys the status and power differential between the individuals concerned.

Hyam has drawn attention to the importance of male sexuality in British imperial endeavours (1986; 1990), indeed, so much so that he has been accused of offering a 'sexual theory of British imperialism' (Berger 1988: 83). But even while stressing the 'sexual opportunities' available to European males in the colonies, including India, Hyam is seen to ignore the unequal power relations obtaining between the men seeking such opportunities and the women providing them (Berger 1988: 84; see also Stoler 1995: 175).[1]

Introduction

In Madras, which forms the locus of the present study, many of these relationships were quite evidently exploitative. Wheeler notes that in the first quarter of the eighteenth century, during the governorship of Joseph Collet at Fort St George (1717–1720), 'the English at Madras possessed slaves in considerable numbers. Many kept slave girls...' (1878: 118–19), and Major Bevan, a contemporary observer of early nineteenth-century Madras, remarked that 'mistresses ... are often sold to their masters by needy relatives' (1839: 18–19). As elsewhere in India, the partnership frequently remained on a 'master-servant basis' (Hawes 1996: 8). Others were housekeepers, and one contemporary witness reports that in some regiments British soldiers were encouraged to form liaisons with local women who lived with and 'act[ed] as servants to the men' (Mrs Sherwood, quoted in Dyson 1978: 89). In addition, native women attached to military personnel who were transferred back home were usually assigned to the soldiers belonging to regiments which came out as replacements (Hawes 1996: 14). Many of these women were therefore drawn into such relationships more out of necessity than choice, and the tie remained an unequal one.

But while the link between empire and sexuality continues to engage students of colonialism, what needs to be appreciated is that these relationships, whether formal or informal, consensual or exploitative, resulted in the birth of children, and in the emergence of a hybrid or métis population.[2] As Nabar points out, Anglo-Indians 'concretised' the encounter between British and Indian; they were, after all, its inevitable 'end-product' (1994: 12). Moreover, this mixed-race group in time forgot the character of the original unions – or suppressed their memory – as it evolved and asserted an inclusive identity of its own.

According to Williamson, the great majority of women 'domicilated' by European men in India were either 'Musulmans' or 'half-casts [of] Portugueze extraction' (1810: 413). The latter would almost certainly have been the case in Madras, where there was a large community of Portuguese (see below). In a letter written from 'Pondamalee' near Madras, a British captain in the 73rd Regiment of Highlanders reported, with some pique, that 'Portuguese wenches' are among the women whom European officers and civilians 'take much delight in supporting as kept mistresses' (Munro 1789: 51).[3] In time, men belonging to other European nationalities (e.g. Armenian, Dutch, French, Flemish, Prussian, Spanish and Italian) also found their way to south India in a variety of capacities so that, according to the Census of 1881 (p.54), by the latter part of the nineteenth century, 'Europeans of other than British nationality' formed just over ten per cent of the total European population of the Madras

Presidency. Like the Portuguese and British, they established relations with local women, or, more commonly as time passed, with the descendants of previous Euro-Indian unions.

The Colonial Science of Racial Hybrids

The métis population which these unions produced was, on the whole, accepted as part of an early official understanding that they would support the activities of the English (Ballhatchet 1980: 96–7). However, the accommodations which had characterized relations between British personnel and the Anglo-Indian population they had helped to create began to change perceptibly towards the end of the eighteenth century, due in no small measure to the elaboration of race theory in Europe and its increasing 'scientificization' during the following century (see Young 1995), in the course of which race came largely to organize the 'grammar of difference' (Stoler 1995: 41). This created a heightened awareness within European ruling circles of racial distinctions between themselves and their colonial subjects. Much theorizing centred on the dangers of miscegenation and the infertility, degradation or moral weakness of racial hybrids. In the second quarter of the nineteenth century Dr Robert Knox, one of the pioneers of race theory, argued that human hybrids were not viable, so that 'separation [between the races] and purity [of race] were the sole alternative to extinction' (Biddiss 1976: 248). When it became evident that the miscegenated offspring of inter-racial unions were not only viable but fecund, rhetorics focused mainly on their character defects. Those who violated established racial categories produced offspring who were seen as flawed, tainted and degenerate (Stoler 1995: 50), a 'raceless chaos' (Young 1995: 25).

These ideas which had evolved in Europe could not help but influence attitudes to and policies toward inter-racial sex and its mestizo products in the colonies. In south Asia, certainly, miscegenation aroused increasing hostility and opposition within the governing classes, and hybrid populations came to be regarded as a danger to the European community. McGilvray reports a 'prevailing repugnance toward racial or cultural hybridization in nineteenth century Ceylon, which led to vehement abuse against Portuguese Burghers' (1982: 245; see also Roberts et al. 1989: 12, 26). Boxer, too, finds that the correspondence of successive viceroys of Goa was 'full of complaints against the real or alleged physical and moral inferiority of mesticos' (1963: 71). Similar attitudes were prevalent in British India (see Bayly 1995; Robb 1995). Anglo-Indians came to be regarded not only as inferior, but as combining the worst qualities of both founding races (see Spear 1932: 61; Younger 1987: 114). Sir Richard Burton's comment that '[n]either British nor Portuguese India ever produced a half-caste at all deserving of being ranked in the typical order of man' was but an extreme expression of a general view (quoted in Dyson 1978: 298; Naidis 1963: 417).

Young suggests that the European fear of miscegenation could be related to the notion that without a clear hierarchy of races, 'civilization would, in a literal as well as a technical sense, collapse' (1995: 95). In the latter part of the nineteenth century, therefore, 'the onus of British colonial policy came to be focussed on an effort to prevent mixing between the British and their subject peoples' (Ibid.: 164). In the Indian context, this official discouragement extended to relations with Anglo-Indians. Thus, inter-racial unions and their miscegenated offspring surfaced regularly, if not very prominently, in the official consciousness. Moreover, these attitudes were reflected in English-language fiction about India, much of it written by colonial Europeans (see D'Cruz 1999; Greenberger 1969; Naik 1994; Narayanan 1986). Like so many other métis populations in the colonies, Anglo-Indians were deemed a 'dangerous conduit of moral contamination and political subversion' (Cooper and Stoler 1997: 24).[4]

But if colonialism 'provided racism with a new and extremely virulent impetus' (Breman 1990: 5), the demands of colonial rule sometimes generated policies which mitigated and even contradicted these racial proscriptions. To take only one example, following the 1857 Bengal army uprising, security concerns led, among other things, to the construction of additional cantonment cities around the country, linked by the most modern forms of communication into a new 'geography of command' (Khilnani 1998: 117). Arising from these developments, Anglo-Indians – though sharing the opprobrium attached to mixed-race groups, and despite their previous exclusion from many military and civil situations (see Chapter 2) – were granted special 'privileges' in employment on the railways and telegraphs, which favoured them over other Indians, and had profound effects on the subsequent course of Anglo-Indian history. Colonial projects, in other words, were by no means all of a kind, but generated a diversity of practices and stratagems.

Then again, Anglo-Indians, no less than other sections of the Indian population, were never passive objects on which colonial rulers simply inscribed their racial ideas. However much inter-racial unions came officially to be frowned upon, they continued to occur. Until the very end of the colonial period many Anglo-Indian women had relationships with and children by (mainly subaltern) European males, while numerous

Anglo-Indian males from poor families sought out or were sought out by Indian women from similarly depressed backgrounds. In the context of everyday colonial life, therefore, official discourses on race and miscegenation were frequently contradicted, ignored or subverted.

Anglo-Indians and the Blurring of Categorical Divides

In both life and fiction Anglo-Indians have been and even today continue to be profusely, not to say extravagantly stereotyped: vulgar, conceited, ill-bred, lacking intelligence, promiscuous (if women) and work-shy (if men), more British than the British themselves, relics of and nostalgic for the Raj – are only a few of the images purveyed.[5] Such negative stereotypes are not countered by presenting more positive portraits – the tactic of what D'Cruz calls the 'image critics' – as if 'a true, unblemished, uncorrupted identity exists' (1999: 319). Rather, these 'arrested, fixated forms of representation' – as Bhabha refers to colonial stereotypes (1994: 75) – need to be understood in their social and political contexts, and to be set against the rich variety and diversity of Anglo-India's cultural repertoire, as these evolved in the course of Britain's imperial rule and have been transformed with India's move from colony to independent nation.

Despite the abundant, essentialized attentions they received in popular discourses, fictional literature and official documents Anglo-Indians – with a few recent notable exceptions (e.g. Hawes 1996) – are hardly present at all in histories of modern India. Perhaps – and this is only speculation – historians would argue that Anglo-Indians were demographically and politically too insignificant to warrant serious attention. Notwithstanding recent attempts to 'revisit the colonial record, push at the edges, unsettle the calmness with which colonial categories and knowledges were instituted as the facts of history' (Prakash 1995: 6), this uncanny silence continues to surround the place of Anglo-Indians in the recent annals of India.

Anthropologists, for their part, have been no less neglectful of this group. Again, I can only assume that in seeking out the exotic – a not uncommon practice in the south Asian context (Inden 1990) – Anglo-Indians have been considered not sufficiently 'other' to attract the ethnographer's attention.[6]

Métis populations like the Anglo-Indians invite serious scholarly attention because, among other things, they blurred the divide between colonizer and colonized, questioning the very efficacy of these labels and challenging carefully wrought images of a 'Manichean world of high colonialism' (Cooper and Stoler 1997: 8; see also Thomas 1994: 2, 187; Tsing 1993: 17; Young 1990: 151). A starkly bi-polar approach to colonialism, which presents colonizers and colonized as virtually homogeneous and exclusive categories, has recently given way to an acknowledgement that each was not only internally diverse, but that they were 'mutually shaped in intimate engagement, attraction, and opposition' (Cooper and Stoler 1997: viii). The work of scholars such as Stoler and Taylor among Europeans and Indo-Europeans in the colonial Dutch East Indies not only underlines the impossibility of viewing rulers and ruled as universal and undifferentiated categories, but – through the prism of the mestizo category – marks an important step away from treating Europeans and colonizers as synonymous (Cooper and Stoler 1997; Stoler 1989, 1991, 1995; Taylor 1983).[7]

In India, too, as Frykenberg has pointed out, the British 'were never ... ever all of a piece' (n.d.: 47). There were significant class divisions among them, which aped and even caricatured hierarchies in Britain.[8] The British elite 'despised and spurned' their own poor, regarding them in many instances as virtually a separate race (see Arnold 1979: 105; Stoler 1995: 125). Indeed, discrimination against those of another race has been seen as a variant of attitudes shown towards the lower classes (Breman 1990: 2). Moreover, both formal and informal distinctions were drawn between the official British – those who represented the East India Company and later the British Government in India – and the non-official British or other Europeans who came to seek employment or trade in the wake of the colonizers (see Renford 1979). Then again, the 'non-domiciled' – those who served only a limited time in the sub-continent before retiring to their homes abroad – were demarcated from the 'domiciled' Europeans, many of whom were born and spent their entire lives in India. While the Anglo-Indians were frequently seen as part of the latter category, or together with them to comprise an undifferentiated 'domiciled community', the lines separating all these sections from one another and from 'native' Indians were porous and imprecise. Thus, despite attempts to create definitive and exclusive racial cum social categories, these distinctions were continuously undermined in the course of colonial rule. British Census commissioners, as well as Anglo-Indian leaders, regularly reported that many members of this métis community were declaring themselves as Europeans, while countless numbers belonging to various Indian groups were 'infiltrating' the ranks of Anglo-India. Such 'migrations', like the sexual and marital unions linking people from what were deemed incommensurable racialized populations, represented an enduring challenge to the notion of a clear-cut dichotomy between rulers and ruled, and to carefully erected category boundaries.

Nonetheless, while miscegenation produced offspring whose ambiguous identities challenged official attempts to enclose them in definitive social or cultural enclaves, no generalized outcomes can be inferred from the existence of such an 'intermediate' status. The manner in which mestizo groups engaged with others and among themselves depended to a large extent on how hybridity was construed in any particular colonial setting. As Klor de Alva suggests, different forms of colonialism 'are likely to create differing senses of mestizaje'(1995: 243). Local circumstances ensured that each experienced its equivocal position in very particular ways, and these can only be known through detailed empirical investigation.

Then again, métis populations which emerged during the colonial encounter, and who, like the Anglo-Indians, are even today officially recognized as distinct social and cultural groups, beg a host of queries about continuities and transformations in the postcolonial world. How does a hybrid community imagine and describe itself to others and to itself? How does it understand its past, contemplate its future, and live in the present? What practices does it posit as marking its 'culture' and so its distinctiveness; what are the ingredients of this 'culture' given the diverse origins of the population, and what changes in these cultural habits have occurred with the withdrawal of the colonial power? In seeking to respond to these and other questions regarding contemporary Anglo-Indians this study aims to provide an ethnographic complement and corrective to the sometimes generalized and unsituated theorizing of certain 'postcolonial critics' (see below).

How were intermediate or métis populations like the Anglo-Indians accommodated in a starkly dualistic model where European-colonizer and colonized-Other were seen as quintessentially separate and distinct? Western social scientists of the immediate pre- and post-Second World War periods concluded that, like all persons of mixed racial heritage, mestizos must be conceptualized as marginal to both solidary groups. Communities of dual racial or ethnic backgrounds were regarded as on the margins of two cultures and two societies, in both of which they were aliens. Until well into the 1960s there was a voluminous literature on marginal situations and 'marginal man', considering, among other things, the psychological difficulties of such a position (see, for example, Park 1930–31; Stonequist 1937). At the end of that decade Gist and Dworkin (1972) made a systematic attempt to explore the concept of marginality comparatively in 'world perspective', with reference to a number of mestizo populations – including the Anglo-Indians – which had arisen out of the colonial encounter. They identified three aspects of marginality – cultural, social and political – suggesting that some hybrid groups might be marginal in all three senses, others in only one or two. While 'marginal man' theorizing had all but disappeared by the mid-1970s, it continued for a time to influence some writings about Anglo-Indians. Cottrell, for example, in comparing recent 'Asian-Western' mixed-race couples in the West with Anglo-Indians in India stresses that the latter are 'socially marginal to the British and socially and culturally marginal to Indians' (1979: 361).[9]

The 'marginal man' was very much an outsiders' view, constructed largely on *a priori* assumptions about the predicament of mestizos who bring together in their persons separate racial or ethnic strains. And although Gist and Dworkin (1972) called their study 'The Blending of Races', their assertions of a universal marginal state for hybrid peoples suggest anything but a successful blending. Moreover, the marginal situation, because it is in effect an innate condition of *mestizaje*, characterizes all members of the group irrespective of social location.

Such a model, in other words, presupposes a view of cultures as autonomous and bounded, so that each social unit is seen to possess its own discrete culture, which provides meaning, continuity and normative order to all its members. From this notion of cultural coherence within particular social categories it follows that those elements of the population which do not belong unequivocally to one of these chaste collectivities – those 'considered halfway between two "pure" cultures' (Glissant 1989: 140) – are deemed to suffer from the absence of an integrating and stabilizing cultural framework; in short, they are marginal.[10]

In anthropology the idea of cultures as bounded and self-perpetuating systems is no longer, if it ever was, an acceptable starting point for analysis. Drummond was among the first to suggest that polyethnic societies (such as those in the Caribbean) can best be understood in terms of an approach which eschews cultural fixity and insularity. Building on Bickerton's (1975) model of overlapping or intersystemic features as crucial for any study of language, Drummond adopts a creole metaphor to argue for the notion of a 'cultural continuum' which highlights diversity and internal variation (1980). While other anthropologists have since utilized the notion of creolization in different ways – Parkin (1993) has identified at least three senses in which the term has been employed – each, in its own guise, eschews the image of 'cultural islands' (Eriksen 1993), a view of cultures as 'well-bounded wholes' (Hannerz 1992: 265–6).[11]

Theorizing the Colonial and Postcolonial

These issues have resurfaced and become pertinent of late in view of the stress now placed on notions of creolization, mixture and hybridity by postcolonial writers. The term 'postcolonial', despite the inference that it signifies a unified field of discourse, has come to assume several disparate though related meanings (see Williams and Chrisman 1993). Let me note only the two most relevant for present purposes, and the by now much rehearsed criticisms of each, since they provide an important theoretical backdrop to this study. Firstly, 'postcolonial' designates certain kinds of literary and literary-critical writings by Asian and African diasporic intellectuals in the West.[12] Though acknowledging the stimulating contributions of these scholars in identifying the limits and frailties of colonial authority, commentators in several disciplines have begun to question what are seen as the largely global, static and de-contextualized categories and theorizing which abound in their accounts. Thus, McClintock asks if most countries can really be said 'in any meaningful or theoretically rigorous sense' to share a single 'common past' or 'post-colonial condition'? (1993: 294; see also Shohat 1992: 103). In another assessment Thomas complains of their 'dogged attachment' to colonialism as a unitary category, and the attribution of general characteristics to what is deemed an undifferentiated concept (1994: ix, 43). Like other critics, he advocates a more historically and ethno-graphically nuanced approach to colonial encounters (Ibid.: 9; see also Young 1990: 146). It is a plea for less reliance on 'subtle readings of currently fashionable European theorists and more on local knowledge of . . . everyday life in the postcolonial hinterlands' (Werbner 1996: 6). Ahmad makes a related point when he notes that the globalized condition of postcoloniality described by many postcolonial authors is never 'fixed as a determinate structure of power against which determinate forms of struggle may be possible outside the domains of discourse and pedagogy' (1995: 9).

In another meaning, 'postcolonial' serves as a shorthand, a 'framing device' for the latter half of the twentieth century, which has seen the emergence of independent nation-states in the wake of decolonization (Breckenridge and Van de Veer 1993). In this descriptive sense it refers to contemporary conditions in former colonies, but such periodization has also been criticized on two quite different grounds. On the one hand, it may suggest a break between the colonial and the postcolonial, an unwarranted assumption where profound inequalities of power continue to characterize relations between erstwhile colonizer states and those they previously colonized. By implying the supersession of the colonial by the postcolonial writers might appear to assert an essentialized contrast between them (Ranger 1996: 273; Werbner 1996: 6; also Pels 1997: 164).[13]

On the other hand, in a different kind of critique, Ahmad argues that such periodization of history only privileges colonialism as the 'principle of structuration' in that history, so that what follows – postcolonialism – 'can only be lived as infinite aftermath' (1995: 7). For McClintock, too, the preposition 'post' renders colonialism the 'determining marker of history' so that the cultures of peoples 'beyond colonialism' are distinguished negatively in their relation to Europe (1993: 293). It is one thing to accept that there are continuities between the colonial past and the postcolonial present, that 'colonialism lives on in postcolonial societies and psyches' (Dirks 1992: 7), but another thing entirely to assume, as Cooper and Stoler suggest is the case in some postcolonial writings, that 'colonialism was the only thing of importance to people who live in what were once colonies' (1997: 33). Such theorizing neglects the possibility, as Nandy has suggested for India, that a large section of the colonial society may have been 'spared the problem of handling the West at the deepest level of consciousness' (1983: 76). Thus, the 'colonial' assumes the status of a totalizing agent, and the 'postcolonial' becomes yet another global, undifferentiated concept – a 'bogus universal', as McClintock puts it (1993: 299). In this book I seek to show that contemporary Anglo-Indian life has been shaped by a complex of factors referable to the colonial past – Anglo-Indians were, after all, nothing if not the offspring of colonialism – as well as to more recent economic and political currents within India itself, and to the global impacts of late capitalist domination by Western powers. But while acknowledging the multifarious environing influences which have shaped Anglo-India today, I consider the diverse ways in which the people themselves have understood, interpreted and responded to them.

Creolized Cultures, Bounded Identities

This brings us to what Shohat refers to as the postcolonialist 'celebration of hybridity' (1992:110). The concept is much favoured in current postcolonial studies, although the possibility that there can be 'diverse modalities of hybridity' is usually overlooked (Ibid.). In some quarters it is seen as 'a generalised condition of postmodernity into which all contemporary cultures are now irretrievably ushered. . .' (Ahmad 1995: 13; also Ranger 1996: 271). There is perhaps some irony in the fact that hybrid groups seem not to figure in these debates, although a number, like the Anglo-Indian, continue to be recognized in the popular imagination and to recognize themselves to be in large part biologically as well as culturally composite. Bear remarks on how Anglo-Indian typologies (in Bengal) slide imperceptibly 'from blood to cultural habits and back to blood' (1998:163), an oscillation I was frequently to note in Madras as well. Thus, while most postcolonial scholars understandably avoid the racialized overtones of colonial language, and treat 'hybridity' as entirely a cultural phenomenon, in the everyday formulations of ordinary people, today as in the past, the concept retains certain neo-racial as well as cultural connotations, and this should not be ignored in our analysis.

Some writers, it has been suggested, tend to assert a colonial moment of binary opposition between colonizer and colonized so that they 'can enjoy the postcolonial confidence that our world today is infinitely more complicated, more fragmented and more blurred' (Cooper and Stoler 1997: 9, 34). However, as I have already intimated, and will demonstrate in the course of this book, the *colonial* milieu in which Anglo-Indians found themselves was no less informed by porous boundaries and fluid identities; this, moreover, in the face of rhetorics – emanating from both Euro-colonial sources and community elites – asserting clearly demarcated groupings and fixed borders. Paradoxically, in contemporary times, which are portrayed by postcolonial writers as quintessentially hybridized and creolized, populations – large and small – continue to enunciate unmixed, pure identities in the idiom of distinctive lifeways. What is apparent is that many peoples now 'want culture' – as Brumann puts it – and, moreover, often assert it in a 'bounded, reified, essentialized and timeless fashion' (1999: S11; see also Sahlins 1999: 403). In what has recently become a torrent of criticism, postcolonial writers have been taken to task for their 'condescension' toward contemporary communities which insist on unmixed identities and solidarities based on collective cultural imaginings (see, for example, Friedman 1997; 83–4; Shohat 1992: 110; Werbner 1997: 240). These critics argue that this kind of essentialist rhetoric cannot be dismissed on the grounds that it is ahistorical and unself-consciously reproduces colonialist stereotypes, for such an attitude confuses local attempts at political mobilization with the postcolonial analyst's own constructs (Thomas 1994: 188). Hall makes a similar point: because essentialism has been 'deconstructed *theoretically*', does not mean that it has been 'displaced *politically*' (Hall 1996: 249, emphasis in the original).

Such a critique applies to the Madras context considered here. Indeed, a dominant theme of the study turns on the dissonance between, on the one side, the fluid, porous, heterogeneous social and cultural field in which Anglo-Indians have been and continue to be located and, on the other, the recurrent characterization of the group and its culture, by persons both within and outside its fold, as fixed, bounded, impermeable and homogeneous. Moreover, *both* the colonial and postcolonial periods were and are characterized by such a tension.[14] In this latter sense, I echo Ranger's observation with regard to Africa, that colonial south Asia – or at any rate urban south India – was 'much more like [the] postcolonial . . . than most of us have hitherto imagined' (1996: 280).

While somewhat discordant, I do not see these proclivities – hybridized social-cultural fields alongside essentialist rhetorics – as mutually exclusive. It is important to retain a creolist image to depict and understand both the colonial and contemporary worlds of a métis community like the Anglo-Indian which arose out of the colonial encounter, as well as to comprehend the transformations it has undergone over time. We do not argue, however, for a notion of creolized that is somehow between and apart from undefiled originary sources. I think Young is right to criticize approaches which, while highlighting mixture, hybridization or creolization, imply 'pure origination of both Western and native cultures . . . two hitherto undifferentiated knowledges' (1990: 150; see also Friedman 1994: 12–13). Creolization as an idea, rather, should imply the 'negation of creolization as a category', and its conceptualization as a natural process (Glissant 1989: 140–1). Amselle offers a similar theoretical framework: an analysis in terms of 'mestizo logics' eludes the question of origins, and postulates an 'originary syncretism, a mixture whose parts remain indissociable' (1998: 161).

Applied to Anglo-Indians, an image of this kind underlines firstly, the historical meeting of separate social and cultural currents (Hannerz 1992: 264). However, we cannot remain oblivious to the inequality of the forces so creolized, a factor which has sometimes been ignored or downplayed (Trouillot 1992: 28). Harris, for example, suggests that Hannerz's (1987) metaphor of separate cultural streams flowing together and merging may be 'unduly benign' in its neglect of 'political realities' (Harris 1995: 109). Secondly, a creolist model assumes the porosity of cultural as well as social boundaries, and acknowledges the heterogeneity of cultural practices within as well as across the lines dividing the constituent groups which comprise the (urban) social order which Anglo-Indians inhabit.

Nonetheless, a focus on the creole need not divert attention from the self-identifications of specific populations, whether or not these deny mixture. Anglo-Indians have, since the early nineteenth century, engaged in an ongoing debate with their British rulers and among themselves regarding the provenance of their 'culture'. Until India's independence their leaders insisted, against the prevailing views of colonial officials, that Anglo-Indians were, by virtue of kinship and lifeways, unequivocally British. With Britain's withdrawal from the sub-continent more fragmented identity claims have begun to be articulated: while those in the middle ranks of the community continue to proclaim a European social and cultural pedigree, at both ends of the class spectrum local (Indian) attachments are increasingly asserted, while elites also share a cosmopolitan outlook with others of similar rank in the wider society.

Thus, critics of the postcolonial writers' attachment to hybridity, in drawing attention to the *contemporary* claims of many *groups* to bounded cultural identities, or to the growth of what Stolcke has termed 'cultural fundamentalism' (1995), should not overlook several important aspects of such political assertions. For one thing, the mobilization of group identities, as already noted, is not only a product of the current (postwar, post-Independence, postcolonial) scene, but was a feature, if a less ubiquitous one, of the colonial period, as well. For another, while a group, *tout court*, or its representatives, may affirm a common identity, there is also a possibility that different sections or classes may insist on quite distinct kinds of cultural belonging, and that these diverse claims can exist contemporaneously or succeed one another over time as circumstances alter. Thirdly, since assertions of cultural identity are not made in a vacuum, the audiences to which they are addressed are obviously vital components of the political context in which they are made. The success or failure of particular identity affirmations must therefore be examined against the background of specific colonial and/or contemporary power alignments.

Finally, between a creolist and an essentialist perspective on culture there should still be ample room for one where the term continues to designate clusters of shared meanings, symbols and practices – 'routines of thought and behavior' in Brumann's phrase (1999). In arguing for the retention of 'culture' as a useful anthropological concept against those who would see it abolished, or used only where it serves as a means of constituting identity,[15] Brumann observes that culture is not always ethnic culture, nor is it invariably relevant to identity formation (Ibid.: S11–12). To emphasize only the manner of its reification is to ignore the equally important 'process of objectification' – the way groups 'describe, redescribe and argue over who they are' (Werbner 1997: 229, referring to Dominguez). It is also to neglect the important mechanisms of the production and transformation of these cultures. To appreciate how the Anglo-Indians have managed to navigate the frequently shifting currents of colonial policy and sometimes equally stormy seas of caste and minority politics in independent India, we have to consider all aspects of this triad: creolization of the cultural field; essentializations of cultural identity; and production/transformation of cultural routines. This study may thus be seen as part of an ongoing conversation about the complex relationship between the colonial and postcolonial in diverse settings, which can be known only through careful empirical investigation.

Researching Anglo-India

Most writings by and about Anglo-Indians – with a few notable exceptions – have treated them as a single, undifferentiated country-wide population. Anglo-Indians resident in Madras certainly see themselves as part of an all-India community, and as sharing a common history and culture with similar groups in other parts of the country. Though not claiming typicality for those resident in this south Indian city, I have no reason to believe that the historical, social or cultural developments to be considered in this book are in any significant way different for settlements in other major urban centres of India.

At the same time, there is something to be said for focussing on a single, localized population. Anthropologically, it makes sense to attempt to make connections among various aspects of Anglo-Indian society and culture in a particular setting – each adding to and deepening our ethnographic understanding. Moreover, aspects of the political and economic history of south India have served to distinguish this part of the sub-continent from elsewhere, and helped to mould the lives of its diverse populations – including the Anglo-Indians – in particular ways. Madras was, after all, the political, economic and administrative centre of one of the three great Presidencies into which colonial India was divided, and is today the capital of Tamil Nadu state. Then, within the Anglo-Indian fold itself, people in Madras sometimes regard themselves and are often regarded as somehow distinct from other sections of the Anglo-Indian community. 'Northerners' occasionally see their Madras compatriots as tainted by too much colonial Portuguese influence (and blood), and so a little less entitled to claim proper 'Anglo' descent. Politically, the Madras community is thought by many elsewhere in India to have gone its own way, in establishing a separate communal association and refusing to this day to amalgamate with the larger northern (Delhi-based) organization, which now has its own branches in Madras. There are therefore good historical (and ethno-historical) reasons for focussing on a particular localized segment of Anglo-Indians although this is not to suggest that they can be treated as an isolate, or that their lives can be understood without reference to the wider community. I will thus refer, for comparative purposes, and wherever the literature allows, to studies of Anglo-Indian groups elsewhere in the country.

I was familiar with Madras from previous research among Indian Christians (Caplan 1987; 1989), in the course of which I met a number of Anglo-Indians, many of whom worship in English in congregations alongside Indian Christians. During this research I became acquainted with approximately 350 Anglo-Indian households – with a total universe of perhaps 1,500 persons – located at various socio-economic levels. I also had numerous conversations with officers of the two main community associations in the city, Anglo-Indian representatives in national and state assemblies, the principals and administrators of various organizations and agencies serving Anglo-India, philanthropists, and other prominent figures in the community, and was present at various meetings and events organized by them. I spent time at Anglo-Indian schools and orphanages, in homes for the elderly in which Anglo-Indians reside, and met with ministers of religious congregations in which they worship. I also attended a number of 'functions' – birthdays, weddings, dances, and other family celebrations, funerals, and Christmas festivities – as well as numerous philanthropic occasions, when charity of one kind or another was distributed to poor Anglo-Indians. Wherever possible, archives were consulted, and documentation, both historical and contemporary, dealing with the community was sought. Finally, I attempted to become familiar with at least some of the works produced by members of this highly literate and articulate community, as well as writings by non-Anglo-Indians about this population.

The next chapter introduces the Anglo-Indian community, traces its emergence in India and Madras, and considers its fortunes against the backdrop of oscillating British colonial policies towards this hybrid group. It points to internal class divisions, and considers how contemporary developments in the wider national and global economies have widened and impacted on these status distinctions.

Chapter 3 then examines forms of colonial boundary-marking, focussing particularly on attempts by those within the ruling circles to demarcate and demean Anglo-Indians, before going on to consider the diverse ways in which these lines of division were breached.

The following chapter turns to the colonial circumstances which prompted Anglo-Indians to regard themselves as British, and others which, paradoxically, encouraged an awareness among them of a separate identity. The latter was and continues to be manifested in vigorous internal politics, based largely on opposition between the main community associations.

Chapter 5 then explores the practices surrounding and impact of the large-scale postcolonial exodus of Anglo-Indians to the West which has reduced the population remaining in India to perhaps half its size at Independence. While people at the bottom of the socio-economic spectrum have neither the skills nor the resources to emigrate, those at the very top increasingly resist doing so. Only within the middle ranks of the community, where people have come to arrange their lives around the hopes or fantasies of 'abroad', do we find what may be termed a 'spirit of emigration'.

The next two chapters, on contemporary families and cultural practices, interrogate the relationship between assertions of a European cultural patrimony and the influences of the local (Indian) cultural environment. Notwithstanding rhetorics idolizing Western nuclear forms, they extol the value of close and extended (if imprecisely defined) families. The centrality of women in the household, which sets Anglo-Indian domestic regimes apart from those in the wider society, is then explored, and this is followed by an examination of changing gender constructs and contrasts.

Chapter 7 discusses cultural practices based on selected elements which Anglo-Indians themselves define as exemplifying their way of life: dress, food and marriage observances. What becomes evident is that these are by no means uniformly distributed throughout the community, but differentially clustered, class positionality being a key determinant. What also emerges from the discussion is that, as the previous chapter demonstrates, Anglo-Indian cultural practices, despite being seen in some (including social science) quarters as derived mainly from Western sources, are much influenced by habits and beliefs in the surrounding society.

The final chapter resumes the main themes of the book.

Notes

1. In Batavia, according to Taylor, many of the initial unions of European men with Asian women 'were disorderly and exploitative' (1983: 171).

2. Terms such as hybrid, métis, mulatto, mestizo, mixed-race, etc. not only have the potential to cause offence, but can be theoretically contentious. Since there is no totally satisfactory solution, I utilize various of these labels, although I regard métis (from métissage meaning the crossing of two races) somewhat more appropriate than others. Spickard has a similar problem with his terminology (1989: 21).

3. It is possible that Captain Munro was referring to Anglo-Indians with his rather demeaning remark that a 'mongrel breed of Portuguese fill the stations of clerks, menial servants and other useful occupations' (1789: 49).

4. Busia, referring to colonial novels of Africa, remarks that the children of inter-racial liaisons were frequently seen as 'the most morally degenerate of beings: villainous, treacherous [who] contrary to genetic laws of breeding, manage to inherit both the most repulsive physical and spiritual traits of their parents' (1986: 367).

5. D'Cruz lists the 'main stereotypes' found in the fictional literature: Anglo-Indians are physically and morally weak; they are stooges and mimics of the British; their women are 'loose'; they are destitute and suffer from an inferiority complex; etc. (1999: 82).

6. Anglo-Indians did feature in sociological debates during the 1960s and early 1970s about marginal groups (see Gist 1972; Gist and Dworkin 1972).

7. Referring to colonization in the Andes, Harris remarks that 'the "Spanish" and the "Indian" ingredients of *mestizaje* are both fictions. Neither is, nor ever was, homogeneous or unified' (1995: 110).

8. Anderson suggests that the colonies 'permitted sizeable numbers of bourgeois and petty bourgeois to play aristocrat off centre court: i.e. anywhere in the empire except at home' (1983: 138). India certainly provided channels of mobility for those socially frustrated in the metropolitan country (see Nandy 1983: 33).

9. Cottrell's data on Anglo-Indians are based on Gaikwad (1967) and Gist and Wright (1973).

10. I am not suggesting that 'marginality' has no descriptive or analytical value. Tsing has recently employed the notion fruitfully to indicate 'distinctive and unequal subject positions within common fields of power and knowledge' (1993: xi). This is quite different from arguing that people are inherently 'marginal' simply by virtue of their mestizo condition.

11. Sahlins has recently ridiculed the implication that the founders of (especially American) cultural anthropology believed that cultures

are unchanging and rigidly bounded. On the contrary, 'the old codgers taught that all cultures are hybrid' (1999: 404, 411). Friedman, moreover, has observed that since cultures 'have always been the product of import and a mix of elements', the assertion that they are creolized is a truism (1997: 80).

12. Postcolonial studies 'has its greatest visibility . . . in departments of English and comparative literature' (Roy 1999: 15).

13. It could be argued that the last two decades of the nineteenth century, when Indianization policies in employment began to take effect, or the post-First World War Montagu-Chelmsford reforms, which consolidated and furthered these policies, represented decisive turning points in Anglo-Indian fortunes, certainly no less than the end of British rule.

14. Fardon suggests a distinction between (a) explanations which regard the world as once having been made up of distinct cultures and societies but is now moving through a hybridized phase; and (b) those which insist that the world never did consist of such bounded units, although people tended to see it that way but do so no more. Those who argue for the latter position, Fardon suggests, need to explore why this change of perception occurred (1995: 5).

15. See, for example, Abu-Lughod (1991); Brumann (1999).

–2–

Anglo-Indians in Madras

As children we used to see our men driving those big engines. And we would feel so proud, and the thought grew up in the children: 'I want to be a driver'.

My daddy was a driver on the railways, working in the harbour, and my mommy was a teacher. I was born in Royapuram and so were my sisters and brother. We lived here in this same street. We all went to school in St Kevin's [Anglo-Indian] school. My children and grandchildren went there too. Royapuram had so many Anglo-Indian families then, but now they've all gone. A wonderful place. God's own country. We were very happy here.

Introduction

This chapter traces the emergence and settlement of an Anglo-Indian population in Madras city, and underlines the significant distinctions within its fold, both past and present. The aim is to counteract the widespread tendency in colonial contexts to essentialize the community, a process which occurred through enumeration, stereotyping and other objectifying procedures which sought to create uniform social bodies, flatten diversity and impose homogeneity (Appadurai 1993: 333). In many colonial discourses – and some contemporary ones – those who comment(ed) on Anglo-India posit(ed) 'a timeless continuity' and an 'internal sameness' (Werbner 1997: 228), an image at odds with its fluidity and adaptability. The chapter considers both the occupational and educational biography of the community in light of fluctuating British policies towards this métis group and the post-Independence aftermath of the colonial legacy. It goes on to note the heterogeneity of class and rank among Anglo-Indians, and points to how contemporary developments in the global economy have created new opportunities for some and driven others further into poverty. The chapter concludes by tracing the changing patterns of Anglo-Indian settlement in the city, which are related to population movements, both residential and commercial, in the wider society and to economic developments – local, national and global – during the past century.

The Evolution of an Anglo-Indian Population in Madras

The Anglo-Indian population is descended from a medley of different ethnic and racial categories, European and Indian. As noted in the previous chapter, there has been a Portuguese presence at San Thome (in what is now south Madras) since the early part of the sixteenth century, making it the first European settlement in the vicinity, and giving rise to a substantial mixed-race population. Many Portuguese were invited to settle in Fort St George, as soldiers and traders, soon after the English factory was established by the East India Company in 1639 (Wheeler 1878: 57). In 1642 the Capuchins were allowed to construct a chapel for them within the confines of the Fort (Mitter 1985: 194; Muthiah 1981: 27; Srinivasachari 1939: 22, 79).[1] Contemporary reports suggested that as many as 3,000 Portuguese had taken up residence, and by 1675 vastly outnumbered the 300-odd English inhabitants (Ranson 1938: 11; Wheeler 1878: 57).

Some of the earliest marriages of English factors and soldiers were therefore with Portuguese women in the Fort – many of whom were, in fact, either of mixed Portuguese-Indian descent or, according to some observers, native converts to Christianity who had adopted Portuguese names (Penny 1904 (I): 26).[2] Indeed, while little was said about such miscegenation, concern was soon expressed about the growing influence of Roman Catholicism in the English settlement. Thus, the Rev Patrick Warner, Chaplain at Fort St George, wrote to the Court of Directors in January 1676, urging them to prohibit the marriages of their employees with Portuguese women, on the grounds that the men themselves 'hardly escape being seduced by their wives and wives' families into popery', while 'the children turn either infidels or popish' (Wheeler 1878: 69). Attempts were made to insist that the children of such marriages be brought up as Protestants, but this would have made it difficult for the men to obtain wives, since, according to Penny, the women preferred to live with the men out of marriage in order to 'retain control over their children's religion' (Penny 1904 (I): 107). The scheme was soon dropped for this, and other reasons, the chief among which was very probably that income from the Portuguese trade had become too significant to jeopardize (see Love 1913 (I)). The importance of the Portuguese traders in early Madras is indicated by the fact that at the founding of the Madras Corporation they contributed three of its twelve aldermen (Frykenberg n.d.: 16). Until at least the end of the eighteenth century what Penny refers to as 'a debased form of Portuguese' was the *lingua franca* on the Coromandel coast (1904: 164; Love 1913 (I): 396; Penny 1908: 154).[3]

The descendants of these initial unions formed a significant part of what later was to be termed the Anglo-Indian community. Their legacy is still evident: a substantial proportion of Anglo-Indians in Madras as in south India generally have Portuguese surnames, a fact which perturbed some Anglo-Indian leaders. One of the most prominent figures in the city during the 1930s and 1940s remarked somewhat plaintively that 'there are, perhaps, more Anglo-Indians in Southern India with Portuguese names than with British – when the situation should be entirely reversed' (Bower 1939: 119).[4]

I have already noted that European men of other than British or Portuguese descent also came to India and established relationships with Indian women, or with the progeny of previous Indo-European unions. The sources of contemporary Anglo-India are thus remarkably 'multi-national' on the paternal side, but it is virtually impossible to say more about the initial maternal progenitors than that they were of diverse local origins. What I found striking during fieldwork was that when discussing their founding ancestors, whether these were identifiable or only guessed at, almost without exception my Anglo-Indian informants would focus exclusively on the family's European male progenitor, disclaiming any knowledge of or interest in the founding female ancestress.

With the rapid increase in the numbers of ordinary British soldiers in India in the course of the eighteenth and nineteenth centuries, the Anglo-Indian population grew significantly. Richard Wilson, the surgeon at the Garrison of Trichinopoly (in what is now Tamil Nadu) during the last quarter of the eighteenth century, referred to the 'numerous male issue of European soldiery in India' (quoted in Love 1913 (III): 180–1). Major Bevan, writing about Madras at the beginning of the nineteenth century, noted how the 'progeny from [the] intercourse of Europeans and natives is very numerous. . .' (1839: 20). According to Hawes, by 1830 the British in India were 'vastly outnumbered by Eurasians of British descent' (1993: 28) and 'the overwhelming majority of Eurasian children born to the British at that time were . . . fathered by "poor whites"' (Ibid.: 44; see also Arnold 1983: 140). We may be reasonably certain that the local women they consorted with were from humble backgrounds, which may go some way to explain the collective amnesia concerning female ancestors among so many Anglo-Indian families.

Most Anglo-Indian writers, when they address the issue at all, under-standably prefer to note the worthy, even distinguished family back-grounds of these women. When John Ricketts came to Britain in 1830 to plead the Anglo-Indian cause before Parliament he was asked at one point about 'the native mothers of East Indians' (as the Anglo-Indians were then called) and replied that in Bengal 'the greater proportion of them are . . . of respectable families, but in reduced circumstances' (Ricketts 1831: 53).[5] A century later, C.N. Weston offered the view that early British officials 'married some of the best women in India' (1939: 145; see also Anthony 1969: 12).

For the moment what is important to note is that social divisions did not arise within the Eurasian population in Madras based on varieties of European descent, as sometimes happened in other colonial settings. Thus, in Ceylon, Burghers of Dutch origin were considered and considered themselves superior to Burghers of Portuguese origin, with the former recognized as a 'successful and articulate middle class', while the latter were regarded as 'the great Burgher residuum: poorer, darker, more numerous, and less European' (McGilvray 1982: 236; see also Roberts et al 1989: 12, 19). In Singapore a hierarchy also emerged between Anglo-Eurasians and Portuguese Eurasians, but, according to Daus (1989), it was the latter who were treated more tolerantly by the British, and who as a result became the successful middle class.

In Madras such rigid dichotomies did not emerge, although Gist and Wright, referring to the Anglo-Indian population in general, report that families with English surnames 'achieve a modicum of prestige' vis à vis other Eurasians (1973: 87). As a result, 'anglicization of non-British names seems to have been a common practice' (Goodrich 1952: 13), and Frank Anthony, a prominent Anglo-Indian leader and chronicler of the community's fortunes, provides a number of examples of this process (1969: 371). There is some evidence of such translations occurring in Madras – I knew a Henriques who had become 'Henricus' at some time in the past, as well as a Suares which had been altered to Swaris.[6] Usually, however, the original Portuguese or other non-English spellings are retained, although in some cases they might be given an anglicized pronunciation: thus, Rodrigues is usually rendered as 'Rodericks', while Gomes is rhymed with homes. But on the whole Anglo-Indians with other than English family names suffer no disabilities in the Madras community.

This is not to suggest an absence of pretensions to hierarchy. While in Madras, I was told by one man with a 'Portuguese' family name that 'the Europeans [i.e. those with Portuguese or other non-English surnames] were traders rather than soldiers. They were fairly well-to-do. They weren't "Tommies" [British soldiers].'

From time to time there are expressions of resentment at the inclusion within Anglo-Indian ranks of persons who would, on the evidence of their surnames, appear to have no claim to British descent. Thus, one letter from a 'non-British Anglo-Indian' to the December 1926 edition of *The Anglo-Indian*, journal of the Anglo-Indian Association of Southern India, based in Madras, notes the 'prejudice against those with non-British names' and points out that

> the worst offenders in this respect are those Anglo-Indians who happen to possess British names, but also have their share of Portuguese or other non-British blood in their veins, as a scrutiny of their family history will show.

But whenever such distinctions are articulated – usually in response to some real or imagined insult addressed to those with non-English surnames – speakers are quick to point out that in Madras there is no antagonism between them because 'they're too mixed up together'. This is, of course, the crux of the matter: from the initial emergence of the community, there have been and continue to be unions between Eurasians of various paternal origins, and all along it has been impossible to distinguish 'pure' lines within the population.[7] If anything, new kinds of population influx have added further to the ethnic heterogeneity of the community. Thus, a small number of Chinese men who found their way to Madras early last century established unions with women in the Anglo-Indian community, as have more recently arrived students from various parts of Africa. Though officially their offspring are not Anglo-Indians – only descendants in the male line of *European* men are so designated – in everyday local settings they are readily absorbed into and regarded as members of the community.

The Emergence of Class Divisions

While diversities of European descent sometimes produced contested claims to status they did not create significant social divisions within the Anglo-Indian fold. Gradations based on wealth and standing, however, have been present in the Anglo-Indian community since its inception.

Some of those writing about the community in the twentieth century have characterized it as uniformly subordinate. For F.E. Penny (1908: 153) this was a question of their racial as much as their class inheritance: 'The Eurasians', she insisted, 'do not as a rule rise above their low-born and low-caste ancestors.' This was a piquant illustration of how in so many British discourses on Anglo-Indians, race and class were blurred to become a 'scrambled social category' (Stoler 1995: 130). In the 1930s, by which time a majority of Anglo-Indians in employment were engaged on the railways, in some other branch of government service, or in the offices of European companies, the sociologist Hedin suggested that 'nearly all Anglo-Indian workers could be described as 'lower white collar class' (1934: 173). By contrast, Wallace – an Anglo-Indian with socialist orientations – insisted that the Anglo-Indian community 'belongs to the working class' (1935: 55–6).

Differences within Anglo-India, based initially on distinctions of paternal rank, grew subsequently into those of occupation, income and standing. The first generation offspring of officers and officials were educated, some of them in Britain, and 'carried the social and economic backgrounds of their fathers' (Hawes 1993: 23–4). Some were employed as senior officials in the administrative and military services. However, in a series of orders issued by the Company at the close of the eighteenth century, Eurasians, who had previously suffered little discrimination in respect of appointments, were banned from senior posts in the civil and military services, and disqualified from all ranks in the army save as fifers, drummers, bandsmen and farriers (Hawes 1993: 198, 203). The reasons for these proscriptive measures have been much debated, and numerous 'theories' suggested by both Anglo-Indian and Western historians. Two seem especially persuasive: first, it was becoming increasingly evident to the British in this period that there were fortunes to be made in India, and it was deemed expedient to exclude Eurasians from this patrimony, since they 'might be recognized' – or might insist on being recognized – 'as heirs to a European inheritance' (Stoler 1989: 154).

Second, British policy-makers were concerned that Eurasians, 'should they be well led or politically organized, could pose a risk to British security' (Hawes 1993: 197; see also Arnold 1983: 140). According to Bishop Heber, British officials 'lament[ed] the increase of the half-caste population as a source of present mischief and future danger to the tranquility of the Colony' (quoted in Abel 1988: 22).

Anglo-Indian writers have unanimously identified these regulations as responsible for depriving their people of 'every honourable career' and of reducing them to the 'status of a proscribed and down-trodden race' (Stark 1936: 59; see also Weston 1939: 103–4). A number of these proscriptions were subsequently lifted, and Anglo-Indians could aspire to posts of intermediate responsibility in the public services (the highest placements were reserved for covenanted members of the Indian civil service who were, by and large, Britons recruited in the UK). Anglo-Indians from 'better families' and with a decent education were able to acquire many of the best positions available to local candidates. Hawes notes that, by the 1830s, Anglo-Indians enjoyed a 'virtual monopoly' of the better paid jobs in the uncovenanted civil service – as clerical officers, surveyors, apothecaries, engineers, and so forth; in Madras, they held seventy-two of eighty-eight such jobs (1993: 152).

Despite the serious setback to the community's economic prospects represented by the Company's proscription on Anglo-Indian civil and military employment, within a few decades some of these regulations had been reversed, and new career opportunities had emerged. In a 'Testimonial' dated 21 January 1848 from the 'East Indian Community' of Madras – signed by 1,285 persons – which was presented to Lord Tweeddale on his departure from the Governorship of the Presidency, mention was specifically made of the 'new sources of employment which have been opened to us in the uncovenanted and other branches of the service under your Lordship's administration, thereby elevating our condition, and which calls for this public expression of our thanks'.[8]

The 1871 Census revealed that some 10 per cent of the city's 'minor professions' (writers, accountants, etc.) and just under 13 per cent of the city's 'learned professions' (ecclesiastical, legal, medical, engineering, etc.) were occupied by Anglo-Indians (Cornish 1874: 356). They were especially prominent, for example, in the Indian Medical Department where they would be attached to European regiments as apothecaries and stewards, working under a European surgeon. Ernst notes that company surgeons 'frequently expressed their unease about the presence of a great number of non-Europeans' (1991: 104).[9] The large increase in the numbers of non-official Europeans in British India in the wake of the East India Charter Act of 1833 brought new sources of competition for better-paid jobs in the subordinate services, which adversely affected the predominance of educated Anglo-Indians (Hawes 1993: 395; Renford 1979). The programme of 'Indianization' which officially commenced in the last quarter of the nineteenth century and was revitalized by the Montagu-Chelmsford Reforms following the First World War, and new educational requirements, further displaced many Anglo-Indians from positions which had been considered theirs almost as of right.

By contrast, the male children of ordinary soldiers found themselves with limited opportunities for schooling or work. Those who were fortunate enough to obtain places in the orphanages and poor schools catering principally for Anglo-Indian children were from the start prepared mainly for menial positions. A Report of the Madras Male and Female Orphan Asylums for 1844–45 emphasized that these boys are 'not educated beyond the standard requisite for the . . . subordinate situations to which they are eligible under Government'. On the whole, then, they 'were trained and fed back into society at almost precisely the same level at which they had been extracted' (Arnold 1979: 111).

At the Madras Male Orphan Asylum a workshop was established for boys with the intention to

> make it an effective school of instruction in the mechanical trades in order, partly, so that the minds of the poorer classes of East Indians will be drawn to these hitherto neglected sources of livelihood.[10]

On leaving these institutions, pupils obtained positions as junior clerks, shipmates, sailors, musicians for regimental bands, etc., or were apprenticed to printers, mechanics, cabinetmakers, and other tradesmen. By the middle of the nineteenth century large numbers of modestly-educated but skilled and semi-skilled Anglo-Indian men found employment in a variety of technical occupations related to central government services. Clarke reports that in Madras many were engaged in the Carnatic Corps of Artificers, which was attached to the Gun Carriage Manufactory, 'where they not only work as artificers, but have their minds stored with scientific knowledge' (1878: 6).

Following the Sepoy uprising of 1857 intermediate positions of moderate responsibility (below Europeans but above Indians), or those requiring technical competence in a variety of employment areas, were reserved for Anglo-Indians, who were deemed more trustworthy than natives (see Arnold 1983: 151–3; 1985: 15). This was certainly the employment hierarchy followed by manufacturing industries in Madras. The Madras Chamber of Commerce, in its quinquennial review of 1902-1907, reported that practically all manufacturing industries were then run by Europeans, and when requiring personnel for posts of responsibility, preferred to hire in the UK on attractive terms (see also Misra 1969: 290). Binny's Ltd. was probably typical: 'Top management, organization and control, and the key executive positions, managerial as well as technical, were traditionally the prerogative of British staff, recruited in the U.K. on attractive terms. . .' (DeSouza 1969: 270–1). The Anglo-Indian community, by contrast, 'held a large proportion of the middle echelon posts, particularly in the Mills and Engineering Works. Their practical approach to problems and their general mechanical aptitude, coupled with a certain relaxed attitude to life . . . provided a characteristic touch' (Ibid.). In the public services, too, Anglo-Indians were excluded from the best-paid appointments. Hawes makes the point that 'at his highest pay level, reached after many years of government service, a Eurasian might earn as much as a junior British covenanted servant' (1993: 169).

On the railways – the first rail link reached Madras in 1853 – a similar hierarchy of responsibility obtained until very nearly the end of colonial rule, when Indianization policies took full effect (Mast 1969: 5; Westwood 1974: 81). From the 1860s domiciled Europeans and Eurasians were selected for training in 'upper subordinate' positions (Bear 1998: 62). Arnold suggests that these employees, though only a tiny proportion of the total staff – 4.4 per cent in 1881, 3.6 per cent in 1904, and 2.2 per cent in 1939 – were 'the railway's labour aristocracy': better provided for in terms of pay, education and welfare (1983: 151).

Higginbotham's Guide to the City of Madras (Bremner 1903: 52) mentions the Locomotive and Carriage workshops of the Madras Railway at Perambur which 'have been an admirable training school for hundreds of Eurasian [boys who] have obtained employment on the railways. . .'. The Indian Statutory Commission (Simon) Report suggests that, in 1930, of 50,000 Anglo-Indian men of working age, 14,000 were employed in the railways (1930, Vol XVI, p.277, quoted in Symonds 1987: 33). Around the same time, according to Bear, virtually all the upper subordinate positions were filled by Anglo-Indians and domiciled Europeans (1998: 9). Anglo-Indian leaders estimated that approximately half of the entire community were either employed by or dependent upon the railways.[11]

In the Anglo-Indian population in Madras today there are very few adult householders who were not themselves employed, or do not count at least one recent forebear (grandfather, father, uncle) on the railway, and many trace several. Those who rose to positions of some responsibility earned considerable respect within the community. Even today, people will often be introduced (or introduce themselves) in public as (retired) 'station master', 'inspector', 'foreman', 'senior driver', and so forth. One man whose father and several uncles had been railway employees identified several positions as constituting the local railway elite:

> The station superintendent of Madras Central was always an Anglo-Indian. Top post. Then, the goods agent-salt quotas, [who] controls the whole of the goods traffic, was always an Anglo-Indian. The joint station superintendent at Vijaywada, [where several railways met] was also an Anglo-Indian. Only Anglo-Indians got those jobs. Pride of the community.

Another area of significant Anglo-Indian employment was the Telegraphs Department (see Brown 1994: 100; Symonds 1987: 33). Although community leaders complained that following the Montagu-Chelmsford Reforms restrictions were being placed on the recruitment of Anglo-Indians into the service (see *Annual Report of the Anglo-Indian Association of Southern India*, 1924), those who worked there even at the end of the colonial period emphasized its distinctive Anglo-Indian ambience. In the words of one former employee:

When I joined [the Department] in '45 in my batch we were 120 recruits, boys and girls, fresh from school . . . I think 10 per cent were non-Anglo-Indians. In those days the office was full of Anglo-Indians, so the [others] also got into that way of moving, more Anglo-Indian than Indian. They even learned to speak our way.

While some Anglo-Indian males were employed as skilled technicians in the factories and workshops around Madras (as welders, fitters, mechanics, etc.), the city's slow industrial growth in the late nineteenth and early twentieth centuries, compared to that of Bombay and Calcutta, restricted employment opportunities until the Second World War, when a range of new industrial enterprises located in the south Indian capital (Hyma 1971).[12] By this time, however, indeed following the First World War, Anglo-Indian males faced growing competition in the employment market from increasingly skilled and better educated members of the general Indian public. Existing practices which virtually guaranteed jobs deemed the preserve of Anglo-Indians (on the railways, telegraphs, customs) even to those with minimal qualifications, could no longer be sustained, so that more and more Anglo-Indian males found themselves unable to find work. Although unemployment was nothing new to men from the most disadvantaged levels of Anglo-Indian society, the feeling grew in leadership circles that it was reaching sections of the community – respectable, hard-working technicians and artisans – who had not previously experienced such hardship. Gidney insisted that by the 1930s more than one-third of the male Anglo-Indian population of working age were unemployed (1934: 36), a figure reiterated by other community notables such as Weston (1939: 118) and Snell (quoted in Brennan 1979: 139).

The situation was partly mitigated by the large-scale entry of Anglo-Indian women into the labour market. Whereas, as we have seen, boys in the charity schools and orphanages of Madras had been prepared for trades, the girls were taught needlework, sewing, ironing and 'any other duties which will be useful to them in their station in life' (*Report of the Madras Male and Female Orphan Asylums and Free Day School for Boys*, 1844–45). A handful found (or were found) employment as teachers or domestics, but reports of the various institutions at which they were educated frequently complained that no suitable vacancies were available for them.

Their near-total exclusion from the employment market began to change in the latter part of the nineteenth century. Women were trained and employed at first in the civil nursing service, established in the early

1870s, and subsequently in the military nursing service, set up some two decades later (see Wilkinson 1958). By the early years of the twentieth century they formed a 'large majority' of the staff in government and civil hospitals, as well as in railway hospitals (Hartley 1938). In the same period Anglo-Indian women were also engaged in some numbers as shop assistants in European-owned retail firms in the major commercial centres of Calcutta, Bombay and Madras. Indeed, the Calcutta Anglo-Indian Association's journal, *The Eurasian* of 17 April 1909 complained about their long hours and low wages, as well as the insulting treatment they received at the hands of many customers.

By the second quarter of the twentieth century the exclusion of growing numbers of Anglo-Indian men from the labour market alongside expanding opportunities for female employment led to a significant increase in working women. They continued to enter (mainly primary school) teaching in English-medium schools, nursing and shop sales in even larger numbers, and turned increasingly to office work. At Binny's Ltd., for example, the company historian informs us that 'the ranks of the lady secretaries, stenographers and typists' was 'a monopoly of [the Anglo-Indian] community' (DeSouza 1969: 271). One woman I knew recalled that in the 1940s, when she worked at Binny's, there were eighty-six stenos, 'all Anglos'. Another, who retired several years ago, related how on leaving school she had applied for a telephone-receptionist's job in Tube Investments (a large European-owned firm) where she spent the next thirty years. 'The building was full of Anglo-Indians.' A third related that she had worked for thirty-eight years as a typist at Best and Crompton, during the time when 'the bosses were all Britishers'. There were some twenty Anglo-Indian 'girls' in the office when she joined the company.[13]

The post-Independence Anglo-Indian community in Madras is, if anything, more economically heterogeneous than before. Though still a small proportion of the total population, the elite comprises a larger and more diverse membership of professionals, government officials and business managers – men and women – who have benefited from what they see as the new opportunities available to educated and enterprising individuals in independent India. Anthony (1969: 352) refers to this category as the 'upper-middle class'. Today, they count among their number medical doctors, lawyers, dentists, engineers, architects, academics, members of the Indian Administrative Service, bank officers, business executives, computer programmers, and so forth. Although less so now than in the years immediately following Independence, Anglo-Indians are also well represented in the officer corps of the armed forces, and quite a number have risen to positions of senior command (see

Anthony 1969: 389–92; Symonds 1987: 31); people often mentioned with some pride that a recent head of the Indian Air Force was from the Madras Anglo-Indian community. One woman I interviewed had spent thirty-five years in the Army Nursing Service, retiring with the rank of Colonel.[14]

The middle echelons, or what I shall refer to as the artisan class, is also more diverse than before – Anthony refers to a similar category as the 'lower middle class' (1969: 352). At one pole, there are those still in secure positions on the railways. Although their numbers and proportions in the service have been steadily declining for the past three-quarters of a century, Constitutional guarantees enabled them to retain their privileged access to railway employment for ten years after Independence (see Symonds 1987: 36). Hence, there are many Anglo-Indians in Madras today who either entered railway service or spent the greater part of their working lives on the railways after Independence. One, not untypical, example is a man from a long line of railway employees:

My father was working as a driver when he expired. It was not the normal practice to give his post to one of the children in those days. I applied for an apprentice fireman's job. You really didn't need much [school] qualification. Only a healthy body. They advertised in the papers. I was called for an interview and was selected. They [those who interviewed him] were local officers [ie. no longer Europeans]. I think it helped if your father was on the railways. And my mother was also a railway nurse. After two years as an apprentice I was promoted as a fireman, then [in time] I got further promotion and retired in 1986 as a line inspector.

Similar guarantees were provided in the Telegraphs Department for a decade after Independence. But one woman's work biography underlines the precipitate decline of Anglo-Indians in this employment sphere at the end of this period:

I joined the Posts & Telegraphs thirty-seven years ago. This was 1959. I was SSLC [high school graduate]. I saw an advertisement for a teletypist. Those days we just applied. We had to sit a test and [if successful] we were selected. Mostly Anglo-Indians were interested. I think Indian women were not yet ready to come out [into the workforce]. Oh God, the P&T was still packed with Anglos! In my batch we were nine – seven boys and two girls – and out of the nine we were five Anglos. The Telegraph Ball was still running and there was a tree at Christmas. These faded out in the '60s, when the Telegraphs stopped recruiting [Anglo-Indians]. There was one more batch after mine which contained Anglos. Then it was dead. No more Anglo-Indians. That's the end of our community in the Telegraphs.

Nowadays, Anglo-Indians with limited formal education but good technical skills continue to find employment in established as well as newly expanding industries around Madras: as fitters, welders, electricians, lathe operators, mechanics and repairmen for motor cars, air-conditioning plant, diesel and petrol engines, etc. With the recent expansion of oil exploration in various parts of India a number of Anglo-Indians have found well-paid work on drilling rigs. One young man, who did a three-year National Trades Certificate course after completing high school, has worked for several foreign companies servicing rigs in Andhra Pradesh, the Andaman Islands and West Bengal.[15]

For those who are able to sell their technical skills and experience to employers in the Gulf states, the possibilities for economic betterment are striking. One young man I met while home on regular leave from his job in Saudi Arabia (after thirty-five days on duty), had recently purchased a new flat with his savings.

I started this job in 1984. Most of the drillers working for this [German] company are Anglo-Indians. The assistant drillers are mostly [other] Indians, and the lower categories, roughnecks, are Philippinos. We work with people from all over. Anglo-Indians stood a good chance because the language of communication was English. They didn't ask for qualifications. If you had a good body [ie. were strong] they took you. When you reach a certain standard they send you out for courses. Here, Indian [oil exploration] companies want graduates. But they're not so good at the job.

Because the rewards are so considerable in comparison to what can be earned at home, there is intense competition for jobs in the Gulf, and not a few Anglo-Indians have harrowing tales to tell about the unscrupulous agents who prey on those seeking such employment. One young man – a well-qualified machinist – had been 'dodged' (cheated) on three separate occasions by people who demanded large advances but ultimately failed to deliver the promised jobs.

The prospects for employment in large organizations in Madras are enhanced if individuals excel in sports.

That is India. If you get selected for a state team any company will give you a job. They all have a sports quota, and if you're a champion you stand a good chance. They'll be fighting over you if you're really good. For the sake of publicity.

A number of Anglo-Indians – men and women – acquired their present positions through such a quota.

New avenues have also opened for those with fewer qualifications or skills. The expansion of the tourist industry has created many opportunities for hotel staff, and a number of young Anglo-Indian men I knew were or had been employed as waiters, stewards, kitchen or bar staff in hotels catering for overseas guests as well as highly paid Indian business executives. According to a senior manager in one of the five-star hotel groups in the city – himself an Anglo-Indian who has risen through the ranks – members of the community are especially sought out for such employment.

It's the Anglo-Indian culture – you know how to move with others, how to speak, when you have to be courteous, humble, and all that. So we'd like to see them have some place. Like they had in the railways in the past. Now the only places where you find a lot of the community getting in is hotels, because very few now get into the railways.

Hotels which attract a cosmopolitan clientele also provide opportunities for a number of musicians who are able to play Western popular music, and several dozen members of the Madras community manage to earn a modest living in this way.

At the lower end of the class hierarchy Anglo-Indian males are more hard-pressed than in the past, as non-Anglo-Indians with equal if not better qualifications are able to compete for all manner of jobs, and members of 'scheduled castes' or 'backward classes' are given preference in public appointments. Anglo-Indians with few skills and little education must fall back on such casual labour as bar-bending on building sites, cycle rickshaw driving (both for the young and fit), house painting (which is very seasonal), or work as security guards – an expanding area of employment as the gap between rich and poor widens. But an increasingly competitive labour market for both skilled and unskilled jobs has meant that nowadays there are many Anglo-Indian men who are jobless or without secure employment.

This is partly mitigated by the steady expansion of Anglo-Indian women into the labour force. Recently, as already noted, the better-educated have begun to secure posts of greater responsibility in banking, industry, computing, higher education, etc. Those with fewer formal skills or qualifications are still to be found in nursing or in shops as sales assistants, though in far smaller numbers than in the past. Many, however, continue to teach in (mainly primary) school, and are even more widely employed in offices as typists, stenographers, telephone operators, and secretaries. In the latter category, increasing numbers are acquiring computer and word-processing skills, which are in growing demand in

Madras and can fetch good salaries. More would do so if they could find the money for training which is very costly.

Others now find employment in the tourist and travel industries (as hotel staff, airline stewardesses, caterers, entertainers, etc.). One young woman who works as a receptionist at a large hotel near Madras airport suggested that she was selected over several non-Anglo-Indian candidates because 'for the hotel line you need someone who looks more modern, not so traditional'. Several women work as hairdressers, beauticians, tailors and cooks, and a few even run their own small businesses in these fields. Those from the poorest households can still find (usually part-time) work as domestics, or untrained teachers, or give tuition to neighbourhood children after school. Several make and sell *idli* (steamed rice cakes) from pavement stalls in the slum settlements where they live. Now, as in the past, a few are sex workers.

The majority of households at the lower end of the Anglo-Indian socio-economic hierarchy, and many in the artisan or middle class, are therefore more likely to rely on regular earnings from female members in employment than they are on income from males. The situation thus has echoes of that described by Taylor et al (1990: 995) in their review of research on black families in the USA, where the involvement of black women in the provider role not only indicates a wider acceptance of women's labour force participation, but arises from the precarious and uncertain conditions that characterize the employment and earning patterns of black men within particular segments of the labour market.

The proportion of extremely poor households, containing unskilled and unemployed or occasionally employed Anglo-Indians has, if anything, risen since Independence. This is partly attributable to the large-scale emigration of Anglo-Indians from the better skilled and better educated section of the community (see Chapter 5) to the West. The upshot of these various developments is a higher proportion of households at the lower end of the class hierarchy now than in the past, and a correspondingly smaller concentration of households in the middle and upper reaches (see also Chapter 6).

In addition, recent liberalization and structural adjustment policies in India have, if anything, made matters worse for the poor. They have contributed to an increasing casualization of labour and higher inflation, particularly steep price rises in basic food commodities and dramatic increases in the costs of housing (see below). Thus, the Anglo-Indian poor, along with those of other communities, have not only been excluded from the benefits of India's recent GDP growth but have been its principal victims.

Anglo-Indian hardship, it must be stressed, is not unique to this community, but needs to be seen in the context of high overall levels of urban poverty in Tamil Nadu. According to studies by the Operations Research Group of the Madras Metropolitan Development Authority, Madras has a severely restricted employment base, which is deemed to be a major cause of a high level of poverty in the city, both absolutely and relative to other major Indian cities (see Noponen 1991: 235). The Madras Institute of Development Studies (MIDS) suggests that approximately half the urban population in the state was, in the ten-year period of its study, living below the 'poverty line', and in most years average consumer expenditure levels fell well below this line (MIDS 1988: 106; see also Vera-Sanso 1994: 83–4).

The notion of a 'poverty line', which provides the official measure of poverty in India, has been much criticized. Calculated on minimal food expenditure to meet basic calorific needs, it is widely regarded as an unsatisfactory yardstick of insufficiency (Brass 1994: 291; MIDS 1988; Vera-Sanso 1994: 83–4).[16] The exclusive focus on food, it has been suggested, ignores a range of 'needs' – from health to education to housing – which people themselves may regard as essential. The interpretation of poverty trends, based on the concept of a 'poverty line', moreover, is hugely contentious.

In their own discourses of poverty Anglo-Indians do not employ these official measures, but rather refer to a range of criteria by which such a designation might be claimed. In a speech in 1973 – a recording of which I heard – the president of the Anglo-Indian Association of Southern India reckoned that while in 1950 about 15 per cent of Anglo-Indians in Madras could be defined as poor, by 1970 the proportion had increased to over 50 per cent, despite the fact that about one-third of these were actually in some kind of employment. Poverty, he stated,

> is a terrible blight on the community. It is reflected in the ramshackle housing they call home. It shows up through their diet, their poor state of health, and the aged appearance of [the] middle aged . . . no statistics can describe the lack of hope that characterizes the unemployed or the despair of the worker whose income cannot provide for the subsistence of his family.

Thus poverty here is defined by a cluster of adverse circumstances and depressed conditions rather than by a single measure of hardship, and the Anglo-Indian poor themselves utilize various of these criteria in their own self-descriptions.

The precise numbers of Anglo-Indian poor are, therefore, extremely difficult to estimate (see Chapter 6). Brennan, who studied the community in Madras in the mid-1970s, suggested that 36 per cent were 'a step away from starvation', while 34 per cent were 'in abject poverty' (1979: 131-2). However, it is not clear what measures she was employing or what sources she was quoting. What seems safe to conclude is that Anglo-Indians share with the city's population at large, and in like proportions, a significant degree of privation.

The Education of Anglo-Indians

In any discussion of Anglo-Indian hardship today it is usual for community leaders and intellectuals to attribute a large part of the blame to the failure of young people (mainly boys) to take education seriously and so acquire the qualifications needed to compete for decent jobs. Yet *en bloc* the community ranked as among the most literate in south India throughout much of the colonial period, second only to the Europeans (see *Census of Madras City*, 1871). There has been some concern for the education of Anglo-Indian children almost since the establishment of the British factory and the emergence of this métis community. It may have originally been driven – in Penny's view – by the rivalry between Protestants and Catholics, or perhaps initially by the Company's disquiet at the preponderance of Catholics in the settlement (see Penny 1904 (I): 164). In any event it rested mainly in the hands of the ecclesiastical authorities.

In 1860 Bishop Cotton proposed a scheme for the establishment of a system of education suited to the requirements of the community and properly endowed.[17] In the same year, Lord Canning acknowledged the need for some more extended and effective means of education for Eurasian (and European) children than then obtained. But whereas Cotton concentrated on the establishment of hill schools for the well-to-do, Canning emphasized schools in the cities for the less fortunate, many of whom were receiving no education (D'Souza 1976: 102–4). In 1879 Lord Lytton revived the momentum created by Cotton and Canning by suggesting that some 11,000–12,000 Eurasian and European children in India – over 40 per cent of those of school-going age – mainly the children of the very poor, were not in school, a situation he regarded as scandalous (Mathur 1955: 114-15). Finally, towards the end of 1881, European schools (which were by this time attended mainly by Anglo-Indians) became a special department of public instruction, formally supervised, and entitled to grants-in-aid. But the level of assistance hardly met the needs of these institutions. In 1924, the president and members of Council of the Anglo-Indian Association of Southern India formally drew the attention of the Governor to the fact that 'no additional grants have been allotted to our High Schools to assist us to meet their increased cost since the Great War'.[18] D'Souza suggests that while the schools were nominally 'backed by moral support and financial assistance from the state', in reality they continued to be essentially a 'voluntary enterprise by Christian denominations' (1976: 104).

In 1932 they were renamed 'Anglo-Indian' schools and, according to Graham (1934: 38), 366 such institutions had a total pupil enrolment of some 56,000 children: 58 per cent of these children were in 153 Catholic schools;[19] 20 per cent were in 79 Anglican schools, while 5 per cent were in 23 schools belonging to other Christian denominations; 8.5 per cent were in 75 railway schools (for the children of railway employees (Sanyal 1930: 215)); with the remaining 8.5 per cent divided among 36 establishments affiliated to different religious or secular institutions.[20]

There is a wide consensus within the community that Anglo-Indians did not reap the full benefits of this elaborate institutional structure and so have been – and remain to this day – unable to compete in the educational and employment market. Community leaders had long recognized that, as the president of the Anglo-Indian Association of Southern India put it in 1924, 'a very small number of Anglo-Indian pupils complete a high school course of education by passing a final examination before they leave school, and . . . a still smaller number proceed to a University'.[21]

For most Anglo-Indian leaders, the origin of this failure lay and continues to lie in late colonial circumstances which, as we have seen, ensured employment for many Anglo-Indians with minimal schooling.

a lad in the 6th Standard of about 14 years of age, with no more than a knowledge of the 3R's, was able to get employment easily on the railways or in the telegraph department (Weston 1939: 108).

Yet despite the widespread belief that, on the one hand, education was the key to good job prospects, and, on the other, that Anglo-Indian males were tempted away from schooling by the promise of ready employment, some figures available to the Anglo-Indian leadership seemed to suggest otherwise. In a survey conducted among nearly 200 unemployed men (176 Anglo-Indians and 24 Europeans) and summarized in the *Annual Report* of the Anglo-Indian Association of Southern India for 1924, it was found that unemployment was more prevalent (64 per cent) among those who completed Standards VII or better than among those who went only as far as Standard IV (9 per cent). Those who collected the figures (and others who sought to interpret them) admitted to being puzzled, but assumed that they were due mainly to post-war demobilization difficulties. The large-scale entry of women into the labour market was also given as a possible reason.

Anglo-Indian girls were also apparently able to secure jobs with little but basic schooling. One woman, who had done her nurses' training in the 1960s, noted the differences between the educational demands on her as compared to her predecessors:

> By the time I came to study there was a lot of physics and chemistry. They weren't there in previous times. You didn't even have to have a high school education. Middle school was enough. I had some aunts who were nurses and they said 'oh, we didn't have to learn all this'. The standard of education for nursing went up [because] as medicine progressed you had to know more. The PUC [pre-university course] became compulsory. So Anglo-Indians have faded out [of nursing].

The general feeling among those concerned with the current situation of Anglo-Indians in the employment market is that whereas, before Independence, leaving school early to enter the workplace could be considered a 'rational' decision, nowadays, it is a recipe for unemployment. Despite constant exhortations by community leaders to complete schooling ('only by education can you come up'), many Anglo-Indians (especially males) from poor and even artisan households still fail to go much beyond primary school, and those who do usually do not go on to finish high school. The majority 'discontinue' on reaching eighth or ninth standard.[22] Those who leave school with, by today's standards, few qualifications or none at all, are therefore seen as persisting in an attitude which has lost its rationale. But many are unable to complete their schooling because of inadequate household finances or simply because they do not fancy their prospects. The head teachers in several Anglo-Indian schools I visited in Madras had similar stories to tell about the lack of commitment to studies of, in particular, Anglo-Indian boys. In the words of one:

> In school, the boys are not as interested in their studies as the girls; you get more boys being detained [kept back] because of their lack of interest. Many of them would like to leave school and take up any job and earn a few rupees a day, rather than go to the end of the road, pass their tenth, twelfth, go to college, have a trade. They prefer something today to long term benefits.

The most frequently cited reason for abandoning school is an inability to cope with the high standards demanded in Tamil. The colonial policy towards Tamil (as towards all Indian languages) in European (later Anglo-Indian) schools was, at best, one of benign neglect which both reflected and perpetuated the attitudes towards Indian culture of the British and, subsequently, the Anglo-Indian leadership. For Lobo, the schools' language policy is at the root of the community's 'general disadvantage' (1994: 29). It was not structured to teach Anglo-Indians an Indian language, and, as a result, many failed to pass Indian language examinations – the key to jobs and higher education, certainly from the post-Reforms period into the present (Ibid.: 16). Although state-supported Anglo-Indian schools are now compelled to offer Tamil, many young people still insist that they cannot cope with the high standards demanded and consequently have to leave school before matriculating. A woman who had quit school without completing her high school certificate remarked 'Tamil is very hard, we all cannot master that language. Where [how] we can learn that language? That's why all our Anglo-Indians cannot go to high school, because of the Tamil!'[23]

But other explanations are also offered. Some give as their reasons for leaving school a lack of interest in studying, or a reluctance to apply themselves seriously. Like the Madras pupils Brennan interviewed in the seventies they 'blame themselves' for their failures (1979: 105-6). Others cite poverty as the principal motive: insufficient resources for fees, books, uniforms or maintenance. But a few also question the value of education in a job market which, they insist, is organized along caste lines. Available jobs in public enterprises, they point out, are reserved in overwhelming numbers for members of Scheduled Castes and Backward Classes, so what chance do Anglo-Indians, who are officially designated a 'Forward' community, have?

At the same time, the character of Anglo-Indian schools has been transformed in the face of wider financial, political and educational pressures. For over sixty years now a growing number of pupils in these schools have, in fact, not been Anglo-Indians (or Europeans). Whereas until the 1920s the admission of non-Anglo-Indians or non-Europeans was limited to a 'trickle' (D'Souza 1976: 285), by the 1930s estimates of this intake ranged from 20 to 40 per cent (Ibid.; Graham 1934: 25).[24] The expanding Indian middle classes saw in these schools an opportunity to educate their children in English, to what were acknowledged to be high standards, and pressed for admission on a fee-paying basis (see Lobo 1994: 16). For these schools, the financial incentives to do so were compelling, since they were not well supported by government or the ecclesiastical authorities. Penny makes the important observation that chaplains and missionaries served somewhat different constituencies and each wanted to promote the interests of the pupils in their own schools. The latter established a widespread system for the education of Indians who had converted to Christianity. 'Thus commenced a rivalry which continued until the Eurasian [Anglo-Indian] schools were for want of money almost beaten out of the field' (Penny 1904 (I): 259).

After Independence, these schools were only allowed to continue as a separate system if they agreed to admit a substantial proportion of their children – 40 to 50 per cent – from non-Anglo-Indian communities.[25] In Tamil Nadu, where there are over forty such schools, the average enrolment of Anglo-Indian pupils (as of 1990) was only between 15 and 22 per cent, and in some schools the proportion was as low as 1 to 3 per cent (Ignatius 1990). To the dismay of some Anglo-Indian educationalists and leaders, many of these schools have, in effect, become institutions for the education of well-to-do members of the Indian public on whom their financial viability depends.[26] Although the government of Tamil Nadu has, since 1974, provided a subsidy for each Anglo-Indian pupil in these schools, this has not kept pace with rising costs, and according to the correspondent (chair of governors) of one of the largest of these schools, it now covers hardly one-fifth of the outlay on a pupil. The effect is to discourage these institutions from admitting the very children whom they exist to educate. Needless to say, it is those from the poorest backgrounds who are most frequently excluded. Although various Anglo-Indian charitable organizations provide 'scholarships' for those most in need, and some of the schools themselves set aside funds to help meet the steadily increasing financial demands of their schooling, the numbers able to be assisted in this way are few, and the amounts available are extremely limited.

At the same time, to maintain a favourable level of examination results, these schools are increasingly tempted to exclude from their rolls Anglo-Indians from those backgrounds whose achievements in examinations tend to lower the overall level of marks and so discourage the parents of potential fee-paying pupils from applying. So whereas there is general agreement about the necessity for changing attitudes towards education – completing high school and going on to further study or training, and raising standards – the historical burdens of policies regarding job recruitment, the schools' attitudes to local languages, and inadequate finances for Anglo-Indian education (among other things), have combined with present-day economic hardship to ensure that those most in need of better educational opportunities have least access to them.

The relatively well-to-do, by contrast, have all along had sufficient opportunities to educate their children. In Madras several well-known institutions, such as the Parental Academy, and later Bishop Corrie's grammar school, were specifically for those who could afford fees. Young Anglo-Indians belonging to such families therefore have for some time had a choice of the best Anglo-Indian schools or, indeed, could select to attend those outside the system, like Don Bosco run by the Catholic Salesian order or the Presentation Order's Church Park school, which have for some time been regarded as among the city's elite educational institutions. From at least the second quarter of the twentieth century the wealthiest families have been able to afford higher education for their children (Weston 1939: 136). Symonds suggests that by 1960 10 per cent of Anglo-Indians pursued such courses, a higher proportion than any other Indian community except the Parsis (1987: 36).[27] With the expansion of the Anglo-Indian professional, executive and business class since Independence, increasing numbers of young men and women from such families complete their schooling and go on to university. This inevitably has lead to an even more pronounced divide than in the past between, at one end of the class spectrum, a well-educated, economically successful, Anglo-Indian elite, and, at the other, an only moderately educated, weakly skilled segment which is unemployed or irregularly employed and increasingly impoverished. The artisan class falls somewhere between these two extremes.

Such a portrayal of class hierarchy is not meant to indicate an absence of individual or family mobility. While many household biographies reveal a continuity of either hardship or (though far fewer in number) affluence through several generations, still others indicate a transformation of fortunes over time. For the most part the latter involve an inter-generational descent into poverty. Already at the beginning of the twentieth century Skipton noted how the 'pauperised lowest class . . . is being continually recruited from the hitherto respectable middle-class' (1912: 19). This process was evident in some of the family histories I collected from Anglo-Indians in Madras. If there is a typical three-generation genealogy of decline it would include a grandfather, born during the colonial period, educated to roughly eighth standard, and employed on the railways; his son, born around the time of Independence, similarly educated and either on the railways, or in some moderately paid but secure technical occupation or minor clerical post; and his young adult grandsons today with similar or slightly better school qualifications, but with only intermittent or low-paid employment.

However, not all histories are of deterioration: some of today's successful Anglo-Indian families have emerged from very humble beginnings. Moreover, of late, there are increasing numbers of both men and women from modest, even depressed, backgrounds who, by acquiring good educational or technical qualifications, which lead on to well-paid positions in the local economy or abroad (mainly the Gulf), are in the process of effecting a steady (and in a few cases dramatic) improvement in their family's economic circumstances.

Anglo-Indian Settlement in Madras

With the growth of Madras beyond the confines of Fort St George, Anglo-Indians lived mainly in 'Black Town' to the north and west of the original English factory. In the course of the late eighteenth and early nineteenth century, they also moved into adjacent areas of the city which had originally been villages acquired by the Company. Thus, *The Madras Observer* for 24 October 1861, in an article on the 'district called John Pereira's', which stretched from the General Hospital to Black Town, noted that it 'is inhabited partly by Europeans and East Asians'. A decade later, the *Census of Madras City* for 1871 (p.74) indicated that while Eurasians were still heavily settled in Black Town, they were also to be found in some numbers in adjacent sections to its west. Their highest concentrations were in the district which included Pursawalkam, New Town (later Periamet), Pudupet and Vepery (see Map). Several years later, the *Manual of Administration for Madras*, no doubt utilizing many of the same Census data, noted that 'to the west of Black Town are the quarters of Vepery and Poothoopett [Pudupet], chiefly inhabited by Eurasians' (Madras Government 1885: 91). When, in 1879, D.S. White decided to propose the creation of an Anglo-Indian Association for Southern India, he called his first meeting in the Prayer Hall in New Town, which was said to be a 'stronghold of the Eurasian community'.[28] Several people I knew had spent their early years in New Town and often remarked on its very Anglo-Indian ambience. One prominent member of the Madras community, who has published several newspaper articles on colourful characters in the neighbourhood, writes how during the war years 'New Town presented a picture of prosperity', but now, 'it has disappeared . . . there are just one or two Anglo-Indian families still there. The inexorable rush of leather merchants have taken over the place now called Periamet' (D'Monte 1994).

By the beginning of the twentieth century, *Higginbotham's Guide to Madras* was claiming that 'Vepery is the chief residential quarter of a large section of the Eurasian community who do not live in Black Town or St Thome' (Bremner 1903: 46). One woman, whom I met when she was in her eighties, had spent her childhood in Vepery in the 1920s, and

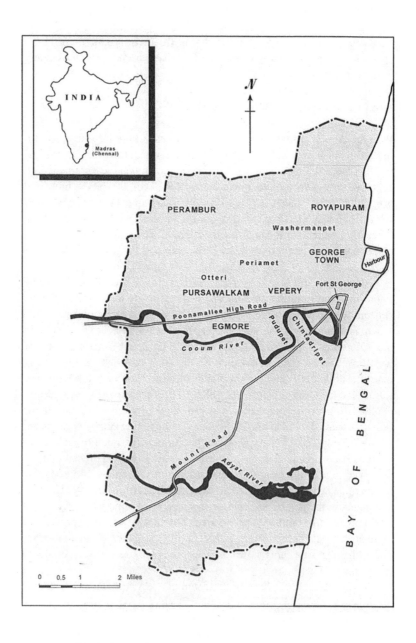

Principal areas of Anglo-Indian settlement in Madras (c. 1948)

commented that 'it felt like 90 per cent of the people around were Anglo-Indians'. There were smaller but substantial concentrations in the neighbouring districts of Pursawalkam and Egmore, as well. The latter, in fact, was the site for the only housing scheme erected in the early years of the twentieth century especially for Anglo-Indian employees of the municipality, and still contains several dozen families. It is referred to by Anglo-Indians in the city as 'the blocks'. In these areas, too, there has been a recent influx of middle-class populations from other parts of Madras, Tamil Nadu or north India in search of building land, houses and business premises, purchasing the properties in which Anglo-Indians have lived as tenants for decades.

With the creation of the first railway terminus at Royapuram north of Fort St George and the completion of nearby Madras harbour in the late nineteenth century, Royapuram became an attractive locus of Anglo-Indian settlement. At the end of the Second World War, the expansion of the harbour and the fishing industry brought new commercial and industrial activity and Anglo-Indians began to move elsewhere as the properties they lived in were bought up.

Following the establishment of the Madras and Southern Mahratta railway workshops in Perambur at the end of the nineteenth century, as well as several large industrial enterprises (e.g. Binny cotton mills) early in the twentieth, the area proved another magnet for Anglo-Indians and increasing numbers settled there. While the population of Perambur more than doubled between 1880 and 1900, it still remained sparsely settled until the middle of the twentieth century (Lewandowski 1980: 48).

Although people were steadily moving away from central parts of the city, George Town – the original Black Town – retained a large concentration of Anglo-Indians until perhaps twenty-five years ago, when a major exodus took place, both abroad and to other parts of Madras. I was frequently to hear reminiscences about people's childhood or early life in George Town, as in other areas of the city. They remembered the names of streets which were 'full of Anglo-Indians' – one elderly man even exclaiming 'Ooo, there was no Indians!' Many could recall the occupants of all the neighbouring houses, the local schools they and their siblings and friends attended, their favourite playgrounds, etc. But, as with so many other central areas of Madras, people were compelled to move away when commercial interests – such as hardware and sanitary merchants in the case of formerly Anglo-Indian sections of George Town – purchased the properties in which they were living.

The church history of Madras provides additional evidence of the pattern of Anglo-Indian settlement in the city. There were, of course, several churches to which Portuguese Catholics had access in San Thome before the establishment of Fort St George. And, as already noted, there were places of worship in the Fort for both Roman Catholics (St Andrews) and Church of England adherents (St Mary's), many of whom were Anglo-Indians. With European and Eurasian settlement outside the Fort new churches and chapels were built. In 1796, Penny tells us, 107 Europeans and Eurasians petitioned the government to erect an (Anglican) church in Black Town, which was consecrated in 1804 as St Mark's (Penny 1904 (I): 650). Others for Europeans and Eurasians in Black Town were built for adherents of the London Mission Society in 1810 (LMS Davidson Street Chapel), for Church Missionary Society devotees in 1818 (Tucker's Chapel) (Ibid.: 260),[29] while the (Anglican) Trinity Church, John Pereira's, was built in 1828. The Old Vepery Church, which had begun life as a Catholic institution, was subsequently taken over by the SPCK, and a new church begun in 1823, which became St Matthias, opened in 1826 (Ibid.: 575-6). Anglo-Indians have also worshipped for many years alongside Europeans in various churches built for the military.[30]

In all the areas served by these churches there were significant concentrations of Anglo-Indians, who have had long associations with most of these places of worship, and who in many of them formed the majority of the worshippers until relatively recently. The Rt Rev Eyre Chatterton estimated that on the eve of the Second World War Anglo-Indians formed one-eighth of the membership of the [Anglican] church in India, and in the civil, as opposed to military, churches comprised the 'larger part of our congregations' (*The Anglo-Indian*, July 1939). Based on his knowledge of the Anglican Church in south India, J.A.H. Bower, grandson of the Rev Henry Bower (see above), wrote that Anglo-Indians formed the 'backbone of our European congregations' (1939: 17). This was certainly the case at St Matthias, Vepery, where – according to several pastors with whom I spoke – Anglo-Indians had, until as late as the 1960s, comprised some 80 to 85 per cent of the congregation. Similarly, Mater Dolorosa (Catholic) Church in Royapuram was, according to the priest and several elderly parishioners, 'an Anglo-Indian parish, completely'. Indeed, while I was discussing the history and composition of this church with its priest-in-charge, an old Tamil gentleman who has been a member of the congregation since 1927 came in and recalled that only his and two other families, and a few Europeans, had not been Anglo-Indians. 'Only to my mother I was talking Tamil.'[31]

Anglo-Indian affiliations to particular congregations, not surprisingly, altered as community and individual fortunes fluctuated over time, circumstances changed, and migrations occurred. In Madras one of the effects of large-scale emigration overseas was to reduce the Anglo-Indian influence in congregations throughout the city. Those which were once entirely or mainly Anglo-Indian are no longer so. Thus, in St Matthias Church, Vepery, they now form hardly one-fifth of the worshippers; in Mater Dolorosa, Royapuram, one-third; in St Patrick's Church, St Thomas's Mount, where Anglo-Indians were once a majority, they are now barely one-quarter of the parish's families; in Sacred Heart Church, Egmore, where previously Anglo-Indians were approximately half the congregation, they are under 20 per cent now; in St Joseph's Parish, Vepery, where they constituted half the parishioners, only one in eight families are Anglo-Indian. These are only a few instances of a fairly widespread pattern.

Church membership has also ebbed and flowed with movements of the Anglo-Indian population within the city itself. Thus, for example, St Francis Xavier Church in George Town had been a mainly Anglo-Indian congregation during the first three decades of this century, and even until the early 1960s Anglo-Indians constituted close to one-half of its worshippers, many of whom were employed in the customs, posts and telegraphs, and railways. By the time I visited it (in early 1992) Anglo-Indians were hardly 5 per cent of the membership. While quite a few left the parish to go overseas after Independence, there has also been a steady movement to other areas of the city, partly to escape what the parish priest described as the over-crowded conditions in this central, densely-populated neighbourhood, but also because the concentration of commercial activity had driven up property prices and put domestic rents beyond the average reach.

Other parishes benefited from internal migrations. At the turn of this century Royapuram's Anglo-Indian population expanded significantly, so that members of the (Catholic) Mater Dolorosa congregation, which had up to then been affiliated as a chapel to nearby St Peter's Church, petitioned the Archbishop of Madras in 1902 to convert it into a Parish church. Several years later their request was granted, the Archbishop acknowledging that 'the numbers of Eurasians and Europeans in Royapuram is increasing'.

In more recent times Our Lady of Lourdes, Perambur, has become an important centre of Catholic worship as Anglo-Indians settled in growing numbers in the area, following the establishment of the railway workshops and other enterprises requiring skilled technicians and artisans. Although they constitute only about one-eighth of the total parish population of 16,000, they form one of the largest Anglo-Indian concentrations in the country and certainly the largest in Madras. Contemporary internal migrations have continued the movement out of inner city districts in which Anglo-Indians had previously concentrated and towards newer neighbourhoods in suburban north Madras.

Since the initial areas of Anglo-Indian settlement were, as already noted, in central districts of the city where pressures on land have been greatest, house rents have probably risen faster in these locations than elsewhere – between two- and four-fold – during the past ten years alone.[32] For example, a couple, their children, and the woman's mother who had been living in a tiny one-room house for over thirty years when I first met them in 1991, had seen their rent nearly tripled by the time I met them again in 1999. Others reported rises of between 30 and 35 per cent between my visits in 1996 and 1999. Households unable to meet the increased rent demands are compelled to find new premises, which means that large sections of the Anglo-Indian population has periodically to relocate. People tend to move to a succession of houses within a neighbourhood, where possible, and eventually to other areas of the city. Since the practice is for landlords to demand an 'advance' of ten months' rent, every move involves the accumulation of what for a family of even moderate means is a large capital sum, and this is usually only possible by going into debt.

While better-off Anglo-Indians tend to live in comfortable, spacious accommodation, with every modern facility, most 'ordinary' families occupy a tiny portion – usually one (or less frequently two) bedroom(s) and a small sitting room ('hall') – of a large house, in which they share bathing and toilet facilities with several other tenants. But while they complain incessantly about the difficulty of finding suitable accommodation, or the high rents and 'advances' they are compelled to pay for it, they also acknowledge the far more precarious situation of less fortunate Anglo-Indians who live in slum hutments ('patch people'), often with broken walls and leaking roofs, without electric light, bathing or toilet facilities; or have no place to call home at all.[33]

During the colonial period only a small minority of Anglo-Indians purchased their own homes.[34] People offer several reasons for this situation. For one thing, a substantial proportion – after the First World War as many as half, as I have noted – were either not in regular employment or were in low-paid jobs. Even those who had steady work occupied at best subordinate positions which earned only modest salaries.[35]

For another, their concentration in railway employment (see above) meant that a good many Anglo-Indians spent at least a part of their lives in one or more railway colonies situated at major railway junctions dotted around Madras Presidency or even further afield – such as those at Villipuram, Golden Rock, Bitragunta, Tambaram, etc. (see also Arnold 1983, Bear 1994). In these, accommodation was related primarily to rank and salary. One woman, now in her seventies, remembers

> I grew up in a railway colony in Tambaram, from the age of seven till nineteen, when I got married. We had railway quarters. We had a verandah, sitting room, a bedroom, a kitchen, bathing and toilet separate. Depending on . . . grade. The top grades had bigger places. They took the rent out of my dad's salary.

One former railway employee, who had risen to the rank of station master, and at the time of retirement was a permanent way inspector, recalled how 'top officers, who were all Europeans, had spacious bungalows. Anglo-Indians were in the middle ranks. So [ours] were smaller.' Others lived for a time in railway quarters, where housing was provided for key staff, but no other facilities. In Madras there were such quarters attached to the Perambur workshops and carriage works, as well as the stations at Egmore, Washermanpet, St Thomas's Mount, Royapuram, etc.

Thus modest incomes and/or 'tied housing' ensured that few railway families had the opportunity to purchase their own living accommodation. The first occasion to do so usually arose at retirement, at which point they were required to move out of employment-related accommodation and most returned or came for the first time to live in major centres of Anglo-Indian settlement such as Madras. At that point, too, those who had been in long-term, secure employment in government offices or larger private firms received lump sum payments from their provident funds.[36] Those who had sufficient resources might purchase property at that time, but only a small minority seemed to have done so. Some explained that the financial demands of supporting large families and children's or grandchildren's education had first call on their retirement savings. A few complained that funds which might have been invested in housing were squandered by profligate forebears (usually fathers) who drank or gambled the funds away. Most, however, indicated that given the avail-ability of housing at reasonable rents until relatively recently even those Anglo-Indians who could have afforded to do so did not think seriously about purchasing their own homes. Now, of course, given the dramatic rises in house prices in the recent past – de Wit (1993: 77) notes that real estate prices rose tenfold over the years between 1981 and 1988 alone – this is no longer an option. A couple who had decided to buy a flat for Rs 13 lakhs (£26,000) in 1994 but had had to delay the purchase, found that it had risen by 50 per cent when they resumed negotiations in 1996. By 1999 people were quoting figures of around Rs 20 lakhs (£30,000 or $43,500) for two-bedroom flats in central districts like Pudupet, while in 'suburban' areas such as Perambur they were said to be selling for Rs 15 lakhs (£21,000 or $30,500). Hence, the retirement benefits earned by a single individual have for some years now been insufficient to meet (the continually rising) costs of home ownership in Madras.[37]

Nonetheless, in recent years there has been a dramatic change in both the attitude toward and the extent of home ownership among Anglo-Indians in Madras. One new house owner remarked

> Now Anglo-Indians want land and a house. In those days most were in quarters . . . they had good houses. But now we're not in the railways, we're in private work. So we're thinking of a house. It's a big investment, and prices double every year or two.

This attitude is most evident among those who have, since Independence, and most especially during the past several decades, obtained advanced educational qualifications, entered professions, and/or found lucrative employment. The huge expansion in the building of condominium-style blocks of flats around Madras has led to new possibilities for home ownership. Individuals with sufficient savings from comparatively high-paying employment abroad now aim to purchase flats outright. One family I visited, one of whose members was employed in Saudi Arabia, had recently purchased one of the fourteen flats in a new block in Perambur. I was told that nine of the purchasers were Anglo-Indians and seven of them had recently been or were still employed in the Gulf.

Furthermore, those with good, steady incomes from employment are increasingly taking advantage of housing loans offered by employers or of government schemes enabling them to take out repayment mortgages.[38] A growing minority of fairly successful Anglo-Indians therefore now live in their own homes. Of the 350-odd households I got to know during fieldwork 15 to 20 per cent owned the houses or flats in which they lived.[39] Since many of these housing developments – and particularly those which are more reasonably priced – are in areas away from the centre of Madras, such as Perambur and newer colonies to the north, there is a steady movement of comparatively successful Anglo-Indians out of districts traditionally regarded as community precincts.

Despite these migrations the Anglo-Indian population of Madras is not concentrated in class-specific enclaves. They tend rather to reside in localities containing people who are economically diverse, and therefore alongside others of dissimilar economic circumstances who, if they are Anglo-Indians, worship at the same churches, and whose children attend the same schools. Apart from a few fairly isolated slum colonies or exclusive neighbourhoods containing a handful of Anglo-Indian families, there is little residential 'concentration' of extremes – either of poverty or wealth. Moreover, Anglo-Indians are not segregated in ethnic neighbourhoods, although there are districts of the city which, as I have shown, have for many years contained large concentrations. Anglo-Indians, therefore, tend to live cheek by jowl with people of different castes, religious backgrounds, and walks of life.

Conclusion

Anglo-Indians are quintessentially the children of colonialism. They are descendants of the initial offspring of unions – formal and casual – involving British and other European men, on the one side, and, on the other, local 'Indian' as well as other women who – especially in the context of south India – came under the inclusive if vague category of 'Portuguese'. Anglo-Indians are thus the inheritors of a diversity of national, ethnic and caste backgrounds. Like other similarly constituted hybrid or métis groups in a colonial context, they were 'subject to a frequently shifting set of criteria that allowed them privilege at certain historical moments and pointedly excluded them at others' (Stoler 1989: 154). This kind of alternation was especially evident in the occupational realm: in the 'early' colonial period, relatively free to follow a range of activities; for a time from the end of the eighteenth century excluded from many civil and most military services under government; from the middle of the nineteenth century allowed favoured if restricted access to positions of intermediate responsibility in central government sectors (railways, telegraphs, customs, etc.) and, from the early years of the twentieth century, in the light of nationalist considerations, increasingly exposed to competition from members of the wider society in virtually all areas of their 'traditional' employment spheres.[40] These latter developments exacerbated the extent of poverty within the Anglo-Indian fold but, at the same time, as women increasingly entered the workplace, they served to mitigate the hardship. Moreover, this latter factor had a profound impact on gender roles in the economy and, as I will discuss in Chapter 6, within the family.

Colonial institutions in which Anglo-Indians (and Europeans) were educated from the late nineteenth century reinforced the policies which shaped Anglo-Indian livelihoods. In the light of the circumscribed positions they were able to fill in selected occupational fields by virtue of belonging to an officially defined intermediate community – and not as a consequence of possessing relevant skills or qualifications – these schools (though offering comparatively high standards of education) came to be seen by many Anglo-Indians as needing only to provide minimal literacy and numeracy. Such attitudes were subsequently to render them unable to cope with the intensely competitive local environment which they were to inhabit in the years before and immediately following Independence. Moreover, in offering a British public/grammar school curriculum and ambience, these schools contributed to positioning this métis group both socially and culturally apart from the mainstream Indian population.

In the post-Independence period Anglo-Indians have gradually lost the protected status they enjoyed in certain occupational niches, and have had to survive in an unsteady economic climate, increasingly subject to global influences which have, if anything, adversely affected those least educated and skilled. Without the protection afforded 'scheduled castes' or 'backward classes' – who comprise the bulk of the disadvantaged in contemporary Indian society – the Anglo-Indian poor feel themselves to be suffering disproportionately. At the same time, the colonial ceiling which confined Anglo-Indians within certain work spaces lifted with the withdrawal of the British, and today there is a small but growing elite – highly educated, cosmopolitan, professional, comfortably off – which, like the upper-middle class in India generally, has benefited from new liberalization and structural adjustment policies.

The result, as I have suggested, is a widening gap between elites and most ordinary people, just as there is in the wider society. Within Anglo-India this class divide is reflected in the housing sector, where a small but expanding number (mainly the elites) own their own homes, while the great majority must rely on generally inadequate and increasingly costly rented accommodation. This housing predicament has its origins in colonial employment regimes which linked housing to certain occupational precincts such as railway colonies, cantonments for the Indian Medical Department, etc. In any case, most Anglo-Indian occupations did not provide the resources, nor encourage an inclination for home ownership, and this attitude only changed significantly some years after Independence, by which time the housing situation in general and the rental market in particular had seriously deteriorated in terms of availability and costs. The reasons for the latter can be related to the expansion – in response to both national and global developments – which have during the last quarter of a century encouraged new commercial enterprises and an influx of populations from other parts of the state, and from other regions of the country. This increased movement into Madras, and especially into central districts of the capital where Anglo-Indians had been settled for generations, has unsettled many families and encouraged, even compelled them, to abandon many of their 'traditional' neighbourhoods and relocate to other parts of the city in search of more affordable housing. Thus, while Anglo-Indians have for many years moved residence in pursuit of new employment opportunities, current migrations are largely involuntary responses to increasing financial pressures over which they have no control.

In creating policies and institutions to educate Anglo-Indians and situate them in the intermediate echelons of a colonial occupational hierarchy, British officials defined and circumscribed, and thus reified this community. It is to the issue of imposed and self-imposed boundaries, and their crossings, that I turn in the next chapter.

Notes

1. This was rebuilt in 1675 as St Andrews Church, but destroyed by the British some seventy-five years later 'when they became suspicious of the activities of the Roman Catholic priests during the wars with the French' (Muthiah 1981: 27).
2. The register of St Thomas's Church in Bombay for the greater part of the eighteenth century shows actual marriages to have been few and far between, and when they did occur in nearly every case the names indicate a British man marrying a woman with a Portuguese name, or sometimes one with no surname at all (Tindall 1982: 138).
3. Taylor reports that in seventeenth-century Batavia, in the Dutch East Indies, 'Portuguese could be heard on the streets, in the markets, in church, and in the households where European men kept Asian mistresses. Its dominance . . . has been explained by the fact that many slaves were bought on the Coromandel and Malabar coasts of India' (1983: 18).
4. Bower himself was the descendant of a captured French soldier (see Note 6).
5. Ricketts pointed out that in Bengal 'the greater proportion of them are Mohamedans' (1831: 53). Boxer remarks that Albuquerque had encouraged his men to marry the 'white and beautiful' widows and daughters of the Muslim defenders of Goa' (1963: 64).

– 53 –

6. Not only Portuguese surnames were sometimes altered: according to *The Anglo-Indian*, journal of the Anglo-Indian Association of Southern India, (November 1934), the Rev Henry Bower (1813-1885), an eminent theologian, Tamil scholar, and founder of a prominent Anglo-Indian Madras family, was himself the son of a captured French soldier by name 'Bowyer or Bouverie' (see also Moore 1986a: 38).

7. There are, for example, among my acquaintances, a Brown married to a Pereira, D'Cruze to Hurtis, Berryman to D'Monte, Fernandez to Roberts, Zscherpel to Lawrence, Gonsalves to Jones, Philipsz to Murray, Vanderputt to Chase, Satur to Broughton, Dubier to Edmonds, Suares to Remington, Vieyra to Pritchard, Thibbles to Rozario, and so on. In Bombay and on the west coast Jews with a European male ancestor would occasionally claim an Anglo-Indian designation which, constitutionally, they were entitled to do (Roland 1989: 113). Moore (1986a: 110) has a photograph (taken just before Independence) of a Bombay police officer who is Jewish and 'considered himself of the Anglo-Indian clan [since Jews] sometimes intermarried with them'. I know of no 'Jewish Anglo-Indians' in Madras.

8. The 'Testimonial' was transcribed from the original by Theon Wilkinson, Wynyard R.T. Wilkinson and Christopher Hawes.

9. As educational requirements for entry were raised the numbers of new recruits began to diminish – see *The Anglo-Indian*, Nov 1926, April 1927; *Memorandum Relative to the Deputation of the Anglo-Indian and Domiciled Community of India and Burma to the Rt. Hon. the Secretary of State for India,* 30 July 1925. The five-man deputation was led by Sir Henry Gidney, president of the All-India Anglo-Indian Association between the wars.

10. Report of the Madras Male Orphan Asylum 1848-49. See also Law (1915).

11. *Memorandum Relative to the Deputation of the Anglo-Indian and Domiciled Community of India and Burma to the Rt. Hon. the Secretary of State for India,* 30 July 1925.

12. This slow growth is attributed by some economists to the European business community which resisted state efforts to encourage development on the grounds of interference in private enterprise (Lamb 1955; Lewandowski 1975).

13. Women reported that most large firms during the 1940s and 1950s required them to leave their jobs at marriage or when they became pregnant. In the course of time most of these employers abolished

such restrictions, although many women decided to give up their jobs after the birth of their first child.

14. A recent edition of *Anglos in the Wind* (1 (4) 1999), a quarterly magazine for Anglo-Indians published in Madras, carried a feature article about another Madras-born retired senior officer in the Military Nursing Services.

15. Those who have worked or are working on rigs, however, report that it can be very short term and unreliable, and others, who have attempted but failed to obtain such employment, usually suggest that technical abilities alone are not sufficient. The mother of one young man who had not been successful offered the view that 'you need to know who's who, [and] to have money to put something in their hand. Only that way. . .'

16. The 'poverty line' is defined as the cost of an all-India average consumption basket which can provide 2,100 calories (in the urban areas), translated to Rs 264.10 per capita per month at 1993–4 prices.

17. Cotton felt that if one thing would be subversive of 'our Indian Empire' it would be 'the spectacle of a generation of natives highly educated . . . side by side with an increasing population of ignorant and degraded Eurasians' (*The Anglo-Indian*, July 1937). There is a view, however, that by the latter part of the nineteenth century the state was less concerned about educating Anglo-Indians than it was in improving facilities for the growing numbers of British in India who were filling median positions in administration but were not paid enough to send their children back home for schooling.

18. *Annual Report*, 1924, Appendix VII 'Address to H.E. Lord Goschen'.

19. Around this time a Catholic European Schools Association was also formed in Madras Presidency, with some forty schools affiliated (see *The Anglo-Indian*, April 1933).

20. Anthony 1969: 109 provides a similar breakdown, although he omits a small category of five 'Armenian/Jewish' schools with some 650 pupils.

21. *Annual Report*, 1924: Annexure I: Memorandum of the Rev H.Y. Necker, 27 December 1924.

22. In a sample survey of Anglo-Indians in Calcutta, conducted in 1957/58, the researchers found that 62.6 per cent had studied beyond primary level but had not matriculated. Another 30.8 per cent had matriculated but not completed university (Anglo-Indian Survey Committee 1959: 7).

23. Exemptions are granted pupils whose parents are in transferable service; they are allowed to choose not to study Tamil. Parents who

can afford to do so can also send their children to private schools which are not subsidized by the state government and where Tamil therefore is not a compulsory subject.

24. D'Souza estimates that in 1916, only 5 per cent of pupils in Bengal's Anglo-Indian schools were not Anglo-Indians; by 1960 the figure had risen to 60 per cent (1976: 287).

25. Roy gives the figure as 50 per cent, Tiwari as 40 per cent (Roy 1974: 59; Tiwari 1965: 191).

26. D'Souza suggests that there may have been fewer Anglo-Indian children in school in 1960 than in the early 1930s (1976: 285).

27. I have not seen any other figures to support this contention, but it contradicts the general perception within the community that Anglo-Indians were poorly represented within the universities.

28. See 'A Brief History of the Anglo-Indians and the Foundation of the Anglo-Indian and Domiciled European Association of Southern India, at Madras: from information gathered from the records of the Association', unpublished, n.d.

29. *The Anglo-Indian*, journal of the Anglo-Indian Association of Southern India, in its edition of June 1926, paid tribute to the late Rev Canon J.W. Foley, who had been in charge of Tucker's Chapel, which, it was noted, had a 'very large Anglo-Indian congregation from various parts of Madras, but chiefly local'.

30. One example is the Garrison (Anglican) Church in St Thomas's Mount (built in 1816). Anglo-Indian Protestants also worshipped in Christ Church, Mount Road, built under the auspices of the Colonial Church Society and consecrated in 1852. In addition, they were to be found in St George's (Anglican) Cathedral (built in 1815) and St Andrew's (Presbyterian) Church (1821), though in smaller numbers.

31. Other Catholic parishes in which Anglo-Indians formed a substantial proportion of the congregation were St Joseph's (Vepery); St Mary's (George Town, much of which comprised the former Black Town); St Francis Xavier (George Town); St Anthony's (Pudupet); Queenship of Mary (Chintradipet); Sacred Heart (Egmore); St Roques' (Washermanpet); and St Peter's (Royapuram).

32. A handful of domestic groups live in some form of public housing where rents are low and have increased more gradually.

33. I met a number of Anglo-Indians who were homeless. A woman whose husband had left her was living with her young son and three (non-Anglo-Indian) friends on a derelict site between several busy roads. Another was sleeping in the grounds of the Government Hospital. A man in his sixties gave his address as 'Platform, Central

Station', while another in his fifties has camped for years on a relative's roof terrace: 'Her husband's mommy married my grandfather's brother, so she lets me sleep at her place. I get up at four o'clock, have a wash, and go out before anyone is awake. I keep my clothes under the stairs.'

34. Of the people who did have domestic properties, many sold them after Independence to finance their emigration abroad.

35. Their low pay (by comparison with Europeans, but not with 'Indians') was a source of sporadic grievance.

36. For the most part, there were no pension arrangements until some years after Independence.

37. This is of course not a problem confined to Anglo-Indians: de Wit observes that Madras has an 'acute housing problem' for its fast-growing population (1993: 76).

38. A few poor Anglo-Indians have managed to be rehoused in slum clearance or other state housing schemes for those on low incomes. I met only one such family.

39. A survey of Anglo-Indians in Calcutta in 1957–8 found that about one-fifth were living in their own premises (Anglo-Indian Survey Committee 1959: 13).

40. Discriminatory and/or Indianization policies have usually been portrayed by community chroniclers as one aspect of Britain's 'betrayal' of Anglo-India. The 'Indian' view, of course, has been that Anglo-Indians were pampered and privileged by the colonial rulers.

Guarding Boundaries – Crossing Boundaries

We [were] confronted with a serious problem of leakage out at the top, and an infiltration on all sides.

I had a lot of interaction with Europeans because a number of Anglo-Indians sang in the choir at St Mary's [in Fort St George]. The British kept a distance from the Anglo-Indians. So far and no further. They drew a line. You keep within that boundary and everything will be fine. It was a very explicit order, even if unspoken. They used to organize picnics for the choir; there was that interaction. And they always treated me very decently. But I knew that I was not fully accepted. Had I been an Englishman it would have been a different matter. I was certainly never invited to join their clubs.

Introduction

The postcolonial condition is frequently represented by its theorists as characterized by, among other things, hybridities and ambivalences. The implication is that contemporary ambiguities contrast with the clear-cut identities of the colonial period. This chapter questions the validity of such a distinction, arguing that the efforts of European colonizers to demarcate subject populations were frequently undermined by the very people on whom they sought to impose their classifications, giving rise to porous boundaries and permeable groupings. Fluidity may thus be said to typify the external no less than the internal environments of Anglo-India.

In the course of the nineteenth century colonial elites sought to formulate elaborate schema for assigning individuals and groups, mainly on the basis of racial criteria, to what were deemed bounded and incommensurable categories. In various spheres of activity – and particularly, as we have seen, where employment hierarchies were concerned – this was the responsibility of what Bear calls the 'colonial copyist', whose work 'was to inscribe the marks of the state on the bodies and lives of

Anglo-Indians and others' (1998: 280). In this chapter I first examine modes of colonial boundary-marking, focussing especially on the ways in which the dominant British, after more than a century of paying little heed to their differences, sought to distinguish and distance themselves from Anglo-Indians. Yet in spite of determined efforts to demarcate and guard the lines of division, they continued to be breached, and this chapter considers the principal ways in which such 'transgressions' occurred. It first examines British discourses on Anglo-Indian women, who were perceived as especially threatening to these exclusive categories of rule through mimicry and sexual enticement. It then considers the censuses and finds not only that many Anglo-Indians, in their desire to claim a 'European' designation, resisted the official labels allocated them by the authorities, but that others seeking to 'infiltrate' the Anglo-Indian fold were involved in similar acts of subversive, even audacious self-definition. Finally, the chapter considers cross-boundary marriages which, in spite of official disapproval, continued to occur throughout the colonial period, further underlining the permeability of lines separating Anglo-Indians from Europeans, on one side, and 'native' Indians, on the other. It ends by considering contemporary forms of cross-boundary unions and their implications for the offspring.

Erecting Boundaries

During the seventeenth and eighteenth centuries British officers and officials employed by the East India Company were much less concerned than were their nineteenth-century successors about drawing rigid social and cultural boundaries between themselves and the local populace. There are countless examples of European men who 'went native', became 'Indianized' – dressing, dining and generally living in the fashion of local dignitaries, adopting what Cohn terms a 'Mughal-Indian style of life' (1987: 425; also Wilkinson 1976: 45). Most 'lived like Indians at home and in the office, wore Indian dress, and observed Indian customs and religious practices' (Nandy 1983: 5). Indeed, like many such early colonists, they 'produced a quotidien world in which the dominant cultural influence . . . was native' (Stoler 1989: 154).

The métis offspring of these unions, and especially those from a reputable paternal background, were in most respects treated as quasi-Europeans, and enjoyed many of the educational and employment benefits available to the well-born, which included being sent to Britain for their education. This is not to suggest an absence of racial awareness or prejudice before the nineteenth century, or that colonial people were invariably made welcome in the metropolitan country. A Captain in the 73rd Regiment of Highlanders stationed at 'Pondamalee' on the outskirts of Madras, in a letter dated March 1780, expresses opposition to transporting to Britain the Eurasian offspring of British officers or civilians and 'Portuguese wenches' because 'the birth which nature has given them constantly exposes them, however unjustly, to ridicule and reproach' (Munro 1789: 50). But the Captain is not only concerned for the sensitivities of the Anglo-Indians thus sent for schooling. He is also worried that they might, by their presence, 'degenerate the race, and give a sallow tinge to the complexion of Britons' (Ibid.: 51). A few years later Martha Graham, in her *Journal of a Residence in India*, also suggests that 'it is a cruelty to send children of colour [i.e. Anglo-Indians] to Europe, where their complexion must subject them to perpetual mortification' (1812: 128).

However, there is a wide consensus among scholars of colonialism in India that from the end of the eighteenth century a transformation occurred in the relationship between British rulers and those over whom they exercised dominion. We have seen how a series of measures introduced by the East India Company severely restricted and diminished Anglo-Indian employment opportunities. Contemporaneously, changing attitudes to colonial peoples – fostered by the growing influence of the Evangelicals and the flowering of European racist philosophy – led to an increasingly negative evaluation and status abasement of the Anglo-Indian population by British elites in India.

By the middle of the nineteenth century these attitudes had hardened to the point where they amounted to an ideology of contempt if not detestation. The 'colonial sin of mésalliance' gave rise to a plethora of pejorative terms for Anglo-Indians, among them 'half and half' and 'chee-chee' (see Note 6) (Kirk-Greene 1986: 278). They were also assigned a host of stereotypes – from mental deficiency brought about by malformation of the 'hybrid' brain to premature depravity on account of excessive sexuality. Their character weaknesses, moreover, were thought to be inherent in their blood.[1]

Such evaluations were reproduced in the fictional literature of the Raj. For the colonial European novelists the tragedy of the Anglo-Indian was racially determined (Younger 1987: 30).[2] In this literature, Anglo-Indian character, as Greenberger has pointed out, is 'uniformly presented as unfavourable', the image 'constantly harsh' (1969: 53). They lack moral fibre, will-power, strength, stamina and honesty, and are 'slave[s] to wild passions' (Naik 1994: 63). Kipling, for one, was repelled by the 'half-caste', the Eurasian who is 'neither flesh nor fowl', those disturbing 'rem(a)inders of the sexual traffic across the racial divide' (Roy 1999: 87). In the view of Gist and Wright, this literature 'rarely depicts . . . Anglo-Indian[s] . . . as admirable persons of unblemished moral character or outstanding intellectual competence' (1973: 44). Indeed, in nineteenth-century novels, there is almost a denial of Anglo-Indian history and existence. Not only is inter-marriage or, for that matter, concubinage disapproved of, but, as Greenberger has noted, whenever a story features a liaison between a European man and Indian woman, the (Anglo-Indian) children born of such a union are not allowed to survive. 'Even true love . . . is not enough to overcome the "impossibility" of such a relationship' (1969: 67). Anglo-Indians were deemed a threat to the 'unique position' of the colonial rulers 'based on racial superiority' (Ibid.: 54). In this regard, any Westernized community was viewed as menacing (Ibid.: 66), a theme developed by Mannsaker. She likens the hostility directed at Anglo-Indians ('those of mixed blood') to that aimed at Bengali *babus* ('those of mixed cultures'), and argues that the British 'tended to dislike and despise those Indians who came closest to the declared aims of their Westernising policies' (1980: 50).[3]

These racial attitudes led to a growing separation between colonial officials and Anglo-Indians, with the latter subject to increasing social exclusion by the British elite. Mrs Fenton, who arrived in India in 1826, noted the 'prejudice existing here . . . against half-castes' (quoted in Steuart 1913: 96), and revealed her own bias in her journal (Dyson 1978: 243–4). Emma Roberts, another contemporary observer, commented that '[t]o be seen in public with, or to be known to be intimate at the houses of Indo-Britons [Anglo-Indians], was fatal to the new arrival in Calcutta; there was no possibility of emerging from the shade or of making friends or connections in a higher sphere' (1835 (III): 97–8). The Reverends Daniel Tyerman and George Bennet, LMS missionaries who toured the Society's stations between 1821 and 1829, including those in south India, wrote about the 'strong prejudices against the Indo-Britons'.[4] The Rev William Miller is also quoted as mentioning the 'proud and overbearing conduct of Europeans in general towards [Anglo-Indians]', while the Rev Beynon referred to 'the manner in which [Anglo-Indians] are treated – their being excluded from all respectable society'. These prejudices did not entirely escape the mission societies themselves. Most, for example, paid their Anglo-Indian missionaries less than Europeans (the Wesleyan Society only half), and gave them no vote or seat on their committees. The LMS, after debating the matter in some detail, opted from the 1830s to pay its Anglo-Indian missionaries on the basis of their 'racial' origin rather than their utility.[5]

By the latter part of the nineteenth century the colonial hierarchy was perceived as a stark divide between the British and their subject peoples, including Anglo-Indians. Many of the latter encountered the separation primarily as an accepted, if unspoken, understanding that members of each 'community', while interacting civilly at their places of employment or in other formal contexts, were expected to live their social lives apart from the other. One prominent pre-Second World War Anglo-Indian author related the story of a European recently arrived in India who was thought to be 'too familiar' with even senior grade Anglo-Indian employees at work, and was ticked off by his superiors and told to keep his distance. '[M]ost of us have experienced this prejudice, which takes many forms' (Wallace 1935: 50). Occasionally this intolerance took a hostile turn, especially if the normal hierarchical relations were inverted. A much-respected contemporary Anglo-Indian leader in Madras recounted how his father's life had been made 'miserable' by a European subordinate on the railways who

> could not stomach having to work under what he called a "WOG Foreman" and would always disobey orders. However father carried on despite all the provocation. But the strain of daily bickering began to tell on him and he would narrate his problems to mother each evening. After a time father took ill and died.

Yet despite attempts on the part of the colonial rulers to erect and guard the boundaries between British and Anglo-Indian, there were constant challenges to these social barriers.

Threatening Boundaries

British discourses of disdain towards Anglo-Indians were frequently focused on women. Emma Roberts, in *Scenes and Characteristics of Hindostan*, notes how 'prejudices against "dark beauties" (the phrase usually employed to designate those who are the inheritors of the native complexion) are daily gaining ground' (1835 (I): 43). We also have Bessie Fenton's remark (in *The Journal of Mrs Fenton*, covering the years 1826–30) that, whereas in the past, 'when European ladies were rarely met with, [Anglo-Indian women] held a place in society which they have now [1827] entirely lost' (quoted in Steuart 1913: 96). Although she writes specifically of Bengal, her comments almost certainly apply more generally in India.

The Anglo-Indian woman was seen as silly, brainless, fast, loose and shameless. An anonymous 'visitor' to Madras in 1811 wrote that European men generally held Anglo-Indian women in contempt, and thought them 'not the most attractive companions', because they were 'proud, cold, and insensible' (Anon. 1821: 22). In letters from Madras between 1836 and 1839, the wife of a district judge asserted that '[t]hese half-caste girls are in the depths of ignorance, indolence, and worthlessness' (Maitland 1843: 273). A century later, a former inspectress of schools in the Bombay Presidency, which included the 'European' schools Anglo-Indian girls attended, suggested that they were, 'as a class, very apathetic, careless and, with a few outstanding exceptions, entirely lacking in ambition' (Graham 1934: 43).

Apart from such images invoking their shallowness, British discourses on Anglo-Indian women were often concerned with their attempts to claim kinship through cultural affinities, mainly in the spheres of language and dress. Despite the diverse origins of the Anglo-Indian population, English had early on become their principal tongue, the language in which they studied, worshipped, and communicated with one another. What could have been regarded as a bridge linking the British and Anglo-Indians (since no other resident community in India claimed English as its first language) was in fact treated by most British in India as a presumptuous incursion into their linguistic (as well as social and cultural) territory. As we might expect, there was (and still is) a wide range of language ability within the Anglo-Indian community, by and large reflecting the speaker's education and class position. The majority of Anglo-Indians, of moderate means and with only an average amount of schooling, spoke and still speak a distinctive kind of local English, with characteristic modes of expression, inflection, slang and humour. It is this 'distinct variant' of English which Maher has labelled an 'Indian language' (1962: 25). And it was this brand of English which the British in India came to scorn and ridicule. Writing in the first half of the nineteenth century, Emma Roberts proclaimed that the English language has 'degenerated in the possession of the "country born" [whose] pronunciation is short and disagreeable, and they usually place the accent on the wrong syllable: [it has] acquired a peculiar idiom' (1835 (I): 42–3). Their characteristic language became a recurrent theme in discourses on Anglo-Indians, and again it was usually women's speaking style which drew most comment. Nichols insisted that the 'Anglo-Indian girl . . . is easy to "spot" [because] she cannot disguise her voice; it has a curiously shrill "overtone", particularly when she laughs' (1944: 224). Upper-class British families, according to MacMillan, were wary of employing Anglo-Indian nannies (despite being much less costly than women imported from England) because of their 'unfortunate' accent (1988: 128). This mode of speech (and sometimes the women who used it) came to be labelled 'chee-chee', and was the butt of endless British mockery.[6] Similarly, the adoption of what was regarded as European costume by Anglo-Indian women during the colonial period was regarded as menacing by British women.[7] Emma Roberts seemed perplexed that 'rich Indo-British ladies attire themselves in the latest and newest fashions of London and Paris', adding somewhat enigmatically that these were 'greatly to their disadvantage'. On the other hand, she was equally dismissive of 'those of an inferior class [who] content themselves with habiliments less in vogue, caring little about the date of their construction, provided that the style be European' (1835 (III): 20). Others saw only ostentation and tastelessness (see Kinkaid 1938: 219–20; Maitland 1843: 273; Naidis 1963: 419). Hawes notes how Anglo-Indian adoption of European modes was treated with contempt, as something of a caricature which was seen to 'diminish British standing in Indian eyes', and European women in the ruling circles consistently sought new styles and materials to escape emulation by Anglo-Indian women (1993: 274–5).[8] In the English-language novels of empire the stereotype of an Anglo-Indian woman included her 'vulgarity in dress' (Mannsaker 1980: 35).

Indeed, in these novels as much as in the general attitude to Anglo-Indians, the latters' greatest fault lay in their 'presumptuous efforts to appear like the English' (Narayanan 1986: 88; see also Naik 1994: 61). For Bhabha, such mimicry involves the borrowing of 'inappropriate objects that ensure its strategic failure', but also menaces by 'disclosing the ambivalence of colonial discourse', threatening to 'disrupt its authority' (1994: 86–8). Thus, women probably drew a disproportionate amount of British hostility aimed at the Anglo-Indian community precisely because they were seen as the principal and most visible 'mimics', constantly holding up a mirror in which Europeans imagined themselves parodied. At the same time, 'class attitudes', as Hawes points out, no less than racial considerations, were 'important influences on British behaviour towards Anglo-Indians' – in view of the fact that the great majority were descended, on both sides, from the poorest sectors of society (1993: 17, 20, 114). Since dress and accent 'were integral elements of class recognition' (Ibid.: 280), such matters received abundant attention in British representations of Anglo-Indian women.

These discourses targeted women because the latter also threatened the boundary between British and Anglo-Indian in a very immediate way: through their 'enticement' of European men. Before turning to marriages across this divide, however, let us consider another way in which the lines demarcating separate populations were breached – namely, during body-counts.

Crossing Boundaries: Colonial Censuses

Colonial censuses, Cohn argues, were about fixing the social categories by which India was to be ordered and governed (1987). In the case of Anglo-Indians, the major concern of those with some interest in measuring their numbers since at least the early nineteenth century was the seeming impossibility of arriving at anything like an accurate count, arising from the continuous flouting of census categories. In 1826 Sir John Malcolm is reported as having stated that 'no correct census has ever been taken of this part of the population' (quoted in Gaikwad 1967: 39), an observation which was to be reiterated by any number of British officials involved in or commenting upon subsequent census results over the years.

By the end of the eighteenth century SPCK missionaries were reporting 'considerable numbers of children born annually in the British settlements in the East Indies of European fathers and mothers who are natives . . . [there are] born annually not less than . . . seven hundred at Madras and on the coast of Choromandel' (see Penny 1904: 507). Yet despite what was assumed to be the rapid growth of the Anglo-Indian population during the course of the nineteenth century – occasioned by a substantial influx of both non-official British and other Europeans (most of them males) as well as British soldiers – Anglo-Indian recorded numbers remained comparatively meagre.[9] The commissioner in charge of the Madras count, for example, referring to the recorded Anglo-Indian figure of 26,374 in the Madras Presidency for 1871, remarked that 'The wonder is, considering how much the Portuguese, Dutch, French and early English settlers intermingled with women of the country, that the numbers should be so few' (Cornish 1874: 73). His surmise was that 'like all hybrid races, probably the tendency [was] to extinction or to reversion to the pure native type' (Ibid.).[10]

Another feature of the Anglo-Indian count which drew comment was the seemingly erratic rise and decline in community figures, both regionally and nationally. So, according to the 1881 census of Madras Presidency Anglo-Indian numbers had fallen by over 17 per cent, to 21,892, since the census of 1871. McIver, in charge of the later count, dismissed his predecessor's explanation, and reasoned that since Eurasians had not suffered from famine mortality, and did not emigrate, the decrease must be 'partly illusory' (1883: 58). He suggested that since much of the decrease occurred on the west coast, it is likely that many Goan Catholics who had been returned as Anglo-Indians in the previous census had been omitted in this, because on this occasion the definition of 'Eurasian' had been more scrupulously applied (Ibid.). In the following decennium Anglo-Indian numbers increased by over 21 per cent, leading the census commissioner to admit that 'trustworthy statistics cannot be obtained', and to bemoan this situation, since 'the question whether the true Eurasian community is increasing or decreasing is of considerable scientific and administrative importance' (Stuart 1893: 309). It was then decided to appoint Eurasians as enumerators of blocks in which Eurasians and 'pseudo-Eurasians' were most to be found. This resulted in a decrease in Eurasian returns in ten of the twenty-two districts of the Presidency during the 1901 census, although only a fall of under 2 per cent in total (Francis 1902: 134). All such remedies were apparently short-lived, however, and failed to provide the reliable figures sought by census officials. Between 1921 and 1931 the recorded Anglo-Indian population in the Madras Presidency again fell by nearly 10 per cent, from 26,023 to 23,492.

On the all-India stage, Anglo-Indian numbers rose with some constancy, although census commissioners were no less suspicious of the figures than their regional counterparts. Between 1891 and 1901 the count increased by approximately 9 per cent (from nearly 80,000 to 87,000), in the following decennium by 15 per cent (to 100,400), and in the one after that by some 13 per cent (to 113,000). These percentage increases far exceeded those of the general population: the latter rise, for example, must be compared to an increase of only 1 per cent in the total population of India (see Hedin 1934: 168).

One of the issues which most exercised officials was the assumed inclination for Anglo-Indians to declare themselves 'Europeans' and thus to distort the figures for both categories (see McIver 1883: 53; Stuart 1893: 308; Thurston 1898: 72–3). In the late nineteenth century European women born outside India still formed a relatively small proportion of the covenanted or non-domiciled European group (1:3.5 in Madras Presidency in 1881), but women were recorded as outnumbering males in the domiciled community (1.04:1). These latter figures convinced the census commissioner for the Presidency that 'a large section of the so-called country-born female Europeans are Eurasians . . . for the women are altogether out of proportion to the well-known facts' (McIver 1883: 55).[11] The commissioner for the Indian census of 1921 also insisted that the figures for the 'domiciled community' (domiciled Europeans and Anglo-Indians) were 'always somewhat doubtful, owing to the tendency of the latter to return themselves as Europeans' (quoted in Hedin 1934: 169).

Following the census of 1931, the commissioner reckoned that, since as many as 55,000 of the 155,555 returned as 'European British Subjects' were born in India, 'we may take 30,000 as the number of Anglo-Indians who should be deducted from the total of European British Subjects and added to that of those returned as Anglo-Indians . . . by this calculation the figure of Europeans in India would be reduced to 125,555 . . . while that of Anglo-Indians is correspondingly raised from 138,395 to 168,400' (Hutton 1933: 426).[12]

British census officials seemed to focus exclusively on individual physiognomic features as the primary explanation for 'passing'. Thus, for Hutton, Anglo-Indians 'not handicapped by excessive pigmentation' were those most likely to return themselves as Europeans (Ibid.). From time to time, those who spoke for and about Anglo-India made similar assumptions. Weston, for example, wrote that 'Instead of being proud of our heritage . . . we have many times denied our origin, especially if we happened to have been born with a fair complexion' (1939: 72). But most Anglo-Indian leaders, while not denying the effects of skin colour, looked to the wider political environment of especially twentieth-century colonial India for an understanding of the forces impelling Anglo-Indians to identify themselves as Europeans. With the approach of Home Rule and then Independence they realized the growing importance of population aggregates and consistently inflated community numbers beyond the official count provided by the censuses as a way of underlining the extent of 'evaporation' of Anglo-Indians into European ranks. Against the 1911 census aggregate of 100,400, Warden suggested a figure of 250,000 for the 'domiciled community' (1915: 4) – the great majority of them Anglo-Indians. Two decades later Sir Henry Gidney told the Simon Commission that at least 40,000 Anglo-Indians were incorrectly classified as Europeans in the 1931 census, and put the '[real] strength of the community' at 'somewhere between 175–200,000' (1934: 32). Since numbers became crucially important for the purpose of drawing up electoral rolls Gidney bitterly attacked the 'thousands' of Anglo-Indians

> who spend their lives pretending to be pure Europeans . . . masquerading under the euphonious name of Domiciled European, squeezing into clubs from which if their coloured relations were known they would be excluded. . . We have seen enough and known enough of the antecedents of many of the Domiciled Europeans to be able to put most of them to utter shame.
> (*The Anglo-Indian*, July 1928).

His successor as president of the All-India Anglo-Indian Association also insisted on declaring a much higher figure for Anglo-Indians than that given by the censuses. In 1941, according to Frank Anthony, despite an official count of 140,422, the real number of Anglo-Indians was between 250,000 and 300,000 (1969: 9).[13] But while he shared his predecessor's disapproval of those who denied their Anglo-Indian identity, the responsibility for these practices, he argued, lay outside the community. For one thing, he reiterated a common complaint that if Anglo-Indians hoped to reach positions of eminence they could only do so as Europeans. Hence, 'they were made and encouraged to call themselves Europeans'. Alternatively, if Anglo-Indians did manage to achieve some prominence in their own right, they were very soon declared Europeans by those (Europeans) who recorded these accomplishments and thereby 'filched' from the ranks of Anglo-India. For another, Anthony accused both the European administration and the leadership of the domiciled European community of having followed a deliberate policy during both world wars of encouraging Anglo-Indians to enlist in the regular armed forces as Europeans. Indeed, during the First World War and for much of the Second World War they could only enlist if they did so as Europeans. Moreover, when they were recruited Anglo-Indians were paid less than Europeans of the same rank which further encouraged the former to make false declarations.[14] Finally, he insisted, the British – in a departure which contrasted with earlier practices designed to distance Anglo-Indians – were fostering 'renegadism' by registering Anglo-Indians on the European electoral rolls. In the Constituent Assembly in March 1946, in an exchange with the leader of the European group, he declared: 'I say you have deliberately emasculated my Community. You do it in order to inflate your electoral rolls in order to get inflated representation in the Legislature' (Anthony 1969: 170–5).[15]

Census officials and the Anglo-Indian leadership were perplexed not only by the tendency for Anglo-Indians to declare themselves Europeans, but by the significant numbers of those apparently not deserving of an Anglo-Indian label who proclaimed themselves as such to the census takers. Thus, in his *Report on the Madras Census* for 1881 McIver referred contemptuously to the 'many Pariahs and Native Christians who have adopted a travesty of European clothes and would return themselves as Eurasians if allowed to do so' (1883: 58). Ten years later the census commissioner again acknowledged the untrustworthiness of the Eurasian figures because 'many persons who are really natives claim to be Eurasians' (Stuart 1893: 309; see also Thurston 1898: 72–3). Francis attributed the abnormal rate of reported growth of the Anglo-Indian community in Madras Presidency in the decade leading up to the census of 1901 to 'Native Christians who had taken to European ways and dress having returned themselves as Eurasians with the idea of enhancing their social position' (1902: 134). These practices presumably persisted, were noted by officials commenting on subsequent censuses as well, and were certainly not confined to the south. In his General Report on the Indian census of 1891 the commissioner made reference to the Eurasian population for the Bombay Presidency and added 'amongst whom there are no doubt a good many Goanese or others with Portuguese patronymics' (Baines 1893: 178). Several decades later similar concerns were still being expressed. Hutton concluded that

> some allowance must be made for the return of Indian Christians as Anglo-Indians. It is possible that a number of the descendants of Portuguese dependents, whose practice it was to take their masters' names and who are found in certain districts in Bombay and Bengal where they are known respectively as 'East Indians' and 'Feringhis' returned themselves at this census [1931], as in previous decades, as Anglo-Indians . . . it is difficult to estimate their number in the Presidency towns. (1933: 430)

Concern at such 'infiltration' was echoed periodically in the Anglo-Indian parochial press. Thus, in a letter dated January 1909 to *The Anglo-Indian Empire*, published in Bombay, a correspondent complained that in Bombay 'East Indians' (Native Christians) and 'Goanese or Natives of Portuguese India' are classified as Anglo-Indians. Several years later *The Anglo-Indian Review* (Journal of the Anglo-Indian Empire League) for February 1916 protested at the tendency for Indians to 'forsake their own racial names and assume names which are those of European races, and thereafter pass themselves off as Eurasians or Anglo-Indians'.

The aspect which most engaged the attention of those who expressed concern was the threat to what were deemed the vested interests of Anglo-Indians from those spuriously claiming such a designation. At least as far back as 1894 the Surgeon-General was asked to do something about the 'pseudo-Eurasians' who were attempting to enter the 'Warrant Medical Service' (Indian Medical Department), reserved for Europeans and Eurasians (see *The Anglo-Indian*, October 1939). Warden later suggested that the threatened influx was on a broad front: 'there are those who are styled Anglo-Indians but who are not such, whom we have seen in "European" schools, in positions on the Railways . . . and on the lists of Anglo-Indian charities' (1915: 66–7).

In Madras, similar misgivings were expressed. Indeed, infiltration was sometimes regarded as more prevalent in the Madras Presidency than elsewhere. In September 1917 *The Anglo-Indian* reported on a Minute presented by the Anglo-Indian Association of Southern India urging the authorities to be vigilant against the adoption by Indians of 'European names and Anglo-Indian characteristics' in order to become eligible for Anglo-Indian privileges. 'This evil', it insisted, should be met by legislation and by individual and collective action. European (later Anglo-Indian) schools were another exclusive preserve thought to be targeted by infiltrators. In an editorial entitled 'The Invasion', the same journal (27 June 1917) argued that one of the main 'gateways' into the Anglo-Indian fold was through the orphanages and poor schools. There were stipends or other advantages provided for Anglo-Indian children which were in the gift of the school authorities, and the editorial alleged that 'at least 50 per cent of the pupils [in these institutions] are pariahs, pure and simple'. Some years later, in a speech to the provincial conference of the Anglo-Indian Association of Southern India, one delegate returned to the same theme, insisting that many 'bogus' Anglo-Indian children were 'enjoying privileges reserved for Anglo-Indian children owing to the laxity of the educational heads and clergy' (*The Anglo-Indian*, March 1940). The Roman Catholic churches and mission organizations were especially criticized, as one letter in *The Anglo-Indian*, October 1934 phrased it, for 'registering all and sundry as Anglo-Indians, no effort being made to ascertain if they are really such'. Although this letter drew a vigorous and indignant rebuttal in the next issue of the journal from the headmaster of one of Madras's leading Catholic orphanage and boarding schools, similar accusations were made from time to time against this and other churches, virtually all of which were run and staffed by non-Anglo-Indians – whether Europeans or Indian Christians. Clergy were also blamed for admitting 'thousands' of children to baptism as Anglo-Indians without appropriate credentials.[16]

During both world wars attention turned to the Auxiliary Force of India (AFI) which was considered another Anglo-Indian preserve. However, according to an editorial in *The Anglo-Indian* of 27 June 1917 this corps was 'packed with coloured men'. A generation later, with the commencement of the Second World War, the journal was reporting an influx of 'masqueraders' into the AFI as a result of the minimum wage of Rs 55 fixed for Anglo-Indians by the Government. After much lobbying the Anglo-Indian Association announced that it had succeeded in persuading the Officer Commanding the Madras contingent to refuse admission to persons of 'doubtful pedigree', and to insist on recruits producing 'nationality certificates' signed by the Association's President (*The Anglo-Indian*, January 1940). Others were not too sure their representations to the authorities had been so successful. Several months later members of the Association were told that 'A good many of the NCOs in the units are masqueraders, and as no self-respecting Anglo-Indian can entertain the necessary amount of respect or regard for these upstarts, in the interests of military discipline, his prudent course is to keep out of the force' (*The Anglo-Indian*, March 1940). In the December issue of the same journal, an advertisement appeared, inserted by one of the Circles (branches) of the Anglo-Indian Association of Southern India, and signed by its chairman.

A WARNING

Ladies and Gentlemen

Guard our Association against harbouring masqueraders and thereby helping them to secure employment in Government and Railway services, and also recruitment to HM regular British Forces and AF(I) Units reserved for Anglo-Indians.

While there were occasional Anglo-Indian voices, such as that of Dover (1937: 115), who ridiculed the 'periodic protests of Eurasian leaders against the assimilation of "foreign elements"', which he described as 'an urge for purity among the impure', most prominent Anglo-Indians saw this influx as contributing to the community's social ills. Nevertheless, this ingression presented something of a dilemma for the leadership. On the one hand, as the foregoing discussion suggests, they thoroughly disapproved of such subterfuge, and recognized the threat it posed to the few occupational and educational privileges available to members of the community. Since this accretion occurred, in Anthony's words, 'at the lowest level', it 'was a drag on the community' (1969: 116), i.e. community status was compromised in the eyes of both respectable Europeans and Indians. At the same time, these additions to Anglo-Indian numbers bolstered their constituencies, both within the various Associations they led, and vis à vis the Government in their struggle for greater representation and influence. In the half-century leading up to Independence there were recurrent claims from within the community that 'infiltration' of bogus Anglo-Indians into the Associations was keeping the genuine articles from joining. Thus, a correspondent to *The Anglo-Indian Empire* (1 May 1909) remarked that 'in Madras a number of . . . bona fide Anglo-Indians fight shy of the Association because of the indiscriminate admission of pure Asiatics'. A similar comment appeared some years later (28 January 1918) in a letter to *The Anglo-Indian*:

there are large numbers of Anglo-Indians holding aloof from the Association ... deterred by the fact ... that those who claim membership therein are not all Anglo-Indian: they do not feel inclined to sit cheek by jowl with the pure and unadulterated pariah though he masquerades in European clothes.

More than twenty years later the same sentiments were still being aired in the journal:

Unless the Association is prepared to unequivocally declare itself hostile to bogus Anglo-Indians and act accordingly it will never win the confidence of many genuine Anglo-Indians who at present keep out of its membership. (*The Anglo-Indian*, March 1940)

Thus, at least some Anglo-Indians felt that the leadership was not pursuing the 'masqueraders' and 'infiltrators' as vigorously as they might have done. Certainly, while protesting adamantly at the 'evaporation' of Anglo-Indians into the ranks of Europeans, and arguing for a compensatory inflation of the community's recorded population as a result, Anglo-Indian leaders did not attempt to calculate the numbers spuriously alleging an Anglo-Indian designation. To do so – and to argue for a corresponding reduction of official Anglo-Indian numbers – would obviously have affected the size of the constituency they claimed to represent.

The community's leadership, and probably most well-to-do members, also had an ambiguous attitude towards the many Anglo-Indians who, whether inadvertently or by design, traversed community boundaries in the opposite direction, 'disappearing' into the general Indian population. Cornish's remark (noted earlier) about the hybrid's tendency to 'rever[t] to the pure native type' (1874: 73) was an attempt to explain Anglo-India's low census numbers in terms of earlier nineteenth-century views on the fate of 'mixed races'. But it highlighted a process which had been previously ignored, and was to remain largely unrecognized throughout the colonial period, both in official British circles and the community itself. Hawes has shown that in the early colonial years, when British men returned to Europe, with few exceptions the Indian companion and her Eurasian children were compelled to remain in India (1996: 8). Gist and Wright suggest that the 'greatest seepage' out of the ranks of Anglo-India probably occurred when 'European or Anglo-Indian fathers did not assume responsibility for their [children's] upbringing and the burden was therefore placed on the Indian mother' (1973: 87).[17]

This practice did not change significantly during the course of the nineteenth and early twentieth centuries when the female partners of

British men (usually ordinary soldiers) were more likely to be Anglo-Indians. Unless there was strong support from families and/or community institutions – schools, orphanages, charities – the women and children thus 'abandoned' might be lost to Anglo-India as they blended into their socio-cultural surroundings. Yet it was not an exodus which Anglo-Indian leaders and intellectuals necessarily wanted to prevent. In a rare mention of this outflow in the pages of *The Anglo-Indian*, an editorial for 7 February 1917 remarked that there are 'hundreds of people of mixed European and Indian blood already submerged beyond recall; submerged among a section of the Indian population worthy in themselves, but who certainly are not exemplars for Anglo-Indians with the blood of Englishmen in their veins'. Several months later a correspondent urged that those who 'practically or closely approximate to the Indian standard . . . should not be interfered with. It is unwise to retard the process of adaptation to the environment' (*The Anglo-Indian*, 4 April 1917). The extent of this 'seepage' cannot be known, but it may very well have been a significant factor in the depression of Anglo-Indian numbers during the colonial period.

In the wake of India's Independence the tendency for Anglo-Indians at the lower end of the class hierarchy to 'melt' into the families and communities of their surroundings has, if anything, probably increased (see below). However, the kinds of census artifice which saw Anglo-Indians at the opposite pole of the socio-economic hierarchy declare themselves Europeans has all but disappeared. The end of the colonial regime displaced the dominant group to which Anglo-Indians had sought affiliation, along with the social cachet attached to European identity. At the same time, the ending of most Anglo-Indian privileges in employment, and the establishment of special concessions for those in the most disadvantaged sections of the wider society,[18] removed the pretexts for other Indians without European forebears to seek recognition as Anglo-Indians.

Madras city which, now as in the past, vies with Calcutta as the largest centre of Anglo-Indian settlement in the country, has experienced a substantial reduction of this population since Independence due to emigration (see Chapter 5). But their numbers are probably even more difficult to establish now than in the past: since 1961 Anglo-Indians have not been counted separately, but have been subsumed within the Indian Christian community. Moreover, census figures for those claiming English as their first language – which some suggest provides a measure of the Anglo-Indian population – are not a reliable indication of their strength since many other people make similar assertions. Census figures for the

Madras city community between 1871 and 1941 never went above 13,500 or below 9,600. Community leaders estimate their numbers at between 10,000 and 15,000 today.

In a recent review of demographic data collection in 'less developed countries' since 1946 Cleland notes the increasing difficulty of conducting 'high-quality censuses', and casts doubt on the accuracy of data regarding the reporting of age or date of birth and the total count (1996: 438). In the Indian context, one of the main problems would appear to be the omission in the censuses of a 'significantly higher proportion of the population than is generally supposed' which results in serious errors in calculating growth rates (Dyson and Crook 1984: 2). What emerges from the foregoing discussion is that the difficulties inherent in gauging Anglo-Indian numbers has all along been not so much a consequence of inadequate counting techniques on the part of census enumerators, as fluid notions of belonging on the part of at least some sections of the population and so the reality of porous boundaries dividing them. It is in the socio-cultural rather than the technological domain that the question of numbers needs to be approached.

The issue of individual mobility has hardly been addressed in Indian studies. Mandelbaum, referring mainly to movement within the caste (*jati*) system, observes that 'leaving one's group and passing as a member of some other . . . is a possible mobility tactic but, insofar as can be known, it is not often done successfully' (1970 (2): 471). In Rowe's view, however, we know little about such movements because individuals are far less likely than groups 'to publish accounts of their activities' (1968: 202). What seems evident is that the dynamic motivating and enabling mobility into and out of the Anglo-Indian fold was, at least during the colonial period, quite distinct from that generally reported for the wider society (see Bailey 1957; Béteille 1965: Silverberg 1968). Whereas most people in India were only able to move as part of (mainly caste) groups once wealth and/or power permitted it, the kinds of machinery for re-classification discussed above were based largely on individual will and circumstance, although these were obviously only activated in specific political, social and cultural environments. Censuses allowed, even invited, the deliberate self-transformation of identities. Hence, if conditions encouraged it and there were enabling mechanisms to abet it, individual mobility undoubtedly did occur even among those belonging to groups which would have expected only to advance as a collectivity. Where populations like the Anglo-Indians emerged which blurred the divide between colonizer and colonized and, moreover, like the Euro-colonial communities out of, alongside and against which they existed, were themselves internally heterogeneous in terms of class, status and physiognomy, the possibilities for personal mobility were much enhanced.

But the decennial censuses were not the only occasions on which community lines were crossed. Indeed, new identities were often only asserted against the background of 'marriages' which had already traversed these indeterminate boundaries.[19] The next section explores the unions of Anglo-Indians with partners outside the community.

Crossing Boundaries: Out-marriages

In Chapter 2 I examined the kinds of relationships involving European men and Indian women which gave rise to the Anglo-Indian population. The female offspring and descendants of the original liaisons between European males and local women soon became a potential source of concubinage and marriage for subsequent generations of European men in India. Indeed, Hawes suggests that 'the frequency of marriage of British men to the Eurasian daughters of men of similar social status has been largely overlooked' (1996: 5). Until well into the first quarter of the nineteenth century many officers married Anglo-Indian women, frequently the daughters of brother officers (Ibid.: 11). The female children of impoverished officers were often placed in military orphanages, and the officials in these institutions took an active part in seeking out suitable European husbands for their charges (Ibid.; also MacMillan 1988: 116). But as the British within the ruling circles increasingly distanced themselves from the Anglo-Indian population, marriage (and concubinage) involving these men and Anglo-Indian (as well as other Indian) women was discouraged and its frequency reduced significantly. With the rise in the numbers of women arriving in India from Britain,[20] a migration encouraged, it has been argued, mainly to police the growing racial divide (Stoler 1991: 64–7), the 'better off in British society were more likely to marry British [than Anglo-Indian] women' (Hawes 1996: 80, 154).

But despite efforts to safeguard the boundaries of the European community, Anglo-Indians presented a constant 'temptation'. It is therefore not surprising that a great deal of British rhetoric focused disapprovingly on the sexual charms and allure of Anglo-Indian women. They acquired a reputation for being 'hot-blooded', and since they were presumed to be 'absolutely riddled with sex and very beautiful' were 'comparatively fair game' for European males (MacMillan 1988: 106). Emma Roberts was both intrigued by and disparaging of the fact that, in spite of 'half-castes' being debarred from Government House, 'the charms of the dark-eyed beauties prevailed . . . [so that] these young ladies form the only individuals of their sex who enjoy greater privileges than are allowed to the masculine portion of the same class' (1835 (III): 97–8).

Even a sympathetic observer like William Huggins, who was sensitive to the social and economic plight of the Anglo-Indians during the first quarter of the nineteenth century, thought their young women too prone to 'lounging, siestas, dressing, dancing, and flirtation' and apt to 'seek marriage greedily' (quoted in Dyson 1978: 221). An anonymously written article in the *Calcutta Review* (1859) suggested that young East Indian (Anglo-Indian) women experienced a high mortality rate, and attributed this 'fact' to early marriages and their 'passionate precipity' (see Bear 1994: 537). While the railway colony, in which many contemporary Anglo-Indians now in their senior years spent at least a part of their lives, evokes immense nostalgia and fond reminiscence, for the colonial British it was a place 'rife with rumours about the infidelities of [mainly Anglo-Indian] railway wives' (Westridge, quoted in Bear 1994: 537). The fictional literature, too, presented the Anglo-Indian woman as a 'siren' who beguiled and tempted men (Moktali 1994: 73), or as a promiscuous husband hunter (Younger 1987: 136).[21] In a recent autobiographical memoir by an Anglo-Indian woman, the author notes that many of the British troops in India 'had taken the cheap literature seriously, imagining they would have easy conquests with Anglo-Indian girls' (Moore 1986a: 138).

Despite their discouragement unions continued to occur across this divide. Men belonging to the British official and military hierarchies sought out (and were in turn sought out by) women from good Eurasian families (Hawes 1996: 19). Remarking on the aspirations of many Anglo-Indian women to marry into European society Emma Roberts commented that they could 'only with the greatest reluctance be prevailed upon to unite themselves to persons of their own class' (1835 (III): 97–8). And while this remark refers specifically to Calcutta, it highlights what was obviously an acceptable ambition – even if not a widespread practice – for Anglo-Indian women in British India more generally, with the full knowledge and consent of their families, to form relationships with Europeans of appropriate rank. Though disapproved of by British authorities, 'mixed' marriages at this social level, though much reduced in number, continued to occur into the twentieth century.

Most unions, as we might expect, involved less well-to-do Anglo-Indian women and European males lower down the colonial class hierarchy – men in the ranks, small merchants, artisans, etc. Girls in orphanages were often pursued as partners by ordinary British soldiers, with the consent and connivance of orphanage personnel (Hawes 1996:

40). Emma Roberts, writing in the early part of the nineteenth century, noted that non-commissioned officers and privates in European regiments, 'if men of character', were permitted to take wives from the Lower Orphan School in Calcutta, which educated and provided for the children of deceased soldiers. But they had to 'choose by the eye alone at a single interview' (1835 (I): 109). At the beginning of the twentieth century Penny observed that Eurasian girls in Madras were 'much sought after as wives by European soldiers, especially if they were educated at the Military Female Orphan Asylum' (1912: 112). F.E. Penny, meanwhile, remarked that a suitor was only allowed to appear at the orphanage after he had been 'seen and approved of by the chaplain' (1908: 212–13).[22]

From the latter half of the nineteenth century Anglo-Indian women increasingly married members of the domiciled European community, the descendants of those who had come to India in various official and non-official capacities after 1833 and stayed on in the country. While a distinction was usually made between domiciled and non-domiciled Europeans – the latter including the British elites who spent only a limited time in India – the difference was by no means clear, and grew less so in the course of the colonial period. People of wealth and standing, even if long resident in India, were likely to acquire the social qualifications which would enable them to be accepted in British elite circles. And they could always 'return' to the United Kingdom. Many non-domiciled Europeans (such as soldiers or railwaymen brought out from Britain), by contrast, might choose to remain in India after completing their service, and thereby to become 'domiciled'.

Anglo-Indians recognized the thin line separating these Europeans from their own ranks. In a 'dissertation' entitled 'Anglo-Indian and Domiciled European' (*The Anglo-Indian,* July 1928) Gidney ridiculed the pretensions of the latter to a separate existence. Not only were they, like the Anglo-Indians, country-born and for many purposes labelled 'statutory natives of India', but

[t]here are very few families that have lived in India for two or three generations, as 95 per cent of them have done, who have not inter-married into Anglo-Indian families, chiefly of the 'albino' variety, and 95 per cent of these people, who spend their lives pretending to be pure Europeans are Anglo-Indians and have mixed blood, but for obvious reasons, they are anxious to remain aloof from their darker brothers.

Gidney thus highlighted the significant overlap created by inter-marriages. A not uncommon union involved time-expired British soldiers who had taken service with the Indian railways, telegraphs or other employment, settled in the country and married Anglo-Indian women (Heathcote 1974: 74; MacMillan 1988: 47). Arnold suggests that the families of domiciled European and Anglo-Indian railwaymen had, by the 1920s, so inter-married as virtually to form a single community (1983: 153). Another was the even more common relationships between Anglo-Indian women and British soldiers which existed well into the twentieth century. Among households at the lower end of the Anglo-Indian class spectrum which I got to know during fieldwork in Madras, perhaps one in fifteen traced kin ties to fathers and grandfathers who had come to India with the British Army during or between the two world wars, and married or cohabited with Anglo-Indian women. In one household I visited my hostess was the daughter of a British soldier stationed for a time in Madras, whose regiment was subsequently transferred:

> I don't know his regiment. I don't know what happened to my father's papers; I only have my baptism certificate. My mother married again. He too was in the army and he too went away. There was one girl from him, my half-sister.

In another instance, the marriage of a young Anglo-Indian woman to a sergeant in the Lancashire Fusiliers was arranged by mutual friends:

> He was quite nice; I can't say anything [critical] about him. The trouble was he was repatriated and [at first] I couldn't go with him because I was expecting a child. Later, I didn't know where he was so I couldn't apply to go to the U.K.

It is perhaps worth remarking that marriages involving Anglo-Indian men and European women occurred far less frequently because for one thing there were very few of the latter in India and for another such unions were judged by the British in India as quite unacceptable in the colonial environment (see Hawes 1996: 87).[23] Ballhatchet notes how it was regarded as of overriding importance that elite English women should be protected from physical contact with Eurasian males (1980: 108–9).

This penchant for (hypergamous) marriage outside the Anglo-Indian fold is undoubtedly to be explained, in part, by the desire for greater economic security and social status. It is also to be understood, in the context of the widespread belief within the community, encouraged in a variety of contexts by early Company policies favouring Anglo-Indians, and subsequently articulated by community leaders, that Anglo-Indians had 'British blood' in their veins, were therefore of British 'stock', and deserved to be regarded as such (see Chapter 4). And the more the British elites sought to distance themselves from Eurasians the greater the latters' insistence on common kinship with the rulers. Marriage was but one obvious way of demonstrating and reinforcing this conviction that the boundaries between the two groups were more imagined than real. Anthony, the late president of the All-India Anglo-Indian Association, who claims some interest in anthropology, even refers to unions between Anglo-Indians and British as 'endogamous' (1969: 8).

Contemporary Crossings

In postcolonial Madras there is still a pronounced inclination among the more affluent Anglo-Indian families for women to marry 'out', but the motives and directions underlying these unions have altered. They are encouraged by the increased possibilities for meeting young men from other communities in university and work contexts. Growing numbers of Anglo-Indian women, as we saw in Chapter 2, now go on to higher education and enter professions and occupations at levels of responsibility. As a result, they frequently find partners from non-Anglo-Indian families of similar or higher class status – mainly well-to-do Indian Christian Tamilians, but from outside the Christian and/or Tamilian fold as well.[24]

These unions can be understood not as assertions of common kinship with members of these bride-taking groups, as in the colonial past, but in terms mainly of a search for improved financial security and status, and the belief that these are unobtainable within the Anglo-Indian community. For the comfortably-off parents of an out-married daughter, the choice seemed inevitable. According to her mother:

> My youngest daughter was going with an Anglo-Indian boy, but then she met this Indian Christian boy and when she learned about the background of his family she fell in love with him. He is a very cultured boy and the parents are very cultured too. When I heard that she wanted to marry a non-Anglo-Indian I was a little upset, but then everybody advised me 'it is better you give her to somebody who would look after her, instead of giving her to an Anglo-Indian boy who might not be able to support her.'

Conversations with Anglo-Indian leaders or intellectuals about marriage would almost invariably come round to what some saw as the haemorrhage of women from better-off families out of the community. After a bemoaning of the growing trend, there would follow the observation that Anglo-Indian males do not make attractive partners because they are not suitably educated, and so unable to obtain good employment. As one former head teacher in an Anglo-Indian girls' school put it:

> We have the problem of better educated girls and less well educated boys. People are thinking of their future, and the future of their children. Who are they going to marry? If [the boys] are not educated, are they going to be husbands fit for their daughters? So it looks like these girls will end up marrying boys of similar education but from outside the community. And it is happening already.

Occasionally, these gender differences in education are construed as a cultural gap, so that there are few common understandings between them. Another head teacher, this one of an Anglo-Indian boys' school, remarked:

> Our girls prefer to marry a Srinivasan or a Somaswamy [non-Anglo-Indian names], who they meet at College or in the office, and who they can talk to on the same wave-length. What can they say to an Anglo-Indian boy who left school after eighth standard?[25]

Moreover, women belonging to the small number of elite Anglo-Indian households which identify themselves as part of a rapidly expanding national, even transnational, network of cosmopolitans, will tend to look for partners in families of like position irrespective of group association. In this network, English is the language of everyday communication; educational and professional accomplishments or success in the modern economy are the principal measures of rank; friendships transcend caste, ethnic or religious affiliation; and lifestyles have a recognizably international character. In such (small but growing) circles, marriages are increasingly being forged on the basis of mutually acknowledged select status and shared elite culture, without reference to ancestry, caste or even religion. Educated and sophisticated Anglo-Indian women fit easily into such a milieu. Not uncommonly, their non-Anglo-Indian husbands have attended Anglo-Indian schools, grown up alongside Anglo-Indians and established close friendships in the community, and are at home in its 'culture', including the speech forms and humour of Anglo-India.

Although, as I noted in Chapter 2, young men in well-to-do families are nowadays increasingly well educated and employed, they are still a small if growing minority, and the overall impression remains of significant numbers of affluent and even middle-class Anglo-Indian women seeking husbands outside the community because of a dearth of 'suitable boys' within it, i.e. young men able to provide both companionship and security in marriage.

There are, of course, barriers to such cross-ethnic marriages, just as there were in the colonial period. But while official policy, on the one hand, and British race and class prejudice, on the other, limited the outmarriages of Anglo-Indian women during the nineteenth and early twentieth centuries, since Independence the principal impediment has been caste. Outside the Anglo-Indian fold, among the educated and prosperous classes in cosmopolitan cities of India, the preference remains for caste-endogamous marriages. While the contours of an endogamous caste in an urban setting may differ from those in the rural area, status and/or purity concerns still combine to exclude Anglo-Indians from the range of potential partners for most respectable high-caste families. This is no less true for Indian Christian than for Hindu caste groups (Caplan 1984). When individuals in these families defy such proscriptions by seeking to marry Anglo-Indian women, the consequences can be severe. There are numerous stories of the family's refusal to attend the wedding of a young man marrying an Anglo-Indian woman, of a son's repudiation, of his wife's exclusion from their home, and so on. Sometimes, relations are restored with the birth of grandchildren, but not invariably.

It is not uncommon for Anglo-Indians to explain this opposition by other groups in terms of the dowry lost to the families when their sons marry 'out'. An Anglo-Indian leader, referring to the marriage of a successful professional woman from a prominent Anglo-Indian family to her equally successful husband from an even more eminent Indian Christian family, remarked on how his parents were furious at the union and refused to acknowledge it for years. This, he suggested, was mainly because, had the young man married in his own community (caste), 'the parents would have been able to demand lakhs in cash, a car, even a house maybe' from their prospective in-laws. But all this was lost because 'Anglo-Indians don't give dowry'. Since dowry transactions tend to operate almost exclusively within, indeed, in effect to define the boundaries of endogamous units (Ibid.) marriage outside the group not only threatens to compromise the status of the family, and the wider lineage and caste, but entails the sacrifice of significant material resources.

At the lower end of the class spectrum a different pattern of external unions has developed. Here, it is mainly Anglo-Indian males who seek partners among women outside their own community. Although relatively undocumented, there is some evidence that such unions occurred during the colonial period, even if they attracted little official attention. Hawes suggests that one option available to poor Anglo-Indian men would have been to marry Indian Christians (1996: 88). Another would have been to find non-Christian partners within the neighbourhoods in which impoverished Anglo-Indians lived (Gist and Wright 1973: 87). And, indeed, early this century Anglo-Indian spokesmen in Madras were exercised by the 'low caste [women] who seek to better themselves by marrying into poor but bona fide Anglo-Indian families. . .'. (*The Anglo-Indian*, 28 January 1918).

Just as Anglo-Indian men without the necessary educational background or training have, from the second quarter of the twentieth century, been increasingly excluded from the full-time work force so they have found themselves at a severe disadvantage in securing wives within the community. Those without qualifications, regular work, a steady income, or proper housing, are perceived as being unable to offer any form of security in marriage. In the families of the poor concern is expressed about ensuring that their daughters would only marry someone with prospects. The father of one girl who, having been assisted by charitable organizations to complete her training, had found a job teaching in a convent school, was insistent that he would not 'give her to a boy who is not working, and she [his daughter] says "I won't get married to anybody unless it's a government servant" [i.e. in a secure position]'. Many young men from hard-pressed families must therefore go elsewhere for their wives.

Their disadvantages are frequently articulated by poor Anglo-Indian males themselves. In the words of one man, who shares a thatched hut with his Tamilian Adi-Dravida ('untouchable') wife:

I couldn't marry an Anglo-Indian because I was jobless. If you want our Anglo-Indian [women] you have to be well-to-do. You should be in a nice position, so you can look after them properly. [But] Indian girls don't command us to 'do this, do that' [demand so much].

Whereas African-American poverty has, according to Wilson and Aponte, 'spawned a sizable and growing black underclass of marginally productive and unattached men, and of [unmarried] women and children in female-headed homes' (1985: 241), in the Madras context male joblessness has not on the whole resulted in either the men or women remaining unattached. Anglo-Indian males from the poorest households and with the poorest prospects seek partners – legal or casual – with low-caste women, Christian and non-Christian, whom they meet in the slum neighbourhoods they inhabit. Rarely, unions of this kind are arranged by parents or other relatives, but generally they are 'love marriages'. To give several examples:

a. Eslyn is married to a Tamilian Catholic woman from an Adi-Dravida background. 'We lived close by one another, so we used to talk and we fell in love. She would give me food [when he didn't have any]. I thought that this girl does so much good, so I asked her to come with me and she was prepared. Her family was cross at first, but it all subsided. Later on [after their first child was born] I married her in a church'.

b. Fitzroy, a casually employed labourer, married an Anglo-Indian woman and when she left him, he married an 'Indian A/D' (Adi-Dravida) who later converted to Christianity. The children of Fitzroy's first (Anglo-Indian) wife all married Hindus. The three children of the 'Indian' wife (including his son Richard, also casually employed) live with Fitzroy. Richard married an Adi-Dravida convert to Christianity. Richard's brother, a part-time waiter in a hotel, married an Anglo-Indian (who left him).

c. Romeo, who drives a cycle rickshaw, has lived with the Hindu Adi-Dravida mother of his three children for twelve years. 'She was staying in the same street where I was. We never got married, but came together.'

While Anglo-Indian women from the poorest families seek, wherever possible, to marry hypergamously within the community, occasionally, though not nearly so frequently as the men, they marry or cohabit with non-Anglo-Indian men from the same social level – the 'rickshaw class', one Anglo-Indian leader scathingly termed it; the 'servant class', in the words of another. The women most apt to establish such liaisons are those in families where one or more members (usually their brothers) are already in relationships with non-Anglo-Indians. Thus, two of Romeo's sisters (example c, above) cohabited for many years with Hindu Adi-Dravida brothers who were Romeo's friends and whom the sisters had met through him. Similarly, Richard's sister (example b, above) married a Hindu Adi-Dravida, whom she had got to know as part of her brother's circle of friends. While caste considerations play virtually no part in marriage calculations at this class level, for many people these unions are only tolerable if the non-Anglo-Indian partner is a Christian, or prepared to convert. Thus, one woman whom I had first met in 1991 when her children were still unmarried, reported when we met again in 1996 that four of the five had 'got married to Indians', but added with some emphasis, 'all church marriages'.

The impression given by virtually all Anglo-Indian leaders and people in positions of responsibility is that the practice of non-endogamous unions (formal and informal) at the lowest end of the Anglo-Indian spectrum in Madras (and possibly other urban centres of India) has reached epidemic proportions and, after emigration, is the single greatest cause of the community's gradual and inevitable 'disappearance'. On several occasions I was told that in some parts of the city where the poorest members of the community are concentrated 'all the Anglo-Indian boys are married to Tamilians'. My own guess, based on the genealogies of households I visited, is that between one-third and one-half of poor Anglo-Indian families have at least one member, and possibly several, who are married outside the community.

Despite their apparent 'disappearance' or 'evaporation' through the establishment of unions outside the community, there is considerable scope for their continued attachment to the community, and for the exercise by their children of various options, one of which may involve a wish to (re-)identify as or with Anglo-Indians, although children of mixed Anglo-Indian and Adi-Dravida parentage now have the possibility of affiliating themselves to the latter category to claim the various state (educational, employment) benefits it can bring (see Chapter 4). Although marriage outside the community during colonial times would have led more frequently to 'evaporation' from its ranks – especially if it meant acceptance into European society – I suspect that this kind of fluidity has been a feature of Anglo-India for some time. The greatly increased frequency of these external unions since Independence has undoubtedly created new 'hybridities', increased the complexity of identity claims, and enhanced the possibilities for and range of such choices. As in the past, however, such agency is more readily available to the better-off than to the poor.

Conclusion

In diverse ways Anglo-Indians, like similar métis populations in the colonized world, 'straddled and disrupted cleanly marked social divides' (Stoler 1997: 225). Constrained by official policies which defined their limited economic and political entitlements, kept at a distance by exclusionary British social practices, and assailed by rhetorics which, through caricature and stereotype, sought to reinforce their separation from European society, many Anglo-Indians nonetheless defied and undermined these laboriously erected barriers. Many assumed new identities as Europeans (even if the very notion of 'European' was itself by no means unequivocal). And, despite efforts to guard their own boundaries, their ranks were apparently infiltrated by unqualified others making claims to what they deemed was privileged Anglo-Indian status. Then again, an indeterminate number of the very poor 'disappeared' back into the surrounding Indian society. These permeable enclosures and fluid identities help to explain the persistent British disparagement of Anglo-Indians in general, and Anglo-Indian women in particular. The latter, through what was perceived as their inappropriate imitation of European mores, were thought to parody and thus threaten the cultural barriers which were meant to separate ruling elites from those over whom they exercised authority. With what was sometimes seen as their powers of enticement, Anglo-Indian women seemed able to move almost at will across officially delineated and carefully guarded racial and ethnic demarcations, thereby underlining the fragility and vulnerability of these ordered colonial categories. Since Independence Anglo-Indian women – mainly but not exclusively from better-off families – have continued to seek marriages outside the Anglo-Indian fold, although their direction and rationale now have more to do with the comparative economic and educational successes of these women alongside a gradual deterioration in the position of Anglo-Indian males since the advent of Indianization in the early years of the twentieth century. This situation, as we have seen, has compelled many of these men to seek partners among the poor outside the community.

Finally, Douglas long ago drew attention to the body as a central metaphor of political and social order (1970; see also Featherstone et al. 1991). In this connection, it has often been argued that the marriages of women out of the group are more strictly controlled than those of men, and that in conditions of stark political inequality women of the subordinate group may be forbidden to men in the dominant group by their own menfolk (Breger and Hill 1998: 23). In the situation we have been examining both European and Indian (male) leaders – at least from the latter part of the nineteenth century – not only severely discouraged their out-marriage, but projected women as representatives of collective integrity.

Political changes during the century – and especially following the Sepoy uprising of 1857 – led to a significant redefinition of 'colonial morality', much of it centred on European women. As in many colonial contexts, they 'became the excuse for – and custodians of – racial distinctions that took the form of class-specific prescriptions for bourgeois respectability and sexual "normalcy"' (Cooper and Stoler 1997: 25; also Stoler 1991: 87). In this regard Euro-colonial elites, as self-appointed guardians of what they deemed were European community borders, portrayed the women of their own society as paragons of restraint and high virtue, as icons of British power, which contrasted with the set of wholly negative images by which they were represented in the early years of the century (Barr 1989: 5; Bharucha 1994: 88–9).[26]

Indian women also carried a heavy symbolic load in the discourses of both Europeans and Indians during the same period. As Chatterjee has pointed out, the colonialists' depiction of Indian womanhood as 'unfree and oppressed' became a trope for 'the inherently oppressive and unfree nature of the entire cultural tradition of a country' (1993: 118). For their part, Indian nationalists assigned to the women the all-important protection and nurturance of the nation's spiritual identity and culture, which were deemed to be located in the home. By separating the domestic sphere from the external world of politics and technology, where European power had so obviously established its hegemony, nationalists were thus able to argue for the existence of an essential, spiritual domain which colonialism had not subdued and, if women played their part and resisted Westernization, could not reach (Ibid.: 120–6). The result, according to Tharu, was the emergence of a 'sacrificial complex' for women involving 'humility, passivity, suffering, the recognition of the mystic strength of tradition together with a strictness of moral purpose' (1989: 263).

By contrast, the Anglo-Indian leadership never assigned to women of their own community a special symbolic guardianship. Since their own borders have been, by definition and historical practice, permeable and elastic, they have had no need nor wish to represent these thresholds in the language of women's bodies. They have remained silent in what may be understood as a potent acknowledgement of their own community's porous boundaries.

Notes

1. Referring to Spanish America, Pagden writes that within a few years of the conquest, the mestizo had become a 'despised breed . . . rejected by a white elite that had come to fear racial contamination too much to wish to acknowledge direct association with them' (1987: 71).
2. Hemenway, in a reference to the quality of this literature, quotes one critic's comment about the 'large number of forgotten and unreadable books' written before Forster's *A Passage to India* (1975: 18).
3. While the suggestion is an interesting one, it does not adequately account for the situation of the Parsis, who were Westernized, but also British favourites (Luhrmann 1996: 84, 111).
4. Christopher Hawes has perused the letters and reports of the two missionaries as well as other south India correspondence in the London Missionary Society records (Church World Mission Archives), and has kindly made some of his findings available to me, for which I am extremely grateful.

5. Boxer notes that the Portuguese in India were prepared to train Indian and mestizo candidates for the secular priesthood, 'but they kept them in strictly subordinate positions as a matter of ecclesiastical and colonial policy' (1963: 66).

6. The derivation of the term 'chee-chee' is obscure (see Spencer 1966: 62–3). However, it goes back at least to the late eighteenth century: *Hobson-Jobson* has a reference to Hickey's *Bengal Gazette* of March 1781 which pokes fun at 'chee-chee misses'. It also writes that 'chee-chee' is a 'disparaging term applied to half-castes or Eurasians and . . . to their manner of speech' (see Yule and Burnell 1886: 142–3). According to Hull, it was also used to describe domiciled Europeans, many of whom had acquired identical language habits (1871: 137).

7. Many of the early arrivals, such as the anonymous author of *Hartly House* (1789), were favourably struck by the splendid costumes of the Anglo-Indians they encountered: 'their persons are genteel, and their dress magnificent' (Anon. 1908: 204).

8. 'It is, I must tell you, the extremity of bad taste to appear in anything of Indian manufacture . . . as none but the half-castes *ever* wear them' (*Journal of Mrs Fenton*, March 1827, quoted in Steuart 1913: 97).

9. The numbers of British and European civilians rose from 2,000 in 1833 to some 80,000 in 1871 (Hawes 1997: 7; Renford 1979: 31). British soldiers in India increased from a few hundred in the mid-1750s to 40,000 by 1858 (Hawes 1997: 2).

10. Cornish was proposing what Young has termed the 'decomposition thesis' of hybrids: namely, 'mixed breeds either die out or revert to one or other of the parent types' (Young 1995: 18) There were several other theories as well (Ibid.).

11. His conclusion, while probably quite credible, does not necessarily follow from his reasoning. Since most domiciled Europeans had by this time been settled in the country for several generations, it would not have been surprising if they exhibited a more 'normal' gender balance than the non-domiciled European community.

12. Mast notes the sudden drop in the number of Europeans on the railways in 1926 compared with figures for previous years, and a corresponding rise in Anglo-Indian numbers. He suggests this was due to a 'transference' to the latter group of some who had formerly 'passed off as Europeans' (1969: 6).

13. His calculations were probably abetted by the Government of India Act of 1935 which defined Anglo-Indians as persons of European descent in the male line whose parents were habitually resident in

India. The definition made no mention of 'hybrid' origins, and thus could equally include 'unmixed' domiciled Europeans.

14. This kind of subterfuge was apparently practiced in various occupational and social contexts (see Lynn n.d. Oral Records, quoted in Hawes 1997: 6).

15. Such grievances were echoed in various contexts: in a letter to the *Madras Mail*, reprinted in *The Anglo Indian* (March 1934), a correspondent urged fellow Anglo-Indians not to 'be ashamed of their parents', nor to abandon their community 'when they obtain successful appointments', and if they remained true to their community 'the census figure [for Anglo-Indians] would be near 500,000'.

16. In his autobiography, one Anglo-Indian refers somewhat contemptuously to Indian Christian converts who, 'by having an Anglo-Saxon name conferred on them at baptism (a regular practice in the case of Roman Catholic converts) and by donning European clothes, were changed overnight from Indians, mostly of the untouchable class, into Eurasians' (Staines 1986: 88).

17. Referring to the Dutch East Indies, Taylor suggests that the majority of mestizo children of soldiers probably were abandoned by their fathers through death, desertion of the Asian mother, or his escape to the Netherlands. 'Such children grew up in the mother's ethnic ward of [Batavia]' (1983: 8).

18. There are reservations for members of 'Scheduled' and 'Backward' castes in a variety of educational and employment spheres.

19. While many of these relationships were formally consecrated in church, others were 'informal' alliances. My use of 'marriage' here is therefore meant to include a variety of domestic relationships.

20. Following the opening of the Suez Canal in 1869 there were fortnightly P&O services to Madras which took about six weeks.

21. In this discourse there is effectively no distinction between sexual promiscuity and the desire to secure European husbands; both are equally condemned. With by now familiar Western logic and double standards, it was deemed acceptable for European men to pursue sexual adventures with Anglo-Indian women, while avoiding marriage, but somehow improper for the women to seek matrimonial unions with such men.

22. It appears that at least for a time in the mid-nineteenth century the military in Madras insisted that the girls their soldiers could marry had to be certified as 'descendants of Europeans', something the Directors of the Female Civil Orphan Asylum were not always able to do. See Report of the Madras Male and Female Orphan Asylums, 1853–54.

23. A similar repugnance for 'hypogamous' unions is reported by Taylor for the Dutch East Indies: 'such a match was regarded as demeaning the woman' (1983: 45). Cottrell, who has made a study of post-Independence Asian-Western couples, notes that the husbands in these marriages are predominantly Asian (i.e. Indian) (1979: 352).
24. In her autobiographical memoir, Moore notes that, after Independence, female members of her extended family for the first time married into a variety of 'Indian communities' (1986b: 158). Both Bhattacharya (1968: 168) and Sen (1988: 250), writing (respectively) about Anglo-Indians in Bombay and Calcutta, report increasing middle-class marriages outside the community (see also Gist and Wright 1973: 78–81).
25. Luhrmann also reports a high proportion of out-marriages by Parsi women in contemporary Bombay, and a reluctance to marry men of their own community. The reason they give is that the men have 'become soft' (1994: 343).
26. Gartrell comments that 'few women have been described so negatively as the British *memsahibs*' (1984: 165).

−4−

Paradoxes of Belonging

We were pro-British because we have English blood in us.

There are Anglo-Indians still talking about 'Indians', as if we are different. That's silly; we are Indians.

Anglo-Indians were denied ancestral knowledge, so it's quite remarkable that we developed a sense of identity at all. From the very beginning we've had to reflect on who we are . . . a group of people trying to understand their experiences, in conditions which perhaps didn't credit them with being more than biological mutants, accidents.

Introduction

While Chapter 2 noted that Anglo-Indians were socially and economically heterogeneous, Chapter 3 drew attention to the porosity of the lines demarcating them from both Europeans and members of the indigenous population. Despite attempts by those within the ruling circles to limit, circumscribe and distance these offspring of métissage, the colonial period was characterized by a considerable measure of fluidity and indeterminacy, as numerous Anglo-Indians (not to mention other Indians) refused and challenged official and 'traditional' categorizations in various ways. And they continue to do so in the present. But if both the colonial and postcolonial environment may thereby be depicted as hybridized in terms of these social practices, in other respects it was and remains anything but. This chapter highlights two kinds of paradox. For one thing, while certain policies deliberately excluded Anglo-Indians from privileged positions alongside Europeans, others ensured their inclusion in favoured statuses not available to other Indians, thus encouraging a particular kind of self-ascription. Throughout much of the colonial period a number of institutions and observances nourished by the European colonial government and Euro-colonial population induced Anglo-Indians to identify themselves unequivocally with, and to an extent as, British. Only in the course of the twentieth century were more qualified and, following Independence, fragmented, modes of belonging posited.

For another, despite, indeed alongside, this colonial rhetoric of identification with Europeans, Anglo-Indians – notwithstanding their diverse origins – came to be aware of themselves and to act together as a separate population. With the approach of Independence, moreover, there emerged a vigorous politics of community which persists into the present, and in spite of a creolized urban social environment, contributes to marking out Anglo-Indians as a distinct collectivity.

The Paradox of British Policies

In many ways, Anglo-Indians were encouraged to see themselves as British. Take the matter of language. Despite the community's diverse backgrounds, and the fact that Portuguese was the *lingua franca* in the early Madras settlement (see Chapter 2), Anglo-Indians were very soon encouraged if not compelled to adopt English as their first language, although, as we have already noted, a significant proportion of those resident in the neighbourhoods of the poor spoke Tamil in everyday contexts and knew little English or none at all.[1] English was the only language taught in the free schools and orphanages established in the eighteenth and nineteenth centuries, as it was in the European, later Anglo-Indian, schools most members of the community subsequently attended.

Policy towards teaching and learning Indian languages in all these schools was, as we have also noted, one of indifference, which only encouraged and perpetuated attitudes within the Anglo-Indian community of disdain for local dialects. Sen, writing about Anglo-Indians in Calcutta, remarks that the 'desire . . . to learn the local language has been lacking among them' (1988: 251). Similarly, Bayer notes how in the past Anglo-Indians in Mysore 'did not take the existence [of the local language] into account' (1986: 114; see also Bhattacharya 1968: 169). Before Independence, most people insist, there was little incentive to acquire more than a passing facility in the language; some who are old enough to remember colonial times suggest that in those days they needed only enough Tamil, as one woman phrased it, to 'communicate with servants, traders and rickshaw drivers'. I was told by a retired civil servant that during her childhood if she or her siblings were heard to speak in the vernacular at home her grandmother would shout 'who's talking in Tamil?' In a letter to *The Anglo-Indian* (April 1931), one young woman expressed dismay that she was not given the option to learn Tamil in her Anglo-Indian school, and this had proved a 'barrier to relations with other Indians'.

What seems evident is that the problem lay more in their negative attitude to local languages than in their ability to learn them. In the report of the Reverends Tyerman and Bennet on their visit to LMS mission stations in India during the early nineteenth century they comment frequently and positively on the aptitude of 'country born' (i.e. Anglo-Indian) missionaries for local languages, and that characteristically, they speak and preach in these with 'facility'.[2] But in the course of the century fewer and fewer educated Anglo-Indians attempted to acquire this fluency while those who had it seemed inclined to disguise the fact, fearing it might be interpreted as a dissolution of the barriers they sought to erect between themselves and other Indians. So, at the turn of last century Nundy observed that 'members of this community sedulously abstained from learning these languages, with the desire to prevent anyone perceiving that there was anything Indian about them' (1900: 65). Echoing this view, a non-Anglo-Indian I knew in Madras, who is a native Tamil speaker, recalled that he was always bemused (and not a little amused) by the 'deliberately childish' Tamil cultivated by many Anglo-Indians he knew before 1947. This, he assumed, was precisely in order to underline who they were (and were not). In Madras, even today, many Anglo-Indians – especially those belonging to the artisan class – insist (sometimes with a hint of pride) that they have no aptitude for Tamil. According to one young man 'in Anglo-Indian schools the person who is often the butt of humour and practical jokes is the Tamil teacher'.

It is worth pointing out that Anglo-Indians supported the movement in the 1960s resisting attempts to make Hindi the official language of India which would, among other things, have meant the downgrading of English (as well as a number of regional languages, e.g. Tamil). In this opposition, they made common cause with those in south India and other parts of the country where Hindi has never been the language of everyday intercourse (see Anthony 1969: 289–313).

During the colonial period, the curriculum in Anglo-Indian schools was based on that formulated in the UK and controlled by the Senior Cambridge examination syndicate (Anderson 1939: 85). The schools' Inspectorate was also in the hands of British officials and, with few exceptions, these establishments reserved their directorial ranks and many of their key teaching posts for Europeans, often especially imported from Britain (Ibid.: 86). Such Englishmen generally modelled these institutions on the public and grammar schools with which they were familiar (D'Souza 1976: 54; Hawes 1997: 4). Children were persuaded to think that their heritage was in the West, urged to 'be loyal to Britain' and 'taught to live as British boys and girls' (Minto 1974: 67). In many of these schools they were compelled to eat European food and wear European clothing, which 'marked them out as members of British society' (Hawes 1993: 113).

Another feature which both defined the Anglo-Indian community and allied it to the Europeans in India was that, since the first generation was baptized as Christian – usually as a deliberate attempt to separate the children from their Indian mothers – their descendants have professed Christianity. Since most Anglo-Indian schools were Christian foundations, many of the teachers were (in the case of Roman Catholic schools) members of religious communities or (in Protestant establishments) clergymen and lay persons 'imbued with missionary zeal' (Minto 1974: 66). Even in those schools not run by the clergy the sole religious influence was Christian. Children were given instruction in the faith and its rituals were a prominent part of their daily routine (Hawes 1993: 109–10).[3] Indeed, Christian moral teachings were seen as the only way to rescue the very large numbers of Anglo-Indian poor from what were regarded as the debilitating effects of living amongst and sharing the life-styles of indigent members of other communities. The *Report of the Madras Male and Female Civil Orphan Asylums* for 1844–45, noted that

> [on first arrival at the school] their morals in many respects did not exceed those of native children, and their habits, which partook of the mixed character of European and native, would have . . . degenerated wholly into the latter, if the benefits of Christian instruction had not been offered.

There was thus a clear religious separation between Anglo-Indians and the bulk of the local population. Moreover, even within the Christian fold, Anglo-Indians were seen to be associated with Europeans, alongside whom they attended English services, while Indian Christians, for the most part, worshipped in the vernacular, often in separate churches or at separate services. In Madras, for example, a number of Protestant churches and chapels were built for the sole use of Europeans and Anglo-Indians, while others were shared with native congregations whose Tamil services were organized at different times. The Company, it appears, was unhappy with this latter arrangement, and in the mid-nineteenth century financed the building of several new places of worship for Indian Christians (Penny 1904 (I): 57; 1922 (III): 92).[4]

Anglo-Indians also possessed a somewhat contradictory legal status under the British which, on the one hand, encouraged them to think of themselves as no different from other Indians, and, on the other, fostered the conviction that they were British and shared the latters' colonial aims.

Thus, John Ricketts, who in 1930 presented a petition to Parliament on behalf of the Calcutta Anglo-Indian community, commented in his evidence on the affairs of the East India Company how, although Anglo-Indians were 'sometimes regarded as natives', they were also 'sometimes recognized as Europeans' (Ricketts 1831: 37). As 'natives', of course, they were denied access to top positions and privileges reserved for Europeans. In their 'European' aspect they were given preference over natives in various appointments where, as we have seen, they occupied intermediate positions and earned privileges akin – if inferior – to British personnel, though denied other Indians. Their legal entitlements were also regarded as distinct from those of other Indians, and stemmed from a recognition of their European links. Anglo-Indians who were one or two generations removed from a European forebear could only be tried before a High Court and therefore not before a 'native' judge (see Renford 1979: 10). The Anglo-Indian and European insane (at least for a time) shared premises while those within the wider Indian society were kept in separate facilities (Ernst 1991: 123). Even Anglo-Indian criminals were deemed to merit treatment similar to that meted out to their European co-prisoners or, at least, distinct from that of other Indians. In November 1927 *The Anglo-Indian* printed an article on 'Present-day Jail Life', applauding the fact that Anglo-Indian and European inmates are kept in a 'clean and commodious' block of cells away from native inmates, but complaining about the 'Magistrates who place Anglo-Indians on an Indian diet'.

The association with British interests was most evident where defence and security were concerned. After the Sepoy rebellion of 1857 it was decided that a local volunteer force of 'unquestionable loyalty to the colonial state' was required (Arnold 1979: 112). This consisted of (mainly domiciled) Europeans and Anglo-Indians, although by the late nineteenth century the latter formed a majority of the force. As part of this unit the Madras Volunteer Guards were established, one of the 'most beneficial results' of the Mutiny, according to Clarke (1878: 55). During wartime the Volunteers took over garrison duties normally performed by regulars (Heathcote 1974: 74), and in peacetime assisted both the military and the police in maintaining law and order. During the First World War they were absorbed into the India Defence Force and in 1920 into the Auxiliary Force of India (AFI).

After 1869 Anglo-Indian railway workers were compelled, as a condition of their employment, to join special railway corps affiliated to the AFI, and which were instrumental in repressing any industrial action on the railways. Since (as noted in Chapter 2), by the 1920s, more than half of all Anglo-Indians were estimated to have become dependent in one way or another on employment in the railways, the community as a whole was seen as aligned to repressive forces in the state. Bower recalls how he once heard a 'very famous Indian politician' suggest that 'grave differences' would exist between Anglo-Indians and Indians as long as the community supported the Auxiliary Force (1939: 152–3). One Anglo-Indian woman, who had been a student in the 1930s, remembered that 'whenever there was a demonstration or some trouble the AFI or the railwaymen were called and they had to go and shoot down these people. So they hated us.'

For the most part, Anglo-Indians refrained from joining Indian railway unions and taking part in strikes: 'They identified themselves with the management in opposition to the Indians' strikes and unions' (Arnold 1980: 252–3).[5] At a meeting of the Golden Rock [Railway] Worker's Union (Golden Rock, near Trichinopoly, was a major railway centre in south India) held on 11 July 1937 the General Secretary of the All-India Congress Socialist Party remarked on how 'very sorry' he was 'to learn . . . that one class of railway workers have largely held aloof from this union. I was told that the Anglo-Indian workers have not joined the union in large numbers' (*The Anglo-Indian*, July 1937). On some occasions, when Indian railway workers struck, they were replaced by Anglo-Indians and domiciled Europeans (see *The Anglo-Indian*, February 1937). Hedin (1934: 175) quotes the *Report of the Indian Statutory Commission* regarding the East Indian Railway strike of 1923 where it is claimed that 'even Anglo-Indian school children cleaned the railway carriages and our lads left their schools to work this railway to enable H.R.H. the Prince of Wales, to travel in comfort and safety when he visited India'.[6]

Since service in railway battalions was forbidden other Indian railway workers, this reinforced the view that Anglo-Indians had a special affinity with the British. Thus, Gidney insisted that in the nineteenth century '[w]e were looked upon and treated in most matters as British; [the Government] confirmed us in that belief, and taught and encouraged us to regard ourselves not only as the "predominant partner", but as a special bulwark of help to Government in difficult times' (1925: 660).

Anglo-Indian Rhetorics of Belonging

Call of the Blood

In light of these institutional arrangements put in place during the colonial period – and in spite of both their equivocal legal status and British attempts to restrict them economically or demean them socially – it is little wonder that those who spoke for and about the Anglo-Indian community identified themselves with the colonial rulers. When Ricketts presented his petition to Parliament he insisted that 'those [Anglo-Indians] who have been educated, are entirely European in their habits and feelings, dress and language, and everything else' (1831: 54).[7] In their Memorandum to the outgoing Governor on his retirement from the Province, the Anglo-Indians of Madras wrote of themselves as 'a Community permanently attached to, and as a body born and bred in the enjoyment of the blessings of [European] civilization'.[8] Three-quarters of a century later, better-off Anglo-Indians were still being associated with European values and ways. In a letter to *The Anglo-Indian* (21 March 1917), a correspondent identified class divisions within the community in terms of their proximity to 'the European standard in appearance, manners [and] customs'.

The Anglo-Indian Association of Southern India, which was established in Madras in 1879 (see below), opened its doors to European members, and thereby sought to dissolve any barriers erected by (usually non-domiciled) colonial elites against what they deemed as socially inferior domiciled Europeans and Anglo-Indians.[9] Between 1891 and 1908, moreover, the Association's (five) successive presidents were prominent Britons, both domiciled and non-domiciled, encouraging belief in Anglo-India's European disposition. In a review of the Association's history on the occasion of its sixtieth anniversary, it is said of one of these European presidents (Rev Canon C. Malden, Garrison chaplain of Fort St George) that 'he wanted us to develop the best qualities of our English blood, and as far as possible, set our face against anything which could identify us with the native races of India' (*The Anglo-Indian*, October 1939).

Although the Association resumed the election of Anglo-Indians to the presidency from 1908, this was the rhetoric favoured by virtually all community leaders and intellectuals until well into the twentieth century. Thus, Warden proclaimed, '[We] are people with British blood, ideals, habits, sympathies' (1915: 9), while Wallace insisted that 'Britishers we are and Britishers we ever must and shall be' (1947 [1930]: 130). During the 'Mutiny', asks Stark, 'had they not answered the Call of the Blood ... and sealed their sonship with the supreme sacrifice?' (1932: 161). And again, 'the tawny sons of Britain helped to man the guns ... ever at the side of their brave fathers ... helping to plant the flag of England on Indian soil' (Stark 1936: 40). When Gidney appealed to young Anglo-Indian men to join the Auxiliary Force his argument was that 'as true and tried sons of Britain we are ready to prove that blood is thicker than water' (*The Anglo-Indian*, 28 June 1921). In countless representations to the authorities urging more favourable treatment for their people, Anglo-Indian spokesmen lost no opportunity to remind the colonial rulers that during the 'Mutiny' Eurasians played an important role in maintaining control of communications and transport, and thus of Britain's military lifeline (see Gidney 1934: 29). Even more recent Anglo-Indian explanations for the community's loyalty during the 'Mutiny' boil down to 'ties of blood, language, dress and habits' (Anthony 1969: vi).

Such pronouncements were widely reflected within the articulate sections of the community across the country and were certainly evident in Madras. Editorials, feature articles and letters in *The Anglo-Indian* from at least the first quarter of the twentieth century, constantly reiterated these views. Thus, 'The proper policy [for Anglo-Indians] is to aim at fusion with the English community' (April 1917); '[F]rom the Mutiny down to the present Anglo-Indians have upheld British prestige and proved themselves worthy of the [British] blood that flows in their veins' (May 1917). Encouraged, no doubt, by war fever, it then insisted that '[Anglo-Indians] cannot help being loyal to Great Britain, simply because their blood is British' (August 1918). And in its Annual Report for 1919, the editorial declared that 'this Anglo-Indian Community has done its share as a British community. It is British in character and will remain British.' In the June 1926 edition of the journal the outgoing president of the Association, reflecting on developments over the preceding twenty-five years, insisted that all along 'we Anglo-Indians . . . regarded ourselves as a branch of the European community'.

Along with such declarations, Anglo-Indians frequently referred to Britain as 'home'. A number of Anglo-Indians I knew in Madras remarked that their parents and grandparents often used such an expression, retaining a largely invented image of the 'homeland' (see Appadurai 1991: 193). Like similar groups elsewhere, they persisted for generations in regarding a land they had never known as their 'true home' (Pagden and Canny 1987: 267). In an editorial in July 1919 *The Anglo-Indian* admitted that many people 'refused to regard India as their own country . . . [but considered it only] as the land of their abode, not their home'. In fact in an earlier issue of the same journal (28 March 1918) a former president of the southern Association introduced his piece with the words: 'when at home in England'. Gidney, for his part, welcomed the formation (in 1923) of an Anglo-Indian Association in London, which he felt 'could do much to advise and help young members of the community coming *home* for education and technical training' (my emphasis).[10] In a recent autobiography of an Anglo-Indian, the writer notes that while Anglo-Indians had made India their home for a time, 'in the back of our minds we knew we would return to our country of origin when it suited us' (Staines 1986: 87). The other side of this rhetorical coin was to recreate 'home' in India. D.S. White, the first president of the Anglo-Indian Association of Southern India, proposed a scheme to settle Anglo-Indians on the land – 'an English village in Southern India is what we have longed for' (White 1882: 2). Several other settlement schemes were later mooted in various parts of the country, though most came to nothing, including one which focused on the Andaman Islands. Another, which came to be known as McCluskiegunj (after its founder, T. McCluskie) initially attracted several hundred settler families but within a matter of a few decades this, like all the others, was unable to realize the goal of providing a 'homeland' for Anglo-Indians. Bear is undoubtedly right to point out that in its ordered layout and organization of social, cultural and religious spaces the railway colony provided a 'kind of home territory for Anglo-Indians' (1998: 15–18). It should be noted, however, that the railway colony was probably an adaptation to India of an arrangement pioneered in Britain (Hawes, personal communication).

Alongside the insistence on 'indissoluble bonds of kinship, inter-dependence and the unity of interests' with the British, in the words of Anglo-India's foremost historian (Stark 1936: 39), went a virtual denial of association with the majority Indian population. In proclaiming their unity with the British they were precluded from 'amalgamating with the natives of the soil or from entering into compacts with them' (Ibid.: 39). Cedric Dover, another prominent Anglo-Indian and the author of several books on the community (much quoted by other Anglo-Indian writers), asserted that the Anglo-Indian 'stubbornly resists the submergence of his identity with the natives of the country, for he is proud of his anglicized customs and remote connection with the ruling race' (1929: 42). According to Gist and Wright 'Anglo-Indian parents commonly indoctrinated their children with attitudes of superiority over Indians and endeavoured to isolate them from intimate association with Indian children' (1973: 39). The Anglo-Indian writer and community leader K.E. Wallace admits as much when he warns that '[i]f in the home we cultivate a strong prejudice against Indians, the child will have a distaste for learning a vernacular, a fact which he may regret . . . when it comes to obtaining employment' (1935: 44).

As we have seen, little attempt was made to relate what was taught in Anglo-Indian schools to the Indian environment. Quite the reverse: according to Anthony, 'pupils were indoctrinated, if not with contempt for themselves, with contempt for things Indian' (1969: 109). Indian languages, religions and ways of life were regarded as having no bearing on Anglo-India's culture, an attitude which persisted well into the twentieth century and, for some, into the post-Independence period. In the autobiography of a now-retired senior police officer from a distinguished Madras Anglo-Indian family, the author admits that '[my] education, culture and outlook [was] thoroughly western, the result of my Anglo-Indian upbringing and background. [There was] almost total neglect at school, church and home of the "Indian" side of that background' (Stracey 1981: vii). In reflecting on their past several Anglo-Indians I knew in Madras acknowledged how, as one woman phrased it, 'we were brought up to look down on the non-Anglo-Indian, to think he was somebody who had no culture'. Another remarked 'most of us were extremely ignorant of Indian culture. We felt very uncomfortable mixing with non-Anglo-Indians.'

The Localization of Belonging

With the approach of Home Rule, which most Anglo-Indian leaders opposed implacably, the nightmare scenario was, according to an editorial in *The Anglo-Indian* (7 February 1917)

> that year by year we will lose touch with English traditions, with English social observances, English literature . . . and will gradually adopt the social conventions and habits of thought, and become subject to the cramping and degenerating prejudices and inducements of the low Indian environment.

Early in the twentieth century there were occasional Anglo-Indian voices urging members of the community to join forces with other Indians – such as Wallace's insistence in 1903 that '[Anglo-Indians] are natives of India. There can be no separate platform for [them]' (*The Anglo-Indian*, September 1918).[11] But for the most part this kind of thinking did not become widespread until after the First World War. As their leaders began to make realistic assessments of political developments increasing calls were heard within the community for Anglo-Indians to identify more with India, and to acknowledge it as their home. To some extent, this was in response to the pleas of Indian nationalist leaders. It is interesting that the first two presidents of the Anglo-Indian Association of Southern India – D.S. White and W.S. Gantz – were members of the Indian National Congress and represented the Association at its annual meetings. But, according to one account in the Association's journal, there were differences of opinion among members, and in deference to what was believed to be the feeling of the majority, the practice of sending delegates to the Congress was discontinued, and it would appear that Gantz's short-lived stewardship of the Association (1889–1891) was at least in part due to his support for Congress (*The Anglo-Indian*, October 1939.) And at least one editor of *The Anglo-Indian* had to resign from his post for championing the nationalist cause (*The Anglo-Indian*, May 1917).

Later, Gandhi deprecated what he saw as the pretensions of Anglo-Indians to a British identity. In an interview (August 1925) with Dr H.W.B. Moreno, General President of the Anglo-Indian League, Calcutta, Gandhi alluded to 'keeping up a false appearance as Europeans', and in December 1927 wrote to Gidney, urging Anglo-Indians 'not to strive for recognition as Europeans' but to 'make common cause with India's masses' (See Gandhi *Collected Works*, 1925 (28): 17; 1927 (35): 387).[12] Moreno, for his part, was persuaded that Anglo-Indians should 'throw in their lot with the Indians' (Gandhi *Collected Works*, 1929 (41): 503), but it was Gidney's pronouncement in early 1926 that Anglo-Indians should 'regard themselves as Indians' which received most attention. It was much commented on by the local press, which noted his 'change of heart', but wondered if the feeling was widespread.[13] The mouthpiece of the Madras Association reported Gidney's remarks without comment, although it continued to editorialize about Anglo-India's British credentials. The Association's *Annual Report* for 1935 made much of the Silver Jubilee of King George V, remarking that '[l]oyalty to the Flag and to the Crown has been an outstanding trait in the character of our people. No community in India rejoiced more than our own.'

It was 1936 before the president, E.H.M. Bower, affirmed the Association's official stance that Anglo-Indians were indeed 'part and parcel of India' and were willing to work with other Indians (*The Anglo-Indian*, October 1936). While some leaders and intellectuals argued for affiliating to Congress, most were suspicious of its programme as this affected Anglo-Indians. Bower thought it was 'growing increasingly socialistic' and, moreover, 'declines to hold that our community has a right to maintain its own . . . mode of living, and its own outlook on the problems facing India'. He saw no reason to criticize Gidney's expression of support (and that of the Anglo-Indian community) for Jinnah 'in his struggle against Congress'. In turn, Gidney had been censured by the Anglo-Indian Civil Liberties Association (based in Calcutta) whose president (a Mr Gibbons) according to Bower, was 'the only Anglo-Indian to have ascended a Congress platform within the past two years'.[14] In the event, the Madras Association refrained from formally committing itself to any particular political organization on the grounds that (in the president's words) 'the best thing we can do is to refrain from tying ourselves to any one party . . . and to show that we are working for the good of India' (*The Anglo-Indian*, February 1940).

As part of this arrival at a new Indian sensibility, community leaders were less constrained about criticizing various colonial institutions. Gidney, for example, attacked British control of Anglo-Indian schools, arguing that 'the imported teacher has never given our boys and girls a true perspective of Indian life and affairs, but has palmed off on to them a spurious superiority-complex in regard to Indians and a painfully unfair inferiority-complex in regard to the white man' (quoted in Anderson 1939: 87). Others joined the assault. In a letter to *The Anglo-Indian* (May 1939) from 'an average Anglo-Indian', the writer repeats Gidney's accusation that their schools have given Anglo-Indians a superiority complex vis à vis Indians, and insists that 'the Indian is in almost every respect our equal'. Furthermore

> The Anglo-Indian with the superiority complex will find that the India of tomorrow has no need for him, while the Anglo-Indian who has learned to respect his Indian brother will discover that the future has a definite place and purpose for him.

Thus Anglo-Indians hesitantly began to examine the possibilities for an alternative identification to that which had prevailed to that point. As the end of British rule approached those who spoke for Anglo-India increasingly acknowledged the realities of their future as one among many minority Indian groups.

In contemporary Madras rhetorics insisting on an 'indigenous' provenance for Anglo-Indians are commonly heard from elites who have of course benefited most from opportunities in post-Independence India. Indeed, they insist that it is only with the departure of the British that they have been able to make progress – economically and socially. The tendency is to play down their 'foreignness' and stress local identity – 'we are very much part of this country, pakka Indian,' as one retired army officer declared. Their own advancement is held up as evidence of the extent to which Anglo-Indians are now accepted by fellow Indians.

This readiness to emphasize rootedness does not signify a belated discovery of original maternal links, nor a denial of their European social and cultural springs, but a desire to acknowledge India as the meeting point for these different influences. For one active member of several Anglo-Indian organizations in the city: 'The fact is that we are really

Indian, and India has always consisted of all kinds of people.' The perception of a receding gap between Anglo-Indian and non-Anglo-Indian interests, even of a certain coalescence reflects, not unnaturally, the experience of people at this class level. Most highly educated and well-placed Anglo-Indians – whether or not married out of the community – associate in a range of occupational and spare-time contexts with people from various ethnic backgrounds who possess similar educational and economic advantages. Even marriage outside the Anglo-Indian fold among the well-to-do does not inevitably imply a denial of community or pose a 'clash' of identities. Where the couple share a language, good education, and other features of common lifestyle – especially religion – they are able to negotiate a *modus vivendi* which takes account of their different backgrounds, and to which their children readily adjust. The student son of a well-educated, highly successful Anglo-Indian mother and a wealthy Indian Christian businessman father purports to be 'very comfortable' in this mixed household.

> People of my generation have no problem with this. I don't think I consciously feel myself to be anything. I'm aware of my Anglo-Indian background; and we have some jokes in the house about the way some Anglo-Indians talk. And I fit in easily when we have some interaction with my mother's family. But I also know about my Indian Christian side. If I go to my grandparents' [father's parents'] place I'm quite happy to go along with their way of doing things. I suppose, if you ask, I'm an Indian and a Catholic, with a bit of Anglo-Indian and Indian Christian thrown in.

Not infrequently, though of different backgrounds, both partners identify themselves and are accepted as belonging to the Anglo-Indian community. I was to discover, somewhat to my surpise, that a number of leading members of community associations, or of organizations (e.g. charities) working for the benefit of community members, were either not Anglo-Indians themselves, but married to Anglo-Indians, or Anglo-Indians married 'out', or the children of only one Anglo-Indian parent, and so forth.

Among the least advantaged members of the community, resident alongside and in continuous interaction with people of diverse caste or ethnic backgrounds but in similar economic circumstances, notions of belonging are no less ambiguous. Blending easily into the society and culture of their surroundings, speaking Tamil in most everyday social (in some cases, even domestic) contexts, there is little in their quotidian demeanor or practices to distinguish them as belonging to a métis community claiming European antecedents. We might expect that the most 'assimilated' are the numerous Anglo-Indian poor who have married outside the community (see Chapter 3), and in many cases such couples and their children are, in the view of some Anglo-Indian leaders and intellectuals, 'lost' to the community. But this is not invariably the case. The key, I was often told, lies in the maternal language: if the mother is Tamilian the children will in all likelihood not speak English, a key indicator of Anglo-Indian identity.

But the evidence from a number of families I visited suggests a more active role on the part of parents (and especially the Anglo-Indian father) in encouraging the children to speak English. In not a few homes they are bilingual at an early age ('The little bugger, he speaks Tamil to his mother and English to me'). But identities involve more than language, and here the choice of school for the children of those who have established unions outside the community is crucial. Some parents, for various reasons – mainly economic – choose or are compelled to send their children to free Tamil-medium 'Corporation' (state) schools (and a few children never go to school despite the fact that there is compulsory education in Tamil Nadu). Although technically eligible for places in Anglo-Indian schools,[15] which are generally regarded as far superior to those managed by the state, the children of mixed (or, for that matter, 'pure') parentage are by no means certain of obtaining such places, nor are parents always able to afford the costs if they do.[16] Several principals and correspondents (equivalent to secretary or chair of governors) of Anglo-Indian schools in the city, with whom I discussed these issues, suggested that as many as half their 'Anglo-Indian' pupils from poorer families in fact have one non-Anglo-Indian parent. The correspondent of one of the largest schools observed that when he was first associated with it some twenty-five years ago there were very few children unable to speak English, since most spoke the language at home – because they were much more likely to have two Anglo-Indian parents. Nowadays the proportion of Tamil speakers is much greater. As many as half these children do not know English when they begin school, a figure repeated by officials in several other Anglo-Indian schools.[17] Given these disadvantages, parents who select an Anglo-Indian school for their children – and are able to find the costs[18] – make a deliberate choice for a distinctive educational ambience, in which not only is the language of instruction English, but the cultural stress Anglo-Indian. They thus retain (or acquire) many of the distinctive traits of their Anglo-Indian parent, and are readily identified, as well as identifying themselves, as Anglo-Indians without necessarily eschewing attachment to the quotidian practices and thought-ways of the non-Anglo-Indian parent. While for some people 'identity' is seen to involve a selection between the two sides of their background, for the majority it is not perceived as a 'choice' at all. Depending on context they stress different kinds of belonging, seeing them not as alternatives but as a creolized field of available possibilities. Thus, children of mixed Anglo-Indian and Adi-Dravida parentage now have the possibility of affiliating themselves to the latter category to claim the various state (educational, employment) benefits it can bring. Occasionally, however, the state narrows the range of options available to individuals of 'mixed' parentage by allocating them to one or other community. To claim certain benefits a certificate is required from the *tahsildar* or local government officer, and it is not uncommon for that official to decide how to categorize the applicant.[19] In general, however, like the well-to-do, 'ordinary' members of the community increasingly resist the dichotomy between Anglo-Indian and Indian, and the notion that the former has no local provenance: I was frequently to hear even from those who readily identified themselves as Anglo-Indian that they were 'first of all, Indians'. Others might prefer to stress religious attachments, such as their Catholic or evangelical credentials.

To the extent that the notion persists of Anglo-Indians as quasi-Europeans it is most likely to be found among the community's artisan class. Indeed, their current disadvantages are frequently explained in terms of victimization for their European associations. Just as often the discrimination they claim to experience (in the workplace and elsewhere) is explained in cultural terms: the pervasive 'corruption' and 'favouritism' all around them is seen as due to the Indian way of doing things, which is fundamentally at odds with the European values and modes of behaviour in which Anglo-Indians have been raised. 'If you plant an apple seed anywhere you get apples, not jackfruit or mangoes.' And the Anglo-Indians, I was told time and again, in so many words, are 'British fruit'. As one man phrased it:

> We are true descendants of Europeans in our colour combination, our blood, our intelligence, and we acquired their ways and habits. It is simply that our culture is different: our way of thinking, our way of moving. Like the Britishers move in England. Their society, their duty to work. It is identical among Anglo-Indians. Our community belongs to that character of upright persons. We are sincere, honest, that's our mannerism. A person who can deliver the goods. To put it in a nutshell, we're British standard. You understand what I'm trying to say?

While certain discourses and practices laid claim to identification with the British rulers (and some, as we see, still do), others, in a different kind of paradox, suggest that Anglo-Indians have for a considerable period constituted and recognized themselves as a separate collectivity with a distinctive character and agenda of their own.

Manifestations of 'Community'

This is not the place to attempt a review of the extensive literature on 'community', but to note merely that while it is regarded as 'one of the *key ideas* of the social sciences' (Hamilton 1985: 8), it is also among the most contested. Until recently social scientists perceived 'community' in terms of essential structural and cultural characteristics which define its limits in a fixed and enduring manner: by such criteria only those who conform to such characteristics fall within the boundaries of the community. There has been a recent turning away from such morphological approaches in favour of a view which regards community as existing in the minds of the people who experience and give meaning to it. In this view, communities are 'constructed', or 'imagined' (Anderson 1983; Cohen 1985).

In the colonial setting, the dominant powers, in seeking to categorize and control others, encouraged not only a certain resistance on the part of people thus designated, but a realization of a shared social location. From the late eighteenth century, Anglo-Indians were encouraged by what they saw as Euro-colonial discriminatory enactments and exclusionary practices to recognize themselves as a distinct community (see Goodrich 1952).[20] Collective activity – frequently directed at alleviating their perceived common handicaps – can therefore be dated from this period.

There are reports of a public meeting of Eurasians in Calcutta as early as March 1825, followed by the formation of an 'East India Club' – and similar sodalities in Bombay and Madras – all of which were short-lived (Goodrich 1952: 146; Moreno 1923: 77). A great deal of debate apparently took place around this time concerning the most appropriate term by which to be denoted – Eurasian, Indo-Briton, and half-caste were a few of the epithets employed. In December 1827 some 200 Anglo-Indians in Madras petitioned the Government of Fort St George to protest the use of 'half-caste' (Hawes 1996: 89), and for a time 'East Indian' gained favour, before being replaced towards the latter part of the century by 'Eurasian' (Moreno 1923: 78). On the eve of the Indian Census of 1911 several Anglo-Indian organizations, including the Empire League, approached the Viceroy Lord Hardinge, and succeeded in convincing him to designate members of this population officially as 'Anglo-Indians'. While the name may have been chosen to emphasize the community's British credentials, this concern to acquire an appropriate label by which to be known was also indicative of a growing realization that Anglo-Indians were seen by others – however they may have regarded themselves – as a distinctive population.

In Madras this realization encouraged attempts to form a community organization. The *Madras Government Gazette* for 8 October 1829 reported that 'Madras is soon to have an East Indian Association . . . a committee has been appointed to frame out its rules. . .'[21] In December of the same year a public meeting was held at which it was decided to form the Madras Philanthropic Association, 'with a view to the present state and condition in life of the descendants of Europeans'. The purpose was to furnish employment and alleviate hardship, and one of its main proposals was the creation of a settlement scheme. A Hyderabad auxiliary was soon formed (*The Anglo-Indian*, June 1938). Another item in the *Asiatic Journal* of 6 February 1830, reported that some of the Association's funds 'may be devoted towards the establishment of a market in the Black Town'. An analogous organization, the Bombay East-Indian Amelioration Fund, with aims not unlike the Philanthropic Association in Madras, was formed in Bombay around the same time, and while there is no evidence that the two bodies coordinated their activities, each apparently kept the other informed (Ibid.).

Similar kinds of liaison operated beween Madras and other major centres of Anglo-Indian settlement. As already noted, John Ricketts presented his 'East Indians' Petition' to Parliament on behalf of Calcutta Anglo-Indians, after extensive discussions among educated and articulate members of the community in that city. On 16 May 1830, at a general meeting of Anglo-Indians in Madras, 'a petition to the British parliament, similar in effect to that prepared by the same class at Calcutta, was agreed to be adopted and forwarded to the Calcutta East Indian Commission for transmission to England'.[22] In a 'Brief History of the Anglo-Indians. . .' (composed by members of the Madras Association from the records of this body) the authors suggest that the Madras petition was to be conveyed by Ricketts. However, the latter was already in Britain, and his petition was presented to Parliament in the spring of 1830, before the Madras document was prepared. It is possible that the chronology is somewhat confused or that the Madras petition was prepared in anticipation of a further delegation to Parliament, or simply that the authors of this 'Brief History' were anxious to stress, as they subsequently declared, that 'the

East Indians of Madras co-operated with their brethren in Calcutta, in sending the petition to Parliament'.[23] Whether or not Anglo-Indians in Madras were directly associated with his petition, they demonstrated a shared concern by greeting Ricketts when he landed in the city on his return from London, celebrating his accomplishments and paying the costs of his stay amongst them (Hawes 1996: 135–6). The authors of the Madras community's history record that

> Mr Peter Ca[r]stairs, the leader of the East Indians in Madras, on behalf of himself and the Community gave [Ricketts] first a public dinner and then a reception ball and supper as the most appropriate mode of congratulating him on, and thanking him for his great achievement both in India and in England.[24]

The same 'history' observes that there is no record of the actual formation of the East Indian Association in Madras and goes on to suggest that 'the idea of petitioning Parliament brought some of the leaders together [but] nothing more was done after that object had been accomplished'.[25]

There is, however, further if sporadic evidence for a desire to act together as a community in Madras. On 19 November 1833 an unspecified number of persons entreated Fort St George for an increase in the proportion of jobs in the uncovenanted services for Anglo-Indians (Hawes 1996: 46, 89). Another petition, dated 21 January 1848, was presented to Marquis Tweeddale on his retirement from the governorship of Madras Presidency (see Chapter 2). It bids him farewell, thanks him for 'the enlightened and liberal policy' which characterized his administration, and notes how much the Anglo-Indian 'condition' has been ameliorated and advanced by his 'acts and deeds'. It was signed by over 1,200 Anglo-Indians in the city, in all probability mainly male heads of household, which suggests that a substantial proportion of the Anglo-Indian population of the city were involved in its preparation. A not dissimilar letter from the 'whole of the East Indian community' of Hyderabad to Lt Gen S.J. Fraser, British resident at the court of HH the Nizam, offering thanks for 'his beneficence and attentions [to the community] on the occasion of his retirement', was published in the *Athenaeum* (Madras) on 13 January 1853. In a carefully guarded reply, General Fraser expressed the hope that 'the invidious distinction which now exists, will cease to be known, and [. . .] you will obtain a large participation in those privileges which are amply due to your merits'. While such expressions of goodwill on both sides were undoubtedly formulaic set pieces on the occasion of changes in higher government echelons, they reveal a shared understanding between group leaders and senior colonial officials that Anglo-Indians formed a distinctive collectivity with common problems and concerns.

In south India a number of organizations – some more ephemeral than others – emerged to represent particular interests and address specific needs within the Anglo-Indian population. I have already referred to the Madras Philanthropic Association and (in previous chapters) to the system of Anglo-Indian (and European) schools. Several others might be mentioned briefly. Thus, in the mid-nineteenth century an 'East Indian Emigration Society' was formed in Madras, to help provide situations in Australia for poor, unemployed but skilled Anglo-Indian men (see *Athenaeum* 6 January 1853; 31 May 1853; 7 March 1857; 14 February 1861; also Chapter 5). In addition, a number of orphanages and poor schools, charitable organizations, and a home for the indigent elderly were established in the course of the eighteeenth and nineteenth centuries, and in as much as they catered for Anglo-Indians (and to a lesser extent domiciled Europeans), served to instill and reinforce among them a realization of common belonging.

One of the more long-lived organizations was the Home Missionary Society of India which established several branches around the country and supported one of the most highly regarded boarding schools in south India from the early part of the twentieth century. Although primarily a Protestant body, the HMSI had some Catholics in its membership and at its schools: it was, according to a report in *The Anglo-Indian*, July 1930, 'an Anglo-Indian organisation for the Anglo-Indian community', whose dual aims were the 'evangelisation of India' and the 'uplifting' of Anglo-Indians. The HMSI has continued to flourish in the postcolonial era and today has several active branches in the city.

Of the formal organizations which have attempted to represent the generality of Anglo-Indians for more than a century, the first was created in Calcutta in 1876. This was followed three years later by the establishment of an Association in Madras, although – as mentioned above – a community association had been mooted as many as seventy years earlier. In the course of the twentieth century other organizations were created either to speak for Anglo-Indians in specific parts of the subcontinent (such as Allahabad, Bombay and Burma), or which sought to represent the interests of the community as a whole. The Anglo-Indian Empire Association (later League), established in 1908 had, by 1916, managed to affiliate over forty district branches, including the Madras Association, although it did not achieve the unification of the main Associations (Abel 1988: 101–2; Renford 1979: 332).[26] Henry Gidney, a member of the Indian Medical Service and an eye specialist, who had assumed the leadership of the League in 1919, incorporated it a few years later into the Anglo-Indian Association of Bengal when he moved to Calcutta. He was also successful in amalgamating a number of separate organizations, which merged in 1926 to form the Anglo-Indian and Domiciled European Association, All-India and Burma and subsequently the All-India Anglo-Indian Association (Abel 1988: 106; Tiwari 1965: 52). Gidney's Association came to see itself – and to be seen by the colonial authorities – as the premier body with the right to speak for all Anglo-Indians in the sub-continent.[27] With the Morley-Minto reforms of 1909 – which granted a separate electorate and reserved seats for Muslims – the British rulers introduced the principle of communal constituencies, thereby inviting if not compelling a number of other minority populations to demand similar 'privileges'. It was Gidney who led the campaign for a separate electorate and in 1919 the Government of India Act, following the recommendations of the Montagu-Chelmsford Report of 1918, created special constituencies for a number of minority communities, including the Anglo-Indians.[28] The Montagu-Chelmsford Reforms also provided for a Central Legislative Assembly and Gidney was nominated by the Viceroy to fill the one seat allocated to Anglo-India.

The Anglo-Indian Association of Southern India (see Note 9 for its later titles) was established in October 1897 to promote the 'social, moral and intellectual advancement of the Europeans and Eurasians permanently settled in India'. Its first president was D.S. White, a civil servant in the Directorate of Public Instruction who, at the time of his retirement, was acting Registrar of Assurances in the Government of the Madras Presidency.

Relations between the All-India and Southern Associations have seldom been harmonious; indeed, almost from their inception these have tended towards opposition. In the 1880s, for example, when the Calcutta-based organization allied itself with the movement hostile to the Ilbert Bill, the Madras Association supported it, in Renford's view 'as a tactical move to win Government approval for other Eurasian demands' (1979: 62).[29] From at least the early part of the twentieth century they grew further apart. While Gidney dominated the All-India Association (1920–42), frequent approaches were made to and by the Madras Association proposing reconciliation and, ultimately, unity. While both organizations consistently proclaimed the desirability of cooperation and of arriving at an accord, numerous meetings and discussions between representatives of the two organizations over a quarter of a century failed to resolve the differences between them. In general, the All-India body favoured amalgamation, while that based in Madras preferred a more federal structure which would allow provincial autonomy.[30]

The fear in the south was that the larger body would absorb their own smaller one, and that a united organization would be dominated by Calcutta – '[its] Governing Body will be practically a Bengal committee', as the Madras Association's *Annual Report* for 1924 put it. The Calcutta schemes were seen to threaten what was described on more than one occasion as a 'loss of identity' (*The Anglo-Indian*, July 1927). At a public meeting in Madras, held in November 1937 to discuss the latest proposals from the All-India body, several prominent members of the Southern Association again spoke out against amalgamation. Anglo-Indians in south India, according to one, were concerned principally if not exclusively with the needs of the community in their own province (Madras Presidency). Only regional associations could therefore appreciate and seek solutions to the problems of their particular constituencies, and thus a substantial degree of local autonomy was essential (see *The Anglo-Indian*, November 1937; *Annual Report* of the Madras Association for 1937). Moreover, the heavy financial demands of the Calcutta body (for 40 per cent of all branch income) would leave the Madras Association without sufficient resources to represent the interests of its own people to the Provincial Government. Some members also saw 'unity' as threatening a takeover of the Madras Association's not inconsiderable assets in the form of land and building ('the habitation').[31]

Amalgamation would also menace some of the privileges enjoyed by the Madras Association. By the 1920s the latter had won the right to nominate two representatives to sit on the Madras Legislative Council, and one member each to the Senate of Madras University, the Madras (city) Corporation, the Advisory Board of the Auxiliary Force and, from the early 1930s, the Board of Film Censors. Generally, these posts were occupied by senior figures in the Association. The leadership could thus emphasize that their own Association was the only one in south India 'respected and recognised by the Madras Government' (*Annual Report*, 1943).

The hostile intentions of Calcutta were seen to be further demonstrated in the establishment during Gidney's presidency of several branches of the All-India body in south India, which competed for members with the Madras organization, which itself had, in addition to its principal Madras city branches, a number of 'Circles' throughout the south.[32] Although the All-India Association had occasionally threatened to open branches in Madras city, it did not do so until 1936, thus challenging the monopoly of the southern body in its very heartland. In its editorial of October 1936

The Anglo-Indian wrote 'This Association had lived in unity and peace for 42 years until the All-India Association came into the Presidency as a hostile body'.

Despite its resistance to what was seen as a takeover, and the sometimes harsh rhetoric of both sides, the Madras Association had all along acknowledged Gidney's immense contribution to the cause of Anglo-India, and his pre-eminent position in the community. Whenever he visited Madras he was welcomed and feted by members of the Madras body. In 1934, the latter decided to remit 7.5 per cent of its membership fees to Gidney to support his work in the Central Legislative Assembly, a policy which was followed throughout the years of dispute and contestation. By 1937, the last year for which figures are available, over Rs 5,500 had been paid, a not inconsiderable amount (*Annual Report*, 1937).

With the death of Gidney in March 1942 and the election in his place of Frank Anthony, all pretence of seeking an amicable resolution of their differences seemed to disappear. Indeed, initial contacts with Anthony soon convinced the leadership in Madras that, by comparison, Gidney had, at least, been interested in dialogue, and was amenable to reasoned argument. They insisted that, just before the All-India president's death, both sides had been on the verge of a breakthrough in their unity talks. The *Annual Report* for 1943 recounted how he 'had conceded complete autonomy to our Association in all Provincial matters'. And in a special pamphlet on 'Anglo-Indian Unity: a review of the position' the author insisted that at a meeting several months earlier Gidney had offered

> (1) Safeguards for our funds (2) Complete autonomous status in the administration of all matters connected with the Community in the Madras Presidency [and] (3) Jurisdiction over all branches of the All-India body in the Madras Presidency.[33]

The new president of the All-India body, it was claimed, repudiated all these proposals: 'Mr Anthony seeks to relegate us to the position of a 'reconstituted branch' of the All-India Association' (*Annual Report,* 1943). Negotiations effectively ceased. Indeed, the All-India body stepped up its activity in the south, and in 1943, the Madras Association's *Annual Report* announced that it had lost one of its Circles through 'hostile propaganda' on the part of the All-India Association, and three years later two more Circles 'defected' to the northern organization, taking some 200 members (*Annual Report*, 1946). Anthony's Association also proposed its own candidates for the Madras Provincial Legislature, drawn from its supporters in the south. In 1945 the *Annual Report* of the southern

Association commented that 'Anthony put up candidates for the Madras Legislative Assembly and his two candidates were elected over those put forward by the South India Association.' The *Annual Report* for the following year records that a memorandum was forwarded to the Viceroy complaining about Anthony's 'interference in our Provincial elections' and attributes his influence as Anglo-India's representative in the Central Legislative Assembly and 'more particularly on the railway voters' as being 'mainly responsible for the failure of our candidates'. In his autobiographical memoir, Anthony himself writes

> Quite frankly, I could not understand Gidney's attitude towards this dissident but ineffective organisation which could only act in a manner subversive of the Community's best interests. . . [In] January, 1946 I undertook a lightning tour of our branches in the South. . . In March the results of the Provincial Assembly elections were announced. Every seat in [the] Legislature was captured by the candidates set up by the All-India body (1969: 168–9).

The rivalry between the two Associations has continued unabated since Independence.

Contemporary Associational Politics

While the issue of uniting the two associations is still discussed (and rejected), one major point of contestation remains the right to represent the community in the central and provincial legislatures. Since Independence it has been the ruling party at the Centre which has nominated two Anglo-Indians to sit as MPs in the Indian Parliament (Lok Sabha); also, the party in power in each state in which there is a large Anglo-Indian population appoints an Anglo-Indian member to its Legislative Assembly. As can be imagined, these posts are fiercely competed for in the community. The Madras Association believes that the All-India body has for decades had an undue influence on Congress governments, and has in effect submitted for nomination to the Lok Sabha only the names of All-India-approved candidates, including Frank Anthony himself, who was an MP for almost half a century until his death a few years ago. For only a brief interlude after the 'Emergency' in the mid-1970s, when Congress was replaced by a Janata government, and following the recent accession to power of a BJP-dominated coalition has Anglo-India not been represented by MPs selected by the All-India Association. Indeed, at the moment of writing, for the first time one of their number is not only a woman but lives in Madras – a member of one of the parties in the

BJP-led coalition – and, significantly, is supported by the Southern Association.

At the State level, the successful MLA must cultivate the leadership of the ruling party, and the bond is as likely to be forged on the basis of personal as of party political linkages. While one or other Association may endorse the candidates, they are not necessarily proposed by them, and the last several Anglo-Indian MLAs in the Tamil Nadu Assembly have represented a variety of organizations (including in one case the Madras Association) or none at all.

The principal theme around which Associational rivalry revolves is poverty. Economic deterioration remains the common thread in their discourses. But the leadership of the Madras Association publicly links the community's presumed deterioration with the coming to power in the All-India Association (based since Independence in Delhi) of Frank Anthony and his inability to represent Anglo-India to the authorities. In a series of letters to newspapers and to prominent figures in the state of Tamil Nadu, leaders of the Southern Association argued that the watershed in Anglo-Indian fortunes was the appointment of the rival Association's leaders to represent the whole of the Anglo-Indian community in Parliament. Until then, as the former claimed in a letter to the *Indian Express* (8 September 1986), 'the community was prosperous and self-reliant. Today it is in shambles, economically, educationally, and culturally, thanks to the leadership of [the two northern MPs].' The latter had failed, morover, as 'social workers' and 'champions of the poor, the needy and the downtrodden'.

The issue of poverty has become a focus of contention in another way, as each Association has taken a different position on the question of 'Backward' status for the community in Tamil Nadu. The assignment of Backward status is a state prerogative, through the Tamil Nadu Backward Classes Commission. Such status entitles the holders to compete for certain reserved places in state government organizations, educational institutions, etc. For the Delhi-led All-India body, which is firmly opposed to seeking such a designation, it is a matter of dignity. According to one of the branch leaders of the All-India Association in Madras, 'the community still has a little pride, so it should not be billed as Backward. [If deemed "Backward"] I may get a few crumbs [benefits] but dignity-wise I'm finished.' Another remarked that Anglo-Indians 'need to rely on hard work, not charity [reservations]'. The community, he thought, should be proud to be deemed 'Forward', on a par with the Brahmins. An ordinary member of one of the All-India Association's branches in the city reckoned that little would be gained from a Backward designation.

The Backward class population is overpopulated. There are hundreds of groups in this category and every day they are bringing more people into the schedule. Since we are a small minority we would get only a few of those reservations if we were declared 'Backward'. So we should be satisfied with the benefits we get: free school and scholarships.

Such attitudes contrast with the Madras Association's position. Community decline, the fault of the Anglo-Indian leadership in Delhi, it is argued, can only be halted by declaring the community Backward and enabling it thereby to enjoy the advantages of such a categorization. Many ordinary Anglo-Indians support the campaign, assuming that it would improve their chances of employment. One elderly woman, whose two sons were without work when I met her, reasoned that 'We're a Forward Community but we're unable to go forward in anything. To be Backward is to come forward; like that it is.'

The Madras Association's stance in favour of Backward status enables its leaders and their allies in other Anglo-Indian organizations to declare themselves the guardians of the poor, and label their opponents in the All-India Association the representatives of the privileged. In numerous public and private contexts I heard comments about the latters' lack of concern for the poor: 'These people are arrogant, they know nothing about the poverty of most Anglo-Indians . . . they only associate with others who are well-off like themselves.' Or: 'Their leaders are very much against the idea of being deemed Backward. It's all very well for those who are well-off.' Discourses of poverty thus constitute an important element in intra-community disputes. Indeed, at one point during fieldwork in early 1996, I found myself caught up in these debates. At a meeting organized by the Madras Association, which I was invited to address on the topic of 'The Anglo-Indian community: past and present', my own efforts to paint a picture of steady progress (which I naively assumed was expected) came to naught. Both the person introducing me before the talk, and another thanking me after it, made plain their own views that the community was sinking further into poverty, that it could only hope to recover if 'Backward' status was granted, and that the Madras Association alone was struggling to achieve this aim. The Association's application for inclusion of the Anglo-Indian community in the list of Backward Classes was turned down in 1995, but its campaign is continuing.

The Politics of Philanthropy

In this section I suggest that the giving and receiving of charity contributes to a shared sense of belonging. Issues of poverty also form an important backdrop to assertions and acknowledgement of leadership positions within the Anglo-Indian community of Madras, through engagement in philanthropic activities. Within this population, as indeed in the wider Indian context, leadership establishes itself very largely by charitable acts (Brass 1990: 96; Dickey 1995: 13; Mines 1994: 184).[34] Anglo-Indians, I was often told, expect service to the group from their leaders, and this is usually glossed as 'helping the poor'. Struggles for public offices (in the Anglo-Indian Associations as well as in other community organizations) are therefore often competed for in terms of how contestants have succeeded or failed in this mission. Challengers for office accuse the incumbents of having achieved little; the latter, in turn, dismiss those seeking office as having done nothing for the poor of the community, and therefore of being undeserving of support. Poverty and its alleviation through philanthropy is therefore the terrain on which contests for influence and reputation within the Anglo-Indian community are continuously waged (Caplan 1998).

Eminent Anglo-Indians or those aspiring to eminence must exercise control of an organization which engages in charitable activities on behalf of the Anglo-Indian poor. Some do this by seeking office in one or more of the well-established institutions, such as the Friend-in-Need Society, the Madras or All-India Associations, the Home Missionary Society, or via the Governing Body of an Anglo-Indian school or the Pastorate Committee of a church with a large Anglo-Indian membership in the city. Those who, for one reason or another, choose or are compelled to remain outside these institutions, will usually attempt to establish an organization of their own. As one prominent Anglo-Indian figure pointed out, 'Every leader needs a group, something to back him up, to enable him to give.' There are thus many clubs and organizations run by prominent individuals or those hoping to become prominent, which sponsor various kinds of welfare: soup kitchens in poor neighbourhoods; 'pensions' for the elderly; financial aid for schoolchildren; school meals; Christmas dinners, hampers and treats, etc. These groups provide a base from which to build or maintain a reputation in the community.

With few exceptions, the charities in Madras serving Anglo-Indians during the colonial period were created, run and funded almost entirely by Europeans; indeed, were an important avenue through which Anglo-Indians encountered colonial authority. Since Independence, the running of these organizations has been assumed by Anglo-Indians themselves, and there has been a proliferation of new philanthropic agencies run for and mainly by members of the community. For the most part they are modest organizations established by prominent families or individuals in the Madras Anglo-Indian community. While some concentrate their efforts on helping poor Anglo-Indians in particular neighbourhoods, others spread their charitable net more widely. Some have been operating for a number of years, others are relatively recent ventures; few are able to survive for very long, and certainly not beyond the lifetimes of their principals.[35]

Charitable groups and institutions in Madras need to rely on their principals – whether elected committee members of major community organizations or founder-officials of what are in effect private philanthropic associations – to provide funds. However, the great majority have relatively few resources of their own to distribute, since there are hardly a handful of very wealthy Anglo-Indians in the city. Those who would seek to sustain or enhance a reputation in the community as philanthropists must therefore depend on their ability to raise funds for their activities.

These funds are raised mainly from and through close personal ties – relatives, friends, neighbours, ex-schoolmates and business acquaintances (some of them from outside the Anglo-Indian community). With the emigration to the West of large numbers of Anglo-Indians over the past forty years (see Chapter 5), philanthropists and their organizations turn increasingly for assistance to family members and friends settled abroad, and to overseas associations formed on the basis of former neighbourhoods, schools or churches in Madras. The utilization of personal links guarantees the bona fides of the organizations and individuals seeking funds, and satisfies the donors that the money will reach the designated beneficiaries.

Anglo-Indian charity is highly personalized not only in its style of raising funds, but also in the manner of their disbursement. There are few formal procedures for identifying the needy, or for verifying their claims of distress.[36] Rather, benefactors usually insist that they are personally acquainted with those on whom they confer benefits, and that there is no need for the systematic investigation of pleas for assistance, as might be undertaken by professional agencies. As one philanthropist told me, 'I have known these people for years; I know all about their families.' Another pointed out that he was a 'local boy ' and knew 'the full history of all our people', while a third, responsible for helping to bring the Anglo-Indian poor of her church to the attention of the parish committee, insisted that I had only to mention the name of any person in her 'zone' and she could tell me 'everything about them'. Indeed, in a small community like the Anglo-Indian in Madras, most persons do know one another, or about one another, and can readily locate others in a network of relations, friends or acquaintances.[37] Moreover, since not a few Anglo-Indian benefactors have themselves come from backgrounds of hardship, if not penury, they can usually trace personal connections to the families they assist. On one occasion, I was asked by a well-known philanthropist to accompany him on a visit to several people whom he regularly helps. In the household of a widow the conversation was mainly about her late husband who had, as a young man, played hockey for the same railway team as my guide. In another household, where a couple were planning, with his financial help, to establish a small business making and selling *idli* (steamed rice cakes) and *dosai* (rice-flour pancakes) in their slum neighbourhood, my host remarked after we had left that the husband, an unskilled labourer, had been his classmate in primary school. In a few cases, bonds of kinship, affinity or godparenthood link philanthropists and the recipients of their charity.

Most appeals for help from the poor involve direct approaches to charitable organizations and their principals. Occasionally they are made in writing, but most requests for assistance are made in person, although the mediation of an influential person will undoubtedly improve the petitioner's chances of success. Alms conferred in the context of a personalized relationship are, however, often difficult to withdraw. Once committed to assisting particular individuals, there is an ineluctable process of being drawn further into the relationship as demands continue and multiply, and the conditions of poverty giving rise to the initial gift are not alleviated. The outcome is that each philanthropic agency tends to develop a particular (though not mutually exclusive) constituency of dependent beneficiaries who consume the greater part of its resources, and effectively exclude others from its charitable favours. Several organizations have recently announced that they are unable to consider appeals for help from new clients.

Charity procedures which are highly individualized inevitably invite various kinds of 'abuse' by the poor. Certain faces would reappear time and again at numerous almsgiving events around the city which I attended, and on several occasions I was asked by individuals not to mention to one agency that I had seen them obtaining help from another.[38] But for most Anglo-Indian philanthropists a personalized system not only ensures their control over every facet of the organization's charitable activity, but guarantees the continuance of a close relationship between themselves and their beneficiaries. Whatever the origins of the gifts they bestow – whether their own resources or those of others – the recipients tend to acknowledge the generosity of those who actually confer benefits directly on them. The charitable relationship here as elsewhere in India is thus a highly personalized one, and even the more bureaucratic organizations are usually identified with their leaders who, as Kakar has suggested, 'are believed to be the sole repository of the virtues and vices of the institutions' (quoted in Mines and Gourishankar 1990: 765). In the Anglo-Indian context, individual beneficiaries of charity almost invariably identify the donor organization by its principal, so that it is the latter ('Uncle A' or 'Auntie B') who provides rather than the organization s/he represents.

While the personalization of charity tends to individualize experiences of poverty, it serves at the same time to unite those in adversity. There is, for one thing, a coalescence imposed by common dependency on assistance and shared deference on the occasions of almsgiving. In a variety of settings throughout the city, the recurrent distribution of 'pensions' and other forms of charity involves an encounter between recipient and donor. While the dispositions of personnel may be different on each occasion, the hierarchical message is similar. During the Christmas season, for example, there are numerous festive presentations of clothing, cash and food hampers, and the spatial structure and tone of these events invariably underline status disparities. The principals and their special guests are usually arrayed in spaces set aside for donors (e.g. on a stage), while the recipients are invited one by one to receive their gifts and adopt the appropriate demeanour of subservience. At one such occasion during the Christmas season of 1995/96, there was a momentary confusion of categories when one of the stalwarts of the donor organization, dressed casually and so not very differently from the generality of beneficiaries, unthinkingly seated himself among the latter, and as proceedings neared their conclusion was asked by the person sitting next to him, concerned that he might possibly have been omitted from the list of beneficiaries, if his name had yet been called. The story was later retailed with considerable amusement to fellow principals of the organization and received with much hilarity.

The symbiotic relationship between the Anglo-Indian poor and their philanthropists suggests that public gifting operates within and serves to define the boundaries of an Anglo-Indian ethnic universe. These philanthropists often attribute their involvement in charity and almsgiving to 'a concern for poor Anglo-Indians'.[39] This kind of statement is meant to indicate that theirs is not an inclusive regard for all those in poverty, but one confined exclusively to members of a particular population and, as we have seen, Anglo-Indian giving is on the whole confined within the community. Willingness to give expresses personal commitment stemming from a shared identity (Werbner 1990). The obverse of this is that the Anglo-Indian poor, while benefiting to some extent from charity proffered by agencies external to the community (the Church is the most obvious example), expect to be the sole beneficiaries of the gifts of Anglo-Indian charities, and to acknowledge the generosity of their principals. Donors and recipients of relief are thus dependent on one another (see van Leeuwen 1994: 607; Seabrook 1985: 5). White's argument (1991: 318) that a narrow 'catchment area' for Parsi gifting – its confinement to the Parsi community alone – helped to define group boundaries, applies to Anglo-Indian charity in Madras as well. Through involvement in such activities the poor and their philanthropists both acknowledge and constitute what Werbner calls the 'recognized limits of trust' and subscribe to 'membership in a circle composed of mutually trusting others' (1990: 306). In an otherwise fluid social universe it may be regarded as one way of declaring a commitment to a bounded community – an expression of 'cultural loyalty' in the words of one Anglo-Indian intellectual – and of asserting a sense of common belonging.

Conclusion

In the colonial context I have been considering, métissage implied porous social boundaries and indeterminate identities. Notwithstanding such a fluid social environment, those who spoke for and about Anglo-India and provided its leadership articulated two seemingly contrary if not contradictory modes of belonging. On the one side, and almost certainly until well into the second or third decades of the twentieth century this was the view of the elites as well as the great majority of those in the artisan class, Anglo-Indians – with few exceptions – proclaimed them-selves British; as Hawes puts it, they sought 'to belong to the British community, rather than to one another' (1996: 74). Apart from anything else, they were 'virtually the children of the Government' (Clarke 1878: 7–8), since their employment in the subordinate levels of civil admin-istration or in European enterprises meant that they were economically and politically dependent on the colonial regime (see Hawes 1993: 157).

Moreover, notwithstanding Euro-colonial social practices and attitudes which distanced and demeaned this métis population, policies set in place by colonial officials in the spheres of education and language, religious instruction, defence and security, etc. prompted Anglo-Indians to associate themselves with the colonizers. In the idioms of blood and culture they identified themselves to themselves and to others as unequivocally British, employing essentialist discourses which denied hybridity and proclaimed purity. Further, while being firmly anchored in India, they metaphorically transported themselves to Britain, which was not simply a longed-for homeland, but an 'imagined state of being or moral location' (Gupta and Ferguson 1992: 10). In Bhabha's perceptive words, they held on to 'certain symbols of the elsewhere' around which a text fetishizing this elsewhere was constructed (1992: 114).

From the time it became apparent that British rule in India was drawing to a close, and certainly after Independence, what rhetorical unity there had been within the Anglo-Indian population of Madras about their sense of belonging was fractured. Different sections of the community began to present somewhat disparate discourses: those at both ends of the class spectrum, where interactions – including marriages – with non-Anglo-Indians are most frequent, insist on more localized identifications. Contemporary discourses emanating mainly from the elite sector, which from the late colonial period had acknowledged the wisdom of aligning itself at least rhetorically with aspirations for independence, have a clear 'nationalist' ring about them. Since such elites have enjoyed the benefits of the post-Independence period, and contemplate a promising future, they promote the idea of belonging to local but urbane circles, seeing themselves as sharing the cosmopolitan lifestyles of other elite Indian groups.

Among the most disadvantaged members of the community, whose day-to-day interactions with non-Anglo-Indians in similar circumstances are intense, identities are more fluid and situational. Despite jeremiads of their 'disappearance' through increased intermarriage since Independence there is considerable scope for continued involvement in community institutions (partly for the benefits they offer), and for the exercise by their children of various options, one of which may involve a wish to (re-)identify as or with Anglo-Indians. These external unions have created new 'hybridities' and increased the complexity of identity claims.

It is mainly within the middle or artisan ranks of the Anglo-Indian population that assertions of a European pedigree can still be heard in contemporary Madras. These claims, however, either meet derision or fall on deaf ears both within the now dominant groups in Indian society, including the elites of their own community, and outside it, where they are meant to be heard by Western governments assumed to be in search of technically qualified and culturally sympathetic immigrant populations. I return to the issue of emigration in Chapter 5. Here it is important to note how essentializing strategies have changed and diversified in the context of an evolving political climate – both before and following Independence.

Alongside colonial discourses associating themselves with their British rulers, Anglo-Indians paradoxically exhibited – a result of both external compulsion and internal dynamic – a remarkable degree of self-awareness and group consciousness from at least the early nineteenth century. In spite of their disparate origins they came to regard theselves as possessing an identity of their own.[40] As we have seen, numerous meetings, activities and resolutions of, at first, various ad hoc groups, and subsequently, more formal associations, 'served as outlets for community opinions and platforms for pleaders of community causes' (Grimshaw 1958: 232). Indeed, from this time on, Anglo-Indians usually employed the term 'community' to describe themselves. In some of the earlier sociological literature on Anglo-Indians, the debate focused on whether their 'marginality' in Indian society – 'poised between the foreign and indigenous "civilizations" of India', as Cressey put it (1935: 264) – rendered Anglo-Indians a 'disorganized' group (Ibid.) or, as Goodrich was to argue, enabled them (because of the discrimination they suffered at the hands of the rulers) to emerge as 'a coherent, self-conscious, minority' (quoted in Grimshaw 1958: 228; see also Goodrich 1952). Naidis (1963) endorses Goodrich's view, as does Grimshaw, who adds that the community fell on hard times in spite of a well-developed group consciousness, and not because of its absence (1958: 231). British policy towards Indian nationalist demands for Home Rule and later Independence in the twentieth century only served to encourage Anglo-India's awareness of a distinctive political existence.

But these imaginings of 'community' have had and continue to have reference to different levels of inclusiveness. Most everyday settings for the expression of Anglo-Indian sensibilities have been parochial, involving relationships within the same city and even neighbourhood. At times, or in certain contexts, Anglo-Indians have seen themselves primarily as part of wider regional collectivities. Thus the Southern Association had a number of affiliated Circles throughout the Madras Presidency, and together their primary reference was the Government and institutions of the Presidency. At the same time, they recognized their opposition to other Anglo-Indians of similar location elsewhere (Bengal, for example) and certainly to those who presumed to speak for all Anglo-India. Hawes suggests that it might be 'more in accordance with reality to perceive the Eurasian population of British India, and its adjacent Indian states, as a series of loosely linked individual communities scattered across the continent, each with its own particular identity' (1997: 6).

In other periods and contexts the focus of interest and concern has been 'national', in as much as the different community associations acknowledged their common position vis à vis both the British rulers, on the one side, and the undifferentiated 'Indian' population (especially, the Indian nationalists), on the other. But while, as we have seen, competing associations and leaders appeared to threaten Anglo-Indian unity and rendered difficult if not impossible the kind of solidarity thought necessary to confront an often hostile colonial regime as well as an independent Indian government beset by numerous sectional claims, from a different perspective these conflicts, as Gluckman pointed out long ago (1955), indicated a vibrant politics of community, and one, moreover, which has persisted into the present. Furthermore, in their commitment to 'ethnic philanthropy' Anglo-Indian leaders and the beneficiaries of their largesse together reiterate a sense of belonging to the same moral universe.

Since Independence, the Anglo-Indian community has been indelibly affected by international migratory movements, which have resulted in a significant proportion of its members leaving Madras (and India) to settle in the West. It is to the latter development that I turn in the next chapter.

Notes

1. By comparison, Dutch was the language of only a minority of the 'Europeans' and Indo-Europeans in the Netherlands East Indies (Stoler 1997: 210).
2. See Chapter 3, Note 4.
3. In a poignant marriage of faith and food, the Madras Military Orphan Asylum, founded in 1789, devised a weekly menu which featured a variety of local rice and curry dishes, but served roast mutton, vegetable and bread for Sunday lunch (Bell 1812).
4. Specific Roman Catholic churches were not set aside for Europeans and Anglo-Indians. However, even when the liturgy was in Latin there were separate English and vernacular services since, as one priest commented, 'preaching was done in both languages'.
5. Renford mentions a United Railway and Government Servants Association, founded in 1874, which had forty branches and 'a considerable number of the 4,000 or so European and 4,000 Eurasians employed on the railways' (Renford 1979: 62). I have been unable to ascertain if there were any branches in south India.

6. An Anglo-Indian and European Railway Workers Union was formed in 1930, and even went on strike for a few months at the Perambur workshops of the Madras and Southern Mahratta railways in late 1932 (See *The Anglo-Indian*, September 1930; December 1932).

7. Hawes points out that the inventories of personal belongings – clothes, books, musical instruments, furniture, etc. – left at death by upper level Eurasians in the early nineteenth century 'indicate reasonably comfortable lives modelled on and conforming to British social behaviour' (1997: 8).

8. Memorandum addressed to Lt Gen, The Most Noble George, Marquis Tweeddale, K.T. & C.B., Governor of Madras, by the East Indian Community of Madras, 21 January 1848.

9. The Association began life as the Eurasian and Anglo-Indian Association of Southern India, changed its name to the Anglo-Indian Association of Southern India in 1907, and to the Anglo-Indian and Domiciled European Association of Southern India in 1928.

10. Speech by Sir Henry Gidney in London, reported in *The Anglo-Indian*, January 1926.

11. Dr K.E. Wallace was for a time president of the Anglo-Indian Association in Calcutta.

12. Bear argues that nationalist politicians refused to build alliances with the Anglo-Indian community which they viewed as 'outside the nationalist project' (1998: 10).

13. For example, the *Madras Mail*, quoted in *The Anglo-Indian*, February 1926.

14. 'Anglo-Indians and the Congress: Mr Bower on the impasse', *The Anglo-Indian*, February 1940.

15. Whereas community organizations (including schools) regard as Anglo-Indian only the child of an Anglo-Indian father, the Tamil Nadu government, when agreeing to provide financial support for Anglo-Indian schools, insisted on the definition being extended to the child of either an Anglo-Indian father or mother.

16. Though technically free, there are numerous 'fees' to be paid (for uniforms, computers, etc.) which many families find difficult to meet. School authorities explain that the amounts given as subvention by the Tamil Nadu government have not kept pace with the costs of education. As a result, many schools favour admitting a greater proportion of non-Anglo-Indian children who can be charged high fees (see Chapter 2). The parents of Anglo-Indian children who are not well-off complain that they find it increasingly difficult to gain admission for their children in Anglo-Indian schools.

17. While the perception is that this is a recent 'problem', there is evidence that it goes back to at least the middle of the nineteenth century. A report in the *Athenaeum* for 29 March 1853 noted that in the Vepery District Free Schools in Madras, attended almost entirely by poor Anglo-Indian children, nearly 20 per cent were, at the time of entry, 'unacquainted with the English language, and a much larger number are in the habit of speaking Tamil ordinarily, both among themselves and at home'. Hawes suggests that similar problems were reported by the Calcutta Free School as far back as the 1830s (personal communication).

18. Most philanthropic organizations for Anglo-Indians in the city offer 'scholarships' to assist children from poor families to attend school. But most cannot afford to offer more than token amounts.

19. One woman, whose mother was an Adi-Dravida and father an Anglo-Indian, complained that her certificate declares her an Anglo-Indian: 'So I could not take advantage of my mother's status. If I had I'd have got a job.'

20. Goodrich argues that prior to 1780 there was virtually no definition of the Anglo-Indian as a category. Whatever prejudices existed were directed against individuals, not against the class 'Eurasian'. In her view, Anglo-Indians thus came into existence as a community only between 1780 and 1830 (1952: 230).

21. See also *References to Madras in the Asiatic Journal 1829–1840,* (December 1831), 1886: 5.

22. *References to Madras in the Asiatic Journal 1829–1840,* (December 1831), 1886: 32.

23. From 'A brief history of the Anglo-Indians and the Foundation of the Anglo-Indian and Domiciled European Association of Southern India, at Madras: from information gathered from the records of the Association', unpublished, n.d.

24. 'A brief history of the Anglo-Indians. . .'

25. It is possible, of course, that the organization referred to initially was the Madras Philanthropic Association.

26. Renford gives the lower figure of forty, while Abel suggests that there were over 150 branches (see also *The Anglo-Indian Review,* IV, 1, 1916; *The Anglo-Indian,* 31 October 1917).

27. There is some dispute as to which of the two principal associations – that begun in Calcutta or that based in Madras – is the oldest. The disagreement turns on whether the present All-India Association is, in fact, a direct descendant of the older Calcutta Association (*The Anglo-Indian,* February 1928).

28. According to Krishna, the British Government, by recognizing the claims of minority communities, established a 'counterpoise policy' which sought to diminish the claims of the majority (1939: 162–3).
29. The Ilbert Bill threatened to withdraw the right of European British Subjects to be tried before a European judge. An association of Europeans was formed around this time to protest the Ilbert Bill (Wolpert 1989: 257).
30. There was never complete unanimity in the Madras Association. From time to time contributions in the Association's journal or annual reports noted differences of opinion, but on the whole the great majority of the membership supported the leadership's stance.
31. It would, of course, be wrong to suggest that these associations reflected the diversity of the Anglo-Indian community. For one thing, most of the membership and certainly the leadership was drawn from a limited circle of the educated and comfortably-off. For another, they seldom involved more than a small proportion of the population. Between 1924 and 1948 the Madras Association's membership averaged 1,100. But in both these regards, the Anglo-Indian Associations were no different from most ethnic or community organizations.
32. The number of Circles in the Madras Association varied, although it seldom fell below six or went above twelve. Some Circles fell into abeyance out of disinterest on the part of the membership. Others came to grief through no fault of their own. Thus, the Negapatam Circle was dissolved in 1928 because of the transfer of the Railway Workshops (and the main source of its membership) from Negapatam to Golden Rock, near Trichinopoly. Similarly, a new Circle established in Jalarpet in 1934 had to close owing to the transfer of all Mail Drivers and Foremen to Arkonam.
33. The Report was written by E.H.M. Bower, the former president of the Madras Association, dated 7 February 1946.
34. Newspapers regularly (and especially as elections approach) feature reports of politicians distributing free clothing (saris or dhotis), toys, cash, ration cards, even land to the poor.
35. A few, which are overseas mission- or church-sponsored, engage in charity as part of their evangelizing programmes.
36. C.S. Loch, in his classic *Reference Book for Almoners, Almsgivers and Others*, noted how important it was to inquire into the circumstances of the poor before offering charity (1883: 10).
37. White similarly points out how in the relatively small Parsi community of eighteenth-century Bombay 'donors and recipients probably knew each other personally' (1991: 318).

38. People seek assistance from several sources partly because no single agency is able to provide more than small amounts of help to any individual, and partly because there is little or no coordination of effort among the donors, making such exploits relatively easy (see also Brennan 1979: 123).

39. Those outside the small circle of philanthropists, however, sometimes point to the less than altruistic motives of some Anglo-Indian benefactors. They see much philanthropic effort as an expression of the urge for recognition and influence in the community: 'Feed the poor, get a name' was how one woman phrased it, and numerous people made similar remarks about individuals who are in the forefront of Anglo-Indian charity. I have even heard philanthropists compared to medieval European squires – 'helping the poor at the gate' – and to more contemporary mafia 'dons'.

40. By contrast, Lewis remarks of the Coloured population in South Africa that because of their heterogeneous nature 'they lacked any strong unifying sense of . . . identity' (1987: 8).

–5–

The Spirit of Emigration

My son has a good job but he wants to go abroad. I'll tell you why. He's got children and he is looking for his children's future. Here only the scheduled castes are given preference in all the vacancies, so whatever qualifications you have, those people are getting pushed up for the top jobs. If we send our children away, with their ability they can come up.

All my friends from many years back have gone and settled in England and Australia, and my heart has ever since been somewhere over there. Only I couldn't make it. So it's sometimes difficult to settle in India.

Maybe the salaries here are not very good. But we should be satisfied in our own country. None of my brothers and sisters are abroad. The next generation, could have a bright future. My son has a good opportunity to go but he doesn't want to leave.

Introduction

Until very near the end of colonial rule Anglo-Indians insisted on close biological, social and cultural ties with the British. The community came to submerge its biography, to borrow Veena Das's phrase, in the biography of the colonial state (1995: 109–10). For much of this period Anglo-Indians imagined themselves as belonging elsewhere. In other words, they could be seen as 'transnationals' – to employ a currently popular term – not by virtue of migration across political boundaries, but through experiencing profound displacement in terms of belonging: by residing in one location but adjudging themselves only at home in another. But while believing themselves biologically, culturally and morally suited to settlement in the West, it was only the end of colonial rule, and the possibilities offered by what was seen as Britain's open door immigration policy, that allowed many to emigrate or, as some phrased it, 'return home' (Gist 1975: 41, 57).[1] Subsequently, against a background of worldwide population movements and in response to changing national policies on immigration in the West, Anglo-Indians began to settle in other countries as well, most notably Australia.

This chapter considers the impact of such an exodus on the 'sending' population. In Madras, people's own explanations for this egression, determination to join it and reactions to being thwarted, alongside a continuous stress on 'abroad' as the only suitable place for Anglo-Indians, amounts to what may be termed a 'spirit' of emigration.

The literature on migration offers few analogous instances of migratory effects which can provide a template for the Anglo-Indian case. Recent work, understandably, is devoted to resisting earlier 'neoclassic' modernization approaches which highlighted 'push-pull' factors, and foregrounded the individual migrant as a rational decision-maker in pursuit of economic opportunities. Modernization theorists viewed the outcomes of such decisions as economically and socially beneficial both to the sending and receiving societies. Those who reject such models rightly draw attention to the unequal structural linkages between those, primarily underdeveloped, regions providing the migrants and other, mainly developed, areas importing them. They focus on the political economy of migration, and seek to move the debate away from individual choice and motivation, to issues of 'dependency' and 'articulation' (Kearney 1986).

In other ways, too, existing studies of international migration in the post-war period provide few clues as to how we might approach the Anglo-Indian case. For one thing, much of the literature on the effects of emigration for sending societies deals with cyclical movements of labour, and assesses the impact of remittances and the investment of monies earned abroad on the economy of labour-exporting families or that of the wider community. Some studies examine the importance of skills acquired by migrants during their periods away, and the manner in which these are applied when they return (Rhoades 1978). Anglo-Indians, however, are permanent emigrants, and so do not import new skills; moreover, those who remain are the recipients of no more than nominal and sporadic remittances. For another, research on permanent migration has tended to concentrate on the 'brain drain', and the signifiance of exporting professionals, scientists and highly skilled technicians from the developing to the developed world (Appleyard 1989). The Anglo-Indians involved in this outflow have all along tended to be moderately educated and skilled, e.g. (male) artisans and technicians or (female) teachers, nurses and secretaries. These are occupations which are in plentiful supply in Madras (as elsewhere in India) and within whose ranks there are serious unemployment and under-employment problems; this can hardly be termed a 'brain drain'. Anglo-Indians therefore do not fit easily into either the category of urban, highly educated and professionally skilled 'new migrants', or the rural, uneducated and industrially unskilled who comprised the 'old migrants' (Helweg 1991). In delineating an Anglo-Indian spirit of emigration, this chapter pays particular attention to the differential access to migration opportunities within the community as well as the diversity of attitudes towards and ideas regarding 'abroad'.

Colonial Migrations

In the latter part of the colonial period there were some modest and sporadic movements of Anglo-Indians overseas. In the mid-nineteenth century an East Indian Emigration Committee was established in Madras to assist Anglo-Indian young men to secure domestic employment abroad. In January 1853 the *Athenaeum* carried several announcements inviting 'East Indian young men between the ages of 16 and 20, willing to engage in Domestic Service as Footmen, Cooks, or Grooms' to present themselves before the Committee (*Athenaeum*, 6 and 13 January 1853). Clarke, possibly referring to the same project, reports that in the 'mid-nineteenth century some 250 poor and destitute [Anglo-Indian] boys were sent out as domestics to Australia' (1878: 30). Several months later the *Athenaeum* carried a report on a group of young men who had been sent to Sydney, Australia by the Madras Emigration Society – which could have been another name for or successor to the East Indian Emigration Committee, or an entirely separate organization – all of whom were 'instantly engaged as artisans, shepherds, or domestic servants' (*Athenaeum*, 31 May 1853).

These efforts obviously continued for several years since in March 1857 the same newspaper carried an article regarding the 'prejudiced reports' circulating about the second batch of East Indian emigrants who were sent out to Australia on the ship *Palmyra*. All had been found employment: 'some were engaged as farm labourers and shepherds in the bush, some as domestic servants, grooms and water-men in the town, and others as labourers on different works'.[2] In addition, twenty-four Anglo-Indian compositors were brought out under contract to the *Sydney Empire* and while they met 'ill feeling and animosity from the generality of the European Compositors', their employer defended their right to be there (see also Moore 1986a: 129).[3]

Other emigration projects were mooted but not all came to fruition. The annual report of the Friend-in-Need Society (FINS) for 1884 includes a brief note on 'Eurasian Emigration to Australia' in which it refers to an enquiry made to the Government of Western Australia to which a positive response was forthcoming. The Government there agreed that 'Eurasians might do well in that Colony' and suggested that an 'experimental batch' of one hundred emigrants be dispatched, only that the cost of their passage and outfit be defrayed in Madras (i.e. by the FINS). The suggestion was circulated to various committees of the Society for comments, most of which were of an 'adverse nature', and the scheme was quietly dropped (Report of the Friend-in-Need Society, 1884).

An immigration policy which discriminated against those who were not of 'pure European' descent ultimately prevented the large-scale movement of Anglo-Indians (and other Indians) to Australia and New Zealand. The Reverend Dr Graham, founder of the St Andrew's Homes at Kalimpong for Anglo-Indian children wanted to send 'the best products of his school' to these colonies (Minto 1974: 74). Boys were taught the rudiments of agriculture, and girls of domestic science, on the assumption that they would go overseas as farm labourers or maids. But Minto tells us that the Whites-only policy of these governments 'was a constant source of irritation and sadness to Graham [since] Eurasians were included in the category of prohibited immigrants' (1974: 74–5).

What seems clear from the foregoing is that emigration was seen as a possible solution to the problem of unemployment and poverty within the Anglo-Indian population. Throughout the nineteenth century the organization of these schemes was largely part of the charitable efforts of Europeans on behalf of Anglo-Indians. Thus, the Madras Emigration Society was established and run by prominent members of the city's British community. Moore mentions a Madras judge (Sir William Burton) as having started a scheme to settle 'poor whites' or Eurasians in Australia (1986a: 129), while in its report on the 'second batch of East Indian emigrants' who travelled to Sydney on the ship *Palmyra*, the *Athenaeum* (7 March 1857) remarks that 'great praise is due Lady Dowling who took a lively interest in the poor emigrants'. Similarly, the Friend-in-Need Society was, at the time its own emigration plans were mooted (see above), run by eminent members of the city's European elite. But even when, in the course of the twentieth century, Anglo-Indians themselves took greater responsibility for the community's poor, through various charitable enterprises (see Chapter 4), emigration continued to be regarded as one solution to unemployment. Thus, in 1930, with the Indian economy in deep recession and Anglo-Indians feeling the effects of the Montagu-Chelmsford Reforms, there were urgent calls for new programmes of emigration to the West, this time by the Anglo-Indian Council in Bombay (*The Anglo-Indian,* January 1931).

While the Antipodes seemed to be the favourite (if frustrated) destination for organizations seeking to assist poorer Anglo-Indians needing employment, there was some settlement elsewhere. Thus, several thousand

Anglo-Indians, mainly originating in south India, were resident in Burma by the early years of the twentieth century. Many had gone there to develop the railways, telegraph and postal systems or in some other official capacity and stayed to settle (see Koop 1960: 19). Better-off members of the community who went abroad during the colonial period tended to make their way to England. Thus a former president of the Anglo-Indian Association of Southern India expressed surprise that 'as far back as 1892', when he visited the UK, 'there were many hundreds of Eurasians earning a comfortable living in London' (*The Anglo-Indian*, 28 March 1918). In 1923 an Anglo-Indian Association was established in Britain, with H.A. Stark as its first president.

Post-Independence Migrations

Alongside the conviction that their roots were in the West, the prospect of Indian independence engendered no little fear within the community that Anglo-India's history of support for the Raj would be repaid in kind by a Congress-led government and, moreover, that whatever economic privileges they enjoyed under the British would be abolished by the new regime. The All-India Anglo-Indian Association in 1942 thus urged the colonial authorities to allow Anglo-Indians the opportunity to emigrate to any part of the British Empire. According to Moore, 'a fever to leave was gripping our people' (1986a: 88). The withdrawal of the colonial rulers was therefore soon followed by the exodus of considerable numbers of Anglo-Indians. Younger states that well over half the population had emigrated by 1982 (1987: 47). Gist quotes unofficial estimates of 50,000 for the number who left the country in the three decades following Independence, which represented between one-fifth and one-quarter of the immediate post-war Anglo-Indian population in India. Anglo-Indian leaders in Madras estimate that between 40 and 50 per cent of the city's community have gone abroad since 1947 (see also Brennan 1979: 265).

Anthony is one among many who have suggested that before 1970 the majority emigrated to Britain (1969: 384). One woman I met recalled that when she started school in 1955 'most of the senior boys and girls were going away to England. They were the first lot that went away. Many people had opted at the time of separation [Independence] to take British passports, and they went off.' The records of the Commonwealth Relations Office in London attest that authorities in the UK were certainly aware of the possibility that large numbers of Anglo-Indians might qualify for and demand the right to settle in Britain. They also reveal an attitude that while this immigration could not be thwarted it should not be encouraged. High Commissions in India (and Pakistan) were therefore advised to err on the side of caution when assessing the claims of Anglo-Indians to UK citizenship under the British Nationality Act of 1948.[4]

With the introduction of legislation in the 1960s and early 1970s designed to reduce drastically the numbers of immigrants entering Britain from Asia and Africa, Anglo-Indians turned increasingly to Australia, which had until that time maintained an immigration policy based on strict racial criteria.[5] Australia began to abandon its Whites-only policy in 1967, and by 1972 had ceased to discriminate against prospective settlers on the basis of ancestry or nationality (Inglis et al. 1992: 1).[6] Immigration from India increased rapidly from this period and according to Helweg Anglo-Indians, at least for a time, were 'given priority', on the basis of 'their Christian identity and British-like values and behavioural patterns' (1991: 30, Note 5; see also D'Cruz n.d.: 8, 14; 1999: 277–9). While figures for the extent of Anglo-Indian migration vary considerably, by the mid-1970s Australia had certainly displaced the UK as the main target of the Anglo-Indian exodus, and continues to do so until today. Their association with Australia has given rise in some quarters, especially on college campuses in Madras, to a new slang term for Anglo-Indians – 'dings' or 'dingos'. Recently, Anglo-Indians have begun settling in Canada and the USA, but the numbers there are still comparatively small.

The issue of emigration looms large in the consciousness of Anglo-Indians resident in the city, and most of the people I met broached the topic in one form or another during the course of our conversations. Only those at the lower end of the class hierarchy who, since they lack the requisite schooling, occupational skills, and high fees required for lodging applications, do not entertain any possibility of leaving, and are not involved in the discourse. Even those technically eligible to settle abroad by virtue of descent, are unable to do so because they lack the capital to fund emigration. Thus, one man I knew, both of whose grandparents and mother were domiciled in Britain, could not leave India: 'It is finances that are holding me up. Cash.'

Increasingly, too, the highly successful minority of Anglo-Indians who have benefited noticeably from educational and economic opportunities in post-Independence India, are less inclined to contemplate emigration, although most are in a position to do so if they want to, and the majority have close relatives abroad, whom they visit from time to time. For the rest, however, and especially those belonging to the artisan class, the hope of leaving India to re-start life in the West (and especially Australia) has touched and continues to touch their lives in a variety of significant ways.

It is worth noting that while many hundreds of Anglo-Indians from Madras spend a period – sometimes years – working in one of the Gulf states, this is not regarded as migration in the same sense as movement to the West. For one thing, permanent settlement is disallowed. Those working in the Gulf are almost invariably on short-term – most frequently two- or three-year – contracts, and while these can usually be renewed when they expire, this is by no means certain. I met any number of Anglo-Indians who had had to return to Madras when their agreements had not been extended. For another, the kinds of employment for which most Anglo-Indians are engaged – catering and tourism workers, technicians, service engineers, maintenance staff, etc. – does not allow them to bring families to the Gulf. Thus, hotel staff – probably the largest single category of Anglo-Indian Gulf workers – are only provided with dormitory-type accommodation, and in any case rents for private dwellings are said to be prohibitively high. The few employees who are in a position to have members of their families with them tend to be in well-paid professional or white-collar occupations, and even they report that the costs of living, and of education and health services in particular, are a disincentive to having their families (and especially young children) join them. Finally, as English-speakers and Christians, Anglo-Indians claim to feel no special cultural affinity to the area. The Gulf is therefore seen simply as a source – much sought after – of lucrative employment, but not a genuine migrant destination. It might, however, provide an individual with the funds and additional experience required to increase his (occasionally her) chances of successful emigration to the West.

Planning Emigration

Some have yet to attempt emigration, but are planning and saving to do so. Aspiring emigrants keep abreast of changes in the target country's selection policies – changing skill demands, age qualifications, regulations regarding family sponsorship and reunion policy, etc. – and there is a constant informal exchange of information within families and the community. In addition, members of the family living abroad keep their relatives in Madras informed of the types of jobs available and other relevant information which can be of assistance in preparing an application. Parents sometimes seek to plan their children's educational and career futures to accord with what these policies are perceived to be.

> In Australia they don't want white collar people, managers in offices. So I tried to fit [the children] in to what was wanted there. 'We need cooks, our

hotels are growing, that's our main business here.' So, the first boy I sent on a one-year catering course, trained him to be a cook. He was the first and landed up in Sydney. Next, my daughter married a boy working in a truck building firm as a fitter. 'We need fitters here.' He got a chance, and they landed in Melbourne. The next boy joined an offshore oil rig because Australia wanted drillers. He started as a maintenance man, painting and fetching tools. He rose to a driller and was able to go to Australia.

Several Anglo-Indians in Madras provide informal assistance in filling out visa application forms. One, who has been involved since the mid-1980s, has recently established an agency (which in 1996 employed a staff of ten) where expertise on (especially Australian) visa procedures is offered, and for a fee pre-application assessments are conducted of the prospective migrant's chances of success.[7] If the person is deemed likely to 'pass' the agency then undertakes (for a further fee) to process the application. Since 1993 it has had a business link with a migration consultant in Australia who provides assistance as well as up-to-date advice on current immigration policies and procedures, and more recently a similar link has been established with a firm in Canada.[8]

With increasing frequency, parents seek to arrange the marriages of their children to Anglo-Indians already abroad or about to emigrate. Several well-known Anglo-Indians with wide-ranging networks of friends and relatives abroad mentioned that they were frequently approached by people in Madras to recommend and arrange introductions to appropriate marriage partners overseas. The fear that Anglo-Indian youth in the West are abandoning the strong religious attachments of the parental generation is a frequent theme in community rhetoric, and this is often given as the reason for parents overseas seeking matches for their children in India. One man, who is sometimes called upon to act as an intermediary, claimed to receive letters from parents in Australia concerned about the marriage prospects of their children:

> They know I'm attached to the church and would like me to recommend a nice Anglo-Indian family. The girl or boy [here] should have good principles; [be] good Catholics. I got several married like that.

Another such go-between commented:

> We're trying to do social service by getting a match for somebody here with somebody in Australia. Especially for a family that has no hope of going to that country. We have contacts there. And it's a genuine problem for people over there to get Anglo-Indian partners, good Christian partners, born-again I mean.

Many Anglo-Indian families, however, seek to arrange such unions on their own, without mediation. Thus, not untypical is the case of a girl who had 'been friends' with a boy in Madras before he left with his parents for Australia. They corresponded and several years on, in her parents' words, 'he came down [to Madras] and married her and took her up'. I was also told about numerous instances of migrants who had returned on holiday to Madras and decided or were persuaded to marry a local young man or woman – frequently a close relative. It is not uncommon for Anglo-Indians to marry their first cousins – cross or parallel – and this practice is, if anything, encouraged when one of the partners is resident overseas. In one family I knew, three (out of a total of seven) siblings had married, in turn, a mother's brother's son (MBS), a mother's brother's daughter (MBD), and a father's sister's daughter (FZD) who were already living in Australia.[9] News spreads quickly about anyone settled overseas who returns for a visit to Madras in the hope of finding a spouse. The mother of three marriageable daughters remarked:

It is God's plan. We have heard of people coming down from Australia around this time [January] to pick a partner. I am praying for A. [her eldest] to find someone. I tell friends and relatives there if they come across anyone suitable, [inform them about] her present qualifications and employment.

Finally, I have also heard about a number of long-standing courtships, even engagements involving two young people in Madras, which were abruptly terminated at the insistence of one set of parents when marriage with someone settled abroad was precipitously arranged.

Whereas the immediate post-Independence exodus is attributed on the one side to the desire to return to their 'homes' in the West, and, on the other, to the fear felt by Anglo-Indians about their future following the withdrawal of the British from India, a different array of motives are said to underlie subsequent emigrations. The most frequent reason given is to improve future educational and economic prospects for children (see also Gist 1975: 41). The belief is widespread that merit, qualifications or experience alone will not secure a job or access to other kinds of resources and benefits in contemporary India, and that what counts is nepotic networks. People in India are assumed to favour only their own kind: members of the same caste, religious community, or kin group. Because, I was often told, Anglo-Indians lack a 'godfather', and in any case would not stoop to such 'Indian' practices, their economic prospects are dim. Moreover, it was repeatedly pointed out, there are now 'massive reservations' for 'Scheduled' and 'Backward' Tribes and Castes, which further narrow the opportunities available to Anglo-Indians in a fiercely competitive economic environment. Therefore, to ensure the future of their children, emigration is seen as the only option.

Aspiring emigrants now also have the example of successful Anglo-Indians abroad. A senior member of one of the Anglo-Indian Associations in Madras remarked: 'I visited Australia and saw for myself that most of the Anglo-Indians are well off. They would never have achieved in India what they have achieved in Australia: good jobs, houses, cars, and a terrific future for their children.' Furthermore, Anglo-Indians in Madras are accustomed to seeing relatives and friends from overseas who return to Madras. One, whose brother lives in the UK, was awe-struck by the affluence displayed by the latter:

> He was coming back every year to see us, all the way from England, whereas I couldn't make a journey to Bangalore. And the money he spends when he comes, you can't understand from where he gets that money.

From time to time those who observe such visitors at first hand comment on the latters' attempts to impress local onlookers by 'putting on Australian accents and showing off their nice clothes'.

Failed Emigrants

Most of the Anglo-Indians I met who belonged to the artisan class had pinned their hopes on settling abroad, but had been frustrated in their attempts. A number were technically eligible for entry into the UK by virtue of what they referred to as the 'grandfather clause' – the 'patriality' rules which entitle the children and grandchildren of British nationals to claim the right to migrate. In virtually every case the father or grandfather had been a British soldier who had been stationed in Madras for a time, and formed a liaison – formal or informal – with an Indian or, more likely, Anglo-Indian maternal forebear. But few of the contemporary offspring could provide details other than his name (and, occasionally, his regiment), which weakened considerably their claims to descent in the eyes of the British authorities. In several instances the family had spent a great deal of time and money to learn the birthplace and other biographical details of a soldier-father or grandfather, but had been unable to do so, and had had to abandon their plans to emigrate on these grounds. As one man put it: 'My father was a Britisher, born in the UK. He came to India and got married to my mother in 1903, or something. Actually I'm lost for records. After my mother died we couldn't produce the documents, so we couldn't get the [emigration] certificate'. Not infrequently, hopes are foiled by the unwillingness of one partner (usually the wife) to leave aged parents or other close relatives who would not qualify for emigration – perhaps by virtue of age or chronic illness – and thus have to be left behind.

> We wanted to go abroad. But mother was alone and we had to stay and look after her. She refused to come with us, because she wanted to be buried in my father's grave.

This can sometimes lead to dissension in marriages, and to lasting bitterness within the household, as the demurring partner is thereafter likely to be blamed for a range of future familial difficulties. But there are few reports of one partner leaving the reluctant other in order to emigrate; the tendency is, rather, to abandon or postpone the intention to leave. Nor is there any history of males migrating to Western countries on their own and either returning to India at the end of a working life, or bringing wives and children to live with them after a time.

Elderly Anglo-Indians who – for perfectly good reasons – passed up an opportunity to go abroad when they were younger, might now voice feelings of regret at what they see as their earlier foolishness. One man remarked: 'we stayed back because life was pleasant for a time [after Independence]. We didn't think it would get so bad. Given a chance now I'd run for it.' A woman, whose children were small when the opportunity to emigrate arose, was reluctant to uproot them, and decided against moving. Subsequently, her siblings and friends left for Australia. 'So foolish, now we sit and cry. Now we are repenting. I am old, and we've finished our days, but the children must come up. But it's too late.' Another woman, who never married, and now lives in an Old People's Home, had been offered a chance to come to Britain soon after her only sister had emigrated. At the time she preferred to stay in Madras with her brother, but after his death was left alone. 'My sister is in London. I always think if only I could be with my sister. Because we're only two. I really did a mistake by not coming with her. Now she too is old, alone and I'm alone.'

Most commonly, however, emigration hopes are thwarted when someone fails to obtain the necessary visa. The agency providing pre-application assessments (see above) estimates that of the forty to fifty assessments conducted each month only fifteen to twenty are deemed to qualify and advised to proceed. A majority of those who attempt the process without benefit of such expert advice have also had their applications turned down, in a few cases more than once, leaving them deeply frustrated and bitter. They explain their failure in various ways. A few acknowledge that they lack the requisite skills. One man told me that he had applied four times for an Australian visa and had been refused each time: 'They said "you can't live up to our points system". They want highly skilled people, but my father couldn't afford to give us an education, so we missed the boat.' Another reckoned he had fallen short of the quota by a mere five points, and was seeking to find ways of making up the small difference. The head of the agency assisting Anglo-Indians to go abroad remarked in the course of a discussion that the principal applicants for Australian visas are usually men because it is their skills which tend to be valued for purposes of allocating the necessary points. The secretarial and stenographic skills possessed by many artisan class Anglo-Indian women are discounted. Only nurses or teachers are likely to be rated by the authorities. Once in Australia, however, it is the women who are more likely to obtain employment quickly, especially, I was told, those with office skills.

Some who have had their applications turned down accuse the authorities in foreign embassies of failing adequately to assess their personal qualities and/or of being duped by their local Indian subordinates who are said to recommend only members of their own [non-Anglo-Indian] communities. One man, who had attempted several times (unsuccessfully) to obtain an Australian visa, commented that 'The High Commissions over here are becoming cheap . . . they are being influenced by [the prejudices of] our communities . . . [it is] the Brahmins and Malayalees who are making the decisions. Australians are there, but they are pulled by the nose.' They are also angry at the costs of Australian visa applications which, according to several people I asked, were virtually free in the 1960s, but which had steadily risen over the years to their current (1999) level of approximately Rs 15,000 (£200). Fees are not returned if the visa is refused. People often sell jewellery and other valuables or take loans to meet the costs.

Anglo-Indians, by virtue of their 'European blood and culture', regard themselves as singularly eligible for settlement in the West. As we saw in Chapter 4 this kind of rhetoric is still current among those within the artisan class who most have to struggle to go abroad. Their attitude was summarized succinctly by a priest (himself an Anglo-Indian) who had assisted many of his parishioners to emigrate – through providing certificates of baptism and letters of recommendation:

> Other communities will be very close, they have their own way of living, and find it difficult to communicate [with their hosts] when they go abroad. But our people can easily integrate wherever they go. They can adapt themselves, because they feel at home with the food, the culture there.

What Anglo-Indians find most difficult to accept is that these 'other communities' – the Gujaratis, Punjabis, Bangladeshis and Pakistanis, as well as migrants from outside south Asia who have settled in the West – are not, as they see it, anything like as culturally qualified as themselves. They are not carriers of a European outlook and way of life or native speakers of English. Indeed, language is sometimes mentioned as a motive for emigration. A woman whose parents had failed in their efforts to obtain an Australian visa insisted that the family had wanted to go abroad because Tamil was too difficult for Anglo-Indians to learn, but 'in foreign [overseas] they've got only one language [which is] our own mother tongue, English'. One couple reported telling their Australian immigration interviewer that they wanted to emigrate because, as Christians, they wanted their children to live under a 'Christian government', and where they would only have to speak English. 'You British,' another Anglo-Indian remarked in the course of a discussion about migration, 'seem ready to accommodate all the foreigners in your country, but *your own kind* you ignore' (my emphasis). One man took up the same theme with relation to what was at the time (1996) recent news about Hong Kong: 'There are fewer Anglo-Indians in India than Chinese in Hong Kong. So I was a little hurt in the stomach that Mrs Thatcher accepted that they could come [to Britain] but we couldn't; because, remember, we are the assets the British left behind.'

They can also be scathing about those Anglo-Indians who have been successful, claiming that among them are the least deserving, and pointing to examples of emigrants who were notoriously work-shy, lacked skills and experience, or – a common accusation – had falsified their educational and technical 'certificates' to obtain a visa. ('There are many people from this area who have gone to Australia, boys who haven't held a job, who know nothing, and in Australia we hear they're on the dole. Bogus certificates. They get false certificates for anything and everything.')

Thus, despite the emigration points schemes operated by several Western governments (and especially the Australians), which Anglo-Indians can understand and respond to, there is also a realization that such a highly rational and seemingly impersonal system can be and is subverted by human intervention. This not only increases the uncertainty of the outcome, but places the reasons for it outside the ready compre-hension of aspiring emigrants. Thus, for example, immigration officials are seen to place differing evaluations on similar qualifications and experience. I frequently heard remarks like this by a father who had encouraged his daughter's career with a view to her emigration: 'My daughter trained as a nurse and worked to get the necessary experience.

But she was turned down by the Australians while her own cousin went there with exactly the same background. I know a lot of people who have similar qualifications, yet some get through while others don't.'

Moreover, internal political considerations in the target countries result in periodic and unforseeable changes in their immigration policies and quotas. Then, since immigration authorities usually give no reasons for their rejection of an application, and particularly as controls have become more stringent, a perception of the process as unpredictable and so outside the supplicants' control has emerged. 'It's a matter of luck' I often heard people conclude. This feeling of impotence in the face of what are seen as capricious immigration rules and procedures leads many people to seek supernatural assistance in their attempts to acquire visas.

The great majority of Anglo-Indians are Catholics, and those familiar with the church in Madras are unanimous in acknowledging their long-standing commitment and generosity to their parishes. Virtually all the priests I spoke to endorsed this view of Anglo-Indians as loyal members of their congregations, but also took the opportunity to report a dramatic increase over the last fifteen or twenty years among them of what were termed 'popular devotions'. These ritual activities, at shrines in and around Madras, are occasions when supplicants seek favours and give thanks for favours granted.

A woman whose daughter had married a young Anglo-Indian from Madras already settled in Canada recounted how she had prayed that he would not change his mind while he waited for the papers to be prepared: 'I prayed to the Infant Jesus, who grants our wishes, and to St Jude, who intercedes for us.'

Certain shrines have become especially popular among Anglo-Indians: for example, that of St Anthony at St Mary's co-Cathedral in central Madras, Infant Jesus in Guindy, south Madras and St Jude at Kottur, about 50 km from the city. The latter shrine attracts busloads of people on the first Sunday of each month, and according to the priest who accompanies these Anglo-Indian pilgrims, 'they pray for visas, for papers to go abroad. And since many families have succeeded, have got their prayers answered, this is an incentive for many more to go there and pray.' Another important place of pilgrimage for Madras Anglo-Indians (as for Indian Catholics generally) is Our Lady of Velankanni, situated over 300 km to the south in Nagapattinam, Tanjore District. Pilgrims generally travel in company with other family members, kinsmen or neighbours, usually by train or bus, but there are also several groups which organize walking pilgrimages to arrive in time for the annual feast of Our Lady in early September. At Velankanni, they seek all manner of boons, including a favourable response to emigration applications. In a report on the Walkers' Pilgrimage one of the group organizers is quoted as saying:

> During the last 25 years at least a thousand have done the walk. From our group, 23 walkers have migrated to Australia, 3 have gone to the USA and many others have secured employment in the Middle East. All of them unanimously attribute their success to the walk. (*Anglos in the Wind*, Vol.1 (2), 1998, p.10).

Increasing numbers of mainly young Anglo-Indian Catholics also spend brief periods at the recently established Divine Retreat Centre in Chalakudi, Kerala. One couple I met told me that while at the Centre they vowed to go to the 'Holy Land' if their efforts to get to Australia were successful. Those who have settled abroad, when returning to visit their families in Madras, almost invariably return to these shrines to give thanks for their own success and pray for that of other family members. For Protestants, the principal arenas for seeking supernatural aid in their personal affairs are the ubiquitous informal prayer groups based around local evangelists, as well as periodic mass crusades and conventions which feature more widely known 'prophets' – foreign and indigenous (Indian Christians). In all such contexts, people not only hear the 'word of God', but, through the agency of these charismatic figures, seek divine assistance in their lives, including the fulfilment of migration hopes (Caplan 1987, especially Chaps 7 and 8).

The Consequences of Emigration

The realization of an individual's or couple's hopes to settle in the West can bring its own problems for the family. Since Anglo-Indian emigration is neither temporary nor rationalized by a 'myth of return', separations are frequently lengthy and sometimes permanent. In some families, moreover, members are dispersed among several continents and the possibility of more than occasional reunions is acknowledged as remote. One couple I met were not untypical in having two sons in Australia, a daughter in the USA and another in Canada. The youngest son is still in Madras but planning to go abroad, probably to join one of his brothers. The parents were undecided about which of their children to settle with. Families usually remain apart for lengthy periods, and parents acknowledge the sadness which such separations can cause. Grandparents, too, frequently remark on how they miss not having their grandchildren nearby, or on the closeness of ties to those in Madras as compared with the somewhat superficial bonds to grandchildren living abroad. 'We talk on the phone every once in a way [while], but it's not the same.'

Most family members who have gone overseas tend to congregate in the same or nearby destination(s). When someone emigrates the general assumption is that he or she will, in turn, 'take up' siblings, and together they will eventually bring over the parents. Less frequently, more distant relatives (uncles/aunts/cousins) help their kin obtain visas. To take one fairly representative case of an elderly couple and their six children (two boys and four girls):

> The penultimate daughter married her second cousin, a long-standing resident in Australia who brought her over. She in turn sponsored an unmarried older brother and together they sponsored their youngest sister, who recently married a young man resident in Australia – sponsored by his own older brother – but whose parents still live in Madras. The three siblings are willing to 'take up' their remaining older siblings, but for the time being the latter have no plans to move since they are employed or married to someone employed in the Gulf and so comfortably enough off. Their parents will not emigrate unless at least one more child joins his or her siblings in Australia.[10]

While the emigration histories of many Anglo-Indian families I met suggest that the great majority meet these expectations of assisting close relatives to go abroad, some quite evidently do not. I was told about Anglo-Indians settled overseas who have all but abandoned their parents, about others who appear to have forgotten their brothers and sisters, or who have made efforts on behalf of one but not another, still others who have helped in-laws to emigrate but not their own blood kin, etc. Even more commonly, people express disappointment at relatives outside the immediate family who refuse to help. 'I wrote my uncle [overseas] to ask if he would agree to sponsor me and he never replied.' While this failure to meet expectations is criticized, sometimes bitterly, allowances are also frequently made on the grounds that relatives abroad are not in a position to help. The tightening of British immigration laws in the 1970s, and the constant changes in Australian immigration quotas during the 1980s as a result of both economic fluctuations and the different policies of successive administrations, have added further obstacles to the realization of the chain migration model (Castles 1992: 57–8). Recent policies, moreover, have tended to encourage a new kind of immigration, of mainly well-educated professionals or persons able to bring with them substantial capital funds, policies which certainly do not favour Anglo-Indians (see Castles 1992; Helweg 1991). Emigration failures which result primarily from such regulations may very well be attributed to neglect on the part of relatives abroad.

Equally if not more sensitive is the issue of financial assistance to those left behind in Madras. While most people appreciate that emigrants in their initial period of settlement may experience economic difficulties themselves, and have their own worries to cope with, the general impression is that those who have settled abroad are 'earning well'. The emigrants who are able to return to Madras on holiday, and are perceived to be spending money freely, reinforce the stereotype of the affluent overseas settler. Reunions of the International Anglo-Indian Federation, formed in 1989, and held every other year in different venues where members of the community are settled, further demonstrate for those in India the wealth of Anglo-Indians in the West, since the costs of travel to and accommodation at these meetings are beyond the means of even the well-to-do in the 'mother house', as one Madras leader put it. In January 1998 for the first time the reunion was held in India, in Bangalore.[11] The meeting drew criticisms for its choice of venue (an expensive hotel), the heavy fees demanded even from participants belonging to the host community, and the apparent unwillingness of the delegates from abroad to engage seriously with the needs of local Anglo-Indians (See *Anglos in the Wind* Vol. 1 (1 and 2), 1998). 'It was just an excuse to have a *tamasha* (party),' I was told by several people in Madras, who pointed to the programme which included a food festival, picnic, fashion show and international ball.

While such reunions attract at most a few hundred participants, the general impression is that virtually all Anglo-Indians abroad are prosperous and should offer assistance to their struggling relatives in Madras. A disinclination to do so is then interpreted as a refusal of kinship, and an inexcusable act of selfishness. According to one priest, 'many went away and forgot their own loved ones. Only very few help, so the people here feel neglected.' And I encountered numerous instances of anger and bitterness occasioned by such alleged inattention. To give a few examples:

(a) D.K., whose brother had left for the UK shortly after Independence, recounted how 'when my children were studying I wrote and asked him to send me £10. No reply. What is stopping this chap?'

(b) I.P., referring to her brother in the UK, commented: 'He's been there three years, but up until now he doesn't help at all. He writes to me once a year and sends me a card, and we send him back that card.'

(c) P.B., speaking about her mother's sister in Australia, stated that 'we're a constant nuisance to them. We're down in life and we expect them to send us some help, so they think "cut the link, that will be better". And that's what they do.'

(d) J.W. recalled how, when her husband had a stroke, she had written to his brothers and sisters in Australia and Canada to ask for help, but they had refused, saying they didn't have anything to spare. 'I didn't dare show my husband the letter, for fear he would abuse me for asking in the first place.'

(e) D.H. was upset on behalf of her maiden aunt, N., who lives with her. N. had helped to raise her own brother's three children. Since leaving Madras for Australia neither her brother nor his children have bothered to send N. any assistance. 'Considering what she has done for them – she brought them up – [they are] ungrateful.'

An Anglo-Indian leader, who is familiar with many such cases, suggested that migrants from difficult economic backgrounds are those most likely to neglect relatives: they 'had a hard life when they were here, so they're the most indifferent to those left behind. I suppose they think "we had it hard, now let them manage for themselves".' At the same time, he pointed out that present circumstances might simply reflect prior strains in family relationships. 'You have to take into account the other side of the story. It is very easy to say "my brother is over there and never sends me any money". But how was the relationship before he went? Maybe they never spoke or visited each other?'

Clergymen, who also have to deal with some of the consequences of such indifference, attest to the occasional dereliction of kin obligations by those abroad, but most report that it is a comparatively uncommon occurrence. In the words of one, himself an Anglo-Indian: 'We have a few cases of people being abandoned, but these are rare, because family ties are still very strong.' And I have numerous examples of Anglo-Indians in Madras who do receive assistance from their close relatives abroad: most frequently it is from children, but also from siblings and other close kin. In some cases help comes in the form of regular cash remittances (to meet rent or other recurrent living expenses), but more commonly it arrives in response to specific requests for aid, as when sums are required to defray unanticipated medical bills or purchase urgently needed items for household or personal use. Relatives overseas sometimes invite close kin in India to spend time with them abroad and of course meet the costs of these trips. When last in Madras I met any number of Anglo-Indians who had recently visited siblings or children in Britain, Australia and elsewhere. One man without children of his own, who had recently lost his wife, was preparing to spend three months in Australia at the behest of several nieces and nephews who had clubbed together to purchase his ticket. Children resident abroad also usually help to meet the expenses of siblings' weddings and of parents' special birthday or anniversary celebrations. The latter, in particular, are observed much as are weddings, with a church ritual reaffirming the original marriage vows, followed by feasting and dancing, for which many relatives and friends are invited. One elderly couple I knew were, when we met in January 1999, awaiting the arrival from Britain of their daughter, who had undertaken to organize and help pay for their fiftieth wedding anniversary festivities.

While such kinds of financial assistance are appreciated, they are sometimes understood as an inadequate substitute, or conscience money to compensate for a failure of kinship obligations. When I met her in 1991, T., a retired teacher, was waiting for her two sons, who had emigrated to Australia several years previously, to send the necessary papers to enable her to join them. When I met her again in 1996, she had still not left Madras. She was living in rented accommodation for which her sons were paying. When I asked why they had still not arranged for her to emigrate, T. replied:

> First came marriage [to non-Anglo-Indians] and then honeymoon and 'money-moon', and all that. Always putting it off. Then they bought a house. And [now they have a] mortgage. 'We'll do, ma, wait ma,' they're writing. I could have died by now [waiting for them].

She then read me excerpts from a letter written by one of her sons:

> My darling mom. I'm sorry I haven't written to you for such a long time. . . I'm ashamed of myself . . . but it won't be long before you will be with us in Australia. The problem is that we used all the money [needed for her passage, the surety, etc.] towards the house. If I'm able to arrange for finance it will be easy for you to come [on family reunion grounds]. Your loving son. . .

She read another letter, this one from one of her daughters-in-law:

> Dearest mom. How are you. . . We here are fine . . . thank you for all the letters written lovingly and regularly . . . [she then reports on the grandchildren] We will send you some snaps. . . I'm still trying for a job. . . [T. interjects, 'the same story for three years']. Christmas is approaching . . . We pray that very soon you'll be spending your Christmases with us .. ['All words,' T. remarks] . . . We are sending Rs [. . .] for two months' rent. Have a wonderful Christmas and a happy new year. Love . . .

Some recipients of financial help do acknowledge that those settled overseas can feel overwhelmed by and resentful of what might appear as constant demands for help. One woman voiced what she thought might be in her daughter's mind:

> My daughter in Australia definitely helps us. But how much can she help? She is the only one of us who has reached abroad, and she asks what the others [her brothers and sisters in Madras] are doing to help the parents. 'If I can help such a lot, the others can help a little. If they can afford to go to a movie, let them cut it out and help the parents. I have my difficulties too. You don't know what the problems are in Australia.' Now we fear if that thought grows, we'll be on the street.

Younger (1987), following Gaikwad (1967), tends to stress the neglect of close relatives in India by those who have gone away, but, without denying its occurrence, these failings have to be seen in the context of a large-scale movement of population, entirely organized and financed by informal Anglo-Indian kinship networks. Such an enterprise could only succeed in a context of strong and close family ties (see Chapter 6).

What also has to be remembered is that Anglo-Indian emigration to the West is permanent, and not one which involves cyclical labour-flows of single males which can generate remittances for investment in family and community assets. It is essentially a movement of families who have to provide for their own housing and maintenance. Moreover, since the first generation of Anglo-Indians abroad belong mainly to the category of moderately-educated, skilled technicians and are not, like more recent 'new' migrants from India and elsewhere, highly educated professionals, they have been among the first victims of economic down-turns in their places of settlement (Castles 1992). The amounts which do find their way back to Madras are therefore modest and sporadic voluntary gifts which may require some considerable sacrifice on the part of those settled abroad.

Resisting Emigration

Anglo-Indian elites have tended not to migrate in anything like the proportions of the artisan class, and, not surprisingly, contribute an alternative, counter-discourse on emigration. I was told that it was mainly the least educated, most incompetent members of the community who have left or seek to leave; that even those who have some skills and position in India are compelled when abroad to accept work beneath their education and station; indeed, many remain unemployed for long periods, or 'despite their qualifications have to settle for an ordinary job', or 'for jobs noone else would do'. Some, I was assured, have given up secure and prestigious occupations in Madras for very much less rewarding ones abroad: 'major-generals have become sheep-shearers'. One man reported that his brother's son had given up a good job and salary to go to Australia. 'He was very comfortable in Pursawalkam. But he sold all his things and went. A foolish decision'. Moreover, while acknowledging the more affluent and comfortable lifestyle to be found in the West, they offer a negative image of migrant life overseas.

Several pointed to the discrimination suffered by all Asians in the West – Anglo-Indians included – as a reason for resisting emigration. As one successful business executive phrased it: 'Discrimination is a natural thing. These white men resent the [Indians]. Maybe [the latter] are happy because they earn a lot of money, while here the salaries and wages are not very good. But we should be satisfied living in our own country. Here no one discriminates against us.' One woman, who had visited her sisters in Australia, commented that 'some people were not so very nice . . . they seemed to feel that we [Indians] were inferior, or something'. For an Anglo-Indian academic, it is only the migrants' poor education and economic vulnerability which accounts for their willingness to tolerate the prejudices of the host societies: 'I don't think anybody who has any self-respect will put up with that sort of situation . . . racism.'

For most elites the reasons for rejecting emigration arise from their economic or professional success. As one retired bank executive put it, 'I'm born and bred here, and well-off; why should I go abroad? I've been abroad and I find that India is good.' Since Independence, many feel, like this man, that Anglo-Indians have enjoyed unprecedented opportunities for self-advancement, and some, at least, have been very fortunate. They are doing well, predict a bright future for their children, and see no reason to abandon flourishing careers, adequate incomes and comfortable homes (usually with servants to help). The fact that most also have some property and would find it extremely difficult to transfer their capital abroad – which in any case would not yield the kind of income required to live comfortably in the West – is an added disincentive to leaving India.

Their anti emigration rhetoric, however, focuses primarily on contrasts between selected aspects of diasporic and Madras-based Anglo-Indian life-styles, which they feel competent to make since most elites have spent time with relatives overseas. Several themes recur in their accounts of these visits, and provide the basis for comparisons. While they readily acknowledge the greater affluence, comfort and 'tidiness' of life abroad, and the superiority of welfare and public service provisions in Western countries, they are rated poorly on several crucial counts which were summarized by one prominent woman in the comment 'morals are zero, freedom is zero, religion is zero'.

To take the last first, most Anglo-Indians, as already noted, regard themselves as devout Christians. This is, above all, defined in terms of regular attendance at church, chapel, assembly or shrine. Moreover, many Anglo-Indian elites play a leading part in the running of their congregations, serving on parish and pastorate committees, in choirs, Women's Fellowships, and so forth. They therefore report unfavourably on their experiences of church attendance in the West (in particular, Australia and Britain), and especially on the religious commitment and attitudes of the younger generation of Anglo-Indians. One elderly woman, all of whose free time is spent in the service of her local congregation (I first met her when she was selling candles during the annual festival), remarked at how appalled she was during a visit to Australia at the deportment of young people in church.

> Here [in India], they're affectionate in private. There they're too open. It's terrible how they express their feelings in public. They behave improperly even in church! And they don't bother dressing up correctly. Going to receive the sacrament like that! It's a little too much for us to take. I cannot manage it. Let me be home.

Another, who was the head teacher of a large Anglo-Indian school, was dismayed at the behaviour of pupils which she observed while on a British Council-sponsored visit to the UK:

> I could never be a teacher in England. I saw some of the classes and I felt very sorry [for the teachers] there. Pupils sat with their legs on the table, and I felt they had no respect. That was in 1961 and I wonder what it's like now. Our students would never sit like that; they stand up when we enter the classroom, and give us that respect. So I stayed on [in India].

Most of those who comment on this or similar kinds of conduct attribute it to a general indifference to religion and the absence of strong moral values in the West, which affects Anglo-Indians no less than others. They point to young couples living together before being wed and to easy divorce after marriage. Children are deemed to require strong guidance or disciplining, which is perceived to be lacking abroad. In India, I was frequently told, if children are disobedient, they can be 'checked', if necessary with 'one rap' (slap), but overseas this is not possible. In

Australia, one man reported, 'anybody sees you hit a child they call the police'. Hence, in the absence of discipline children grow up without a sense of right and wrong, or a sense of appropriate behaviour. In the words of one well-to-do couple:

> Children-wise it's good over here. We can have control over them. Over there they go out on their own . . . So many people come from there and say 'my daughter is living on her own, and my son is gone like this'. By hearing things like that we feel scared to go there. But we don't have any problems like that. Children don't get corrupted here. They have fear [respect] for parents.

The comments of elites also concern what they term the 'lack of freedom' in Western societies. Several things are implied by this. For one thing, it refers to what is deemed the social isolation of individuals and families. In Australia, I was told, 'everyone is so reserved', while in Britain, 'they don't have much of going out; each one in their home'. They compare this situation to the ease with which people move among networks of relatives and friends in Madras. 'In India you have the freedom to go about, alone, anytime; you can spend your time chatting, and loafing and wandering.' Moreover, 'there are a lot of friends who you can call on for help. That's a rich heritage in this place.' Furthermore, in the West 'you can't just walk into anybody's house, like you do here. You've got to find out if they're going to be there; if they have time for you. People here can be visited at any time, and there is no need to arrange in advance for an appointment.'

Lack of freedom also suggests an image of non-working parents in the West isolated from their working children. Those too old to find work abroad, in particular, insist that children 'are quite busy there and don't have time for you.' A woman who had been on several visits to her sister in Australia had decided against emigrating herself because 'Australia is just a busy life. Here the children have free time, and can walk over.' Many people who had visited, even lived abroad for a time, reported feeling lonely and isolated while there. A woman in her seventies, still an active member of her church and several community organizations, had gone to the USA to visit her daughter and son-in-law. She recalled having to 'sit and wait' for them to return from work and feeling alone all day. 'You don't have this warmth and friendship there. Each one is busy. How much TV can you watch?' Another, who lived for a time with her son in Australia, had returned to Madras after two years (and has since died). According to her daughter:

They would all go out to work and she was expected to stay at home. She had to wait for them to take her around, and only on the week-end they would drive out. She felt she was more independent here, quite capable of moving around on her own. She was able to walk, travel by bus, anytime she wanted. She loved visiting and missed all that there.

But these are very much the minority views of elderly Anglo-Indians or those who have benefitted from educational and employment opport-unities in post-independence India, and envisage the same or even greater prospects in the future for their children. The great majority of Anglo-Indians – particularly those within the artisan class – continue to subscribe to a discourse which regards emigration overseas as the only way to alleviate a life of hardship and despair for individuals and families. Just as importantly, these Anglo-Indians insist that settlement abroad beckons as the most obvious solution for a community which they feel is out of place in India and belongs by kinship and cultural affinity to the West.

Conclusion

Anglo-Indians, like many former colonial subjects, have been caught up in the transnational migrations which are such a marked feature of the postcolonial world. It is vital to understand these contemporary move-ments of population against the background of global capitalist structures and dependency relations. But the demonstration and analysis of such a world system must also leave room for complementary perspectives which take account of those regions and classes at or near the end of the long chain linking dominant Western cores to their remote peripheries. It is clear that the latter do not passively accept the structural constraints imposed by the former, and only by attending to the diverse ways in which migrating communities – like the Anglo-Indians – make sense of and respond to the variety of global and local imperatives can we more fully appreciate the dynamics of population movements to the West.

This chapter has sought to identify a spirit of emigration within a major section of the Anglo-Indian community in Madras. This can be traced to the colonial period, during which the British, despite policies which distanced and proscribed the Anglo-Indians, were at the same time instrumental in fostering an attitude among them of a special bond with the colonial power and a status as virtual Europeans. Many thus imagined themselves as transnationals for whom 'home' was in Britain.

With India's independence, this sense of belonging, alongside a fear of the consequences of their association with the Raj, concern for their economic future, and increasing problems of unemployment and under-employment, have led many Anglo-Indians to attempt emigration. People at the very bottom of the social spectrum, however, who face a daily struggle for survival in an increasingly competitive environment, have neither the skills nor the financial wherewithal to leave the country, and do not seriously entertain any hopes of settling overseas. While the educated and successful have left in some numbers, those remaining increasingly associate with and regard themselves as part of a cosmopolitan but Indian ambience. They see little reason to leave the country, though many have the qualifications to do so; they prefer to remain, comparing their own lives favourably with those they observe when they visit foreign places. Such Anglo-Indians disdain and reject the emphasis on 'abroad', and offer a counter-discourse on life in India as opposed to the West. In one respect it may be read as an assertion of their 'Indian' identity and rootedness. While it may not be the first time a critique of 'European' social and cultural patterns is heard within the community, it is undoubtedly more widespread and frequently articulated nowadays than it was during the colonial period.

By contrast, those belonging to the artisan class, with a modicum of education and a diversity of moderate if sometimes inadequate or inappropriate skills, have come to arrange their lives around the hopes or fantasies of emigration. They seek or encourage their children to acquire what are thought to be the appropriate qualifications and abilities demanded by immigration officials; they retain close links with kin overseas whose support can be crucial for a successful application; arrange marriages to partners abroad; and engage in ritual practices which are deemed to bring rewards in their quest for emigration. Such would-be emigrants continue to insist on their European qualifications; they are, like a significant proportion of the community was in colonial times, transnationals of the mind. They have thus evolved an ethos and attitude which is, in many respects, out-focused, and which insists, as one Anglo-Indian woman put it, that 'life is only abroad, not here'.

But if predominantly artisan class Anglo-Indians continue to inhabit an imagined European landscape, their everyday lives – as well as those associated with other sections of this urban community – are not thereby placed in abeyance or discontinued. The next two chapters, on families and cultural practices, explore the interplay between assertions of a European cultural genealogy and the inevitable influences on their cultural practices of the Indian environment in which Anglo-Indians have been and continue to be located.

Notes

1. 'People like me who came to England in the 1950s [from a former colony] have been there for centuries; symbolically . . . there for centuries. I was coming home' (Hall 1991: 48).
2. The article notes that these young men preferred Australia because they could 'put their hands to any work without shame or compunction, whereas in India [if they did the same work they] would . . . be discarded by their kith and kin, and also by countrymen' (*Athenaeum*, 7 March 1857).
3. According to several newspaper reports arrivals from India were frequently met with cries of 'cooly'.
4. Christopher Hawes, personal communication. See Note 5.
5. In January 1948 the Australian immigration authorities disembarked over 400 Anglo-Indian officers and other ranks who had served during the Second World War in the British and Indian armies – together with their families – from amongst the 1,200 passengers on the *SS Asturias* bound for Canberra. (Christopher Hawes, personal communication. Dr Hawes has perused the reports on this incident in the Public Record Office (DO35/3421: PRO) and kindly summarized some of them for me).
6. According to Rivett, from the mid-1960s it was possible for 'light-skinned' members of mixed-race communities like the Anglo-Indians to enter the country (Cited in D'Cruz n.d.; see also D'Cruz 1999: 278).
7. The Australian system allocates points for skills, age, family connections already in the country, etc.
8. The individual who established the agency is well-known within the community in Madras and even elsewhere in India. People contemplating emigration and others who have not been successful sometimes criticize him because whereas his services were once offered without charge he now operates strictly as a business, and fees have risen steadily during the past several years. In 1999, people were quoting figures of around Rs 6,000 (£85) for an assessment.
9. Young unmarried Anglo-Indian males, even if they can afford the fare, nowadays complain of the near impossibility of obtaining a visitor's visa for Australia. The reason, I was told, was partly the fear on the part of immigration officials that they will 'jump ship', or, even more likely, marry while abroad, and claim the right to settle.

10. While most elderly persons would not qualify for visas on their own, they are eligible under family reunion policy, provided most of their children are already abroad.
11. Previous meetings were held in Britain (1989), Canada (1992), Australia (1995) and New Zealand (2001).

–6–

Close Families and Matrifocal Households

We bring up our children like that. We want our parents to be with us. We don't like to part with them, no matter how old they may be. Maybe one or two families neglect their parents, but most of the people I know care for their parents. [Abroad] they don't have the genuine love, like we have in this place.

In previous days there was more love and affection. Families were united; they had caring. Now each one is so isolated. There's confusion [within] families.

I was at home until the age of five, and then I was sent straight to the boarding. Three of us [siblings] were there. We didn't come out until after ten years. We couldn't afford to come home, because there wasn't enough to eat. My mommy used to come and visit us maybe once a month.

Introduction

In *The Development of the Family and Marriage in Europe* (1983), Goody notes that contrasts between the social systems of 'East' and 'West' have for many years been phrased in terms of how the domestic domain is organized in each. Utilizing Guichard's (1977) schema – applied to the engagement between Arab and Christian in medieval Spain – Goody notes how these structures are differentiated by mode of descent, nature of kin groups, stress on conjugality, marriage tendencies and position of women (see Goody 1983: 11). In India, the colonial encounter may also be assumed to have involved the juxtaposition of two quite different domestic regimes. To adopt/adapt several of Goody's key distinguishing features: local traditions tended to be characterized by unilineal (mainly patrilineal) descent (the core members of the household are thus related patrilaterally), with the resulting importance of extended kin groups and comparative unimportance of the couple, and a separation of the sexes accompanied by gender inequality. That associated with the British and other Europeans emphasized bilineality, the centrality of the conjugal pair (with the corresponding weakness of extended kin groups) and gender equality along with no separation of the sexes.

While this is a rather crude rendering of the distinctions – real or imagined – it does suggest the kinds of contrasting structures which met in colonial India. It is therefore of no little interest to inquire into the kind of domestic regime which emerged among the offspring of the unions between Europeans and Indians. This chapter examines the configuration of contemporary Anglo-Indian families, and explores some of the influences – colonial and postcolonial – which have shaped their development. It underlines the dissonance between, on the one side, a persistent rhetoric claiming a clear distinction between their own European-derived family regimes and those associated with other Indians, and, on the other, quotidian domestic practices which situate members of this community very firmly in their local surroundings.

The Composition of Households

To begin the discussion I should point out that the numerical data presented here are not based on a random sample or systematic survey of households. They are, rather, derived from observations of and discussions with the members of some 350 domestic units over a decade, and detailed genealogies from some 200 of these. My remarks, therefore, are meant to be suggestive and not statistically definitive.

The 200 households for which I have information contain a population of 938 persons, or an average of 4.6 per unit. Thirteen (6.5 per cent) are single-person households; the great majority (127 or 63.2 per cent) contain between two and five persons; fifty-eight (28.8 per cent) contain six or more persons.[1] People report that sibling groups have become smaller in each succeeding generation and the genealogical evidence from the great majority of households confirms the trend. In many cases the difference is dramatic. A middle-aged man who is one of eleven siblings, all of them comfortably off, remarked:

> It wasn't unusual to have so many children, whether you were Catholic or Protestant. In our family, there was seventeen years between the eldest and youngest. It was exciting coming from a large family, but we saw how it could cause problems. Now all my brothers and sisters have between one and three children. We are still Catholics but it is a deliberate choice.

Another man, a widower, at the opposite end of the economic spectrum, reported a not dissimilar trend:

I had sixteen children. Almighty God! Those were golden days. But I have [only] thirty-four grandchildren. My third daughter, who I live with, has one boy.

The great majority of people are not only conscious of the deliberate reduction in family size, but are agreed that it relates to a more precarious economic environment and, in particular, to the necessity of concentrating resources on the education of fewer children. In a discussion about family size with an artisan-class couple and their teenage son, the conversation went like this:

Wife: We were eleven children, and my father could afford to give us only middle or high-school education. Each of us has got one or two children.

Husband: My [seven] brothers and sisters are the same. They have two or three children only.

Son: I meet with other Anglo-Indians, and they all have very small families. So it must be a trend. No one has more than one or two brothers and sisters. Only a lot of aunties and uncles.

Wife: Now he [son] fights with us because he has no one to play with. 'You had so many brothers and sisters,' he tells us, 'and I have no one.'

Husband: The times are like that. The Pope is against family planning, and we listen, but we do our own way. So we can give them proper education one or two children is enough.

Even in the recent past family size was not entirely a matter of pre-planning. The death of young children was a fairly regular occurrence, especially within the most disadvantaged sections of the community. The examples below, all relating to women now past their child-bearing years, reveal the scale of loss that could occur.

F.A. had thirteen children. 'I lost four, three girls and a boy, due to financial troubles. I couldn't afford to buy the food they needed. They got sick.'
H.J. had eight children and lost six. 'I got only one boy and one girl [who were] the third and fourth [born]. When [the others] were small they died – TB, motions [cholera?], and all. Medicines, doctors we couldn't afford.'
A.B. had eleven children and lost eight. 'Two or three months they lived and then died. Some fatty hearts, some the pock (smallpox). Three girls stayed living.'

Figures of household size, of course, tell us nothing about their composition. But before turning to consider this I should note briefly the economic circumstances of the 200 households in my 'sample'.

(1) About one-eighth (12.5 per cent) may be categorized as comfortable/ upper middle class in terms of secure, well-paying employment and adequate income.

(2) At the opposite end of the spectrum, just over one-fifth (22.7 per cent) of these households must be classified as 'very poor' – with only irregular, low-paid work and so no reliable source of income. Most receive some form of charitable assistance.

(3) The remainder of households – nearly two-thirds (64.6 per cent) – fall somewhere between these poles. Those with some access to regular but unskilled employment tend not to generate sufficient income for their everyday needs and approach the poverty end of the spectrum. Perhaps slightly under a third of households (31.3 per cent) would answer such a description. The remainder – about a third (33.3 per cent) – have adequate, if modest earnings from skilled, secure occupations and can be labelled what I have termed an artisan class.

All told then, over half these households (54.0 per cent) are either poor or very poor. In Chapter 2 I briefly considered the problem of gauging and estimating poverty; here I would only say that the distribution in this sample of 200 domestic units almost certainly does not reflect the spread of incomes in the total number of households (some 350) which I visited during the research period. Since I did not obtain sufficient census data for those outside the sample I cannot be certain of their circumstances, but I would guess that a higher proportion tended towards the middle ranks than is suggested by the distribution in the sample. Because of my interests in poverty and charity at different points during the research period, I undoubtedly concentrated more on domestic groups at the lower than at the upper end of the class hierarchy.

Returning now to household composition, below I employ an abbreviated version of the familiar classification of household types utilized by any number of anthropologists of India (following Kolenda 1968). The figures refer to my 'sample' of 200 households.

(1) Single-person units (eleven or 5.5 per cent): these contain unmarried or previously married but separated or widowed persons living on their own. I should also note that a number of people who might otherwise be living in single-person households (or did so in the past) are resident in several homes for the elderly in Madras. They have been omitted from the household count.

(2) Nuclear or sub-nuclear households (seventy-six or 38.0 per cent): these contain a set of unmarried siblings and either both their parents or a widowed/separated parent.[2]

(3) Supplemented nuclear (seventy-one or 35.5 per cent): In these households the nuclear core is supplemented by one or more unmarried, separated, or widowed relatives of the married couple other than their unmarried children (Wadley and Derr 1993: 393). In the households which I know the most common addition is the widowed mother of the wife. This matrilateral bias tends to demarcate Anglo-Indian from other Indian supplemented nuclear groups, and is also a distinguishing feature of their joint households.

(4) Joint households (thirty-five or 17.5 per cent): These are households in which two or more married couples, related lineally or collaterally, reside. Several of these are, in fact, 'supplemented joint', meaning that other relatives in addition to the core members are included in the co-resident group (see below).

(5) Other households (five or 2.5 per cent): Such units do not fit easily into any of the above categories: they consist mainly of (unmarried and/ or widowed) siblings living together, and in one case two unrelated widows sharing a household.

Uberoi has recently decried the tendency in studies of Indian families to focus on the predominance of either nuclear or joint units, which 'fails to capture the complexity of the data and results in contradictory readings' (1993: 384). Even the more elaborate classificatory scheme suggested by Kolenda (1968) and utilized above, which provides a more nuanced picture of household forms in a given population, does not account for the array of everyday influences impinging on the ways in which domestic units configure themselves.

The 'developmental cycle' (Fortes 1958) was offered as a processual supplement (and antidote) to the static typological approach of earlier family and household analyses. The intention was to allow for transformations in domestic groups as personnel advanced through their own life cycles. The approach attracted something of a following in the Indian setting, where the Hindu joint family has an iconic status, and where in the view of some analysts every domestic group strives to develop from a nuclear towards a joint unit. Gray and Mearns suggest that such a simple model is inadequate to account for the 'major trends in [south Asian] household formation and transformation' (1989: 32). Others have also rejected the idea of a general sequence of household development, positing instead a diversity of ways in which domestic groups evolve in India (Uberoi 1993: 386–7). Certainly, the notion of a common 'developmental cycle' of the Anglo-Indian household would not convey the variety and complexity of the domestic field.

Close Families

There is no consensus on the ideal form of household. While some members of the community suggest that Anglo-Indians, 'like the British', favour living in nuclear groups, most – even if they actually reside in a variant of the nuclear household (see above) – express no clear preference, although the scant literature on the Anglo-Indian family predisposed me to think that they would do so. Thus, Gupta, writing in the late 1960s, finds that for Anglo-Indians in Lucknow 'the nuclear family [is] their ideal and characteristic form of household' (1968: 19). Although Bhattacharya (1968), referring to the Bombay community in the same period, reports that the great majority of households consist of husband, wife and unmarried children, he does not indicate if this is also regarded as the optimal form of the family.

Although no one I knew suggested that the joint family is the Anglo-Indian ideal, I was surprised by the very positive, even enthusiastic, tones in which many people speak about it, often based on their own experience of joint living. In one household, which includes a widow, her two unmarried children and two married daughters along with the latters' husbands and children, the eldest married daughter commented:

> We are able to live together in a joint family. We have our ups and downs, and we have to adjust [to each other]. But no one wants it any other way. My husband's family is also joint. Although he lives here, his [married] sister stays together with his parents.

Nor is the joint household a recent phenomenon. Here is how one man, now in his seventies, remembers his own domestic arrangements around the time he was married some fifty years ago.

> My family was a joint family. We were all joint together, brothers and sisters, after marriage. I was with my wife. My sister had her [husband and] three children, my brother his [wife and] daughter; two children of another sister who lived outside Madras were down with us studying. And others [children of his other brothers and sisters] came to stay for holidays. At one stage we

were about twenty people in the house. It was the best. We were the envy of most people in Perambur. Model family.

It may be that with the removal of the British from India the status accorded the nuclear unit – because of its association in Anglo-Indian minds with the colonial rulers – was downgraded, and greater importance attached to the joint family. But this is only speculation and it is impossible to say whether the proportion of joint households has increased since Independence.[3] However, if the recollections of elderly people, like the man quoted above, are to be credited – and there are quite a few others with similar reminiscences – joint living has not only been highly valued but not infrequently practiced within the Anglo-Indian community since before the end of the colonial period. In more than half of the joint households in my 'sample' the core couples are linked matrilaterally – parents co-residing with one or more daughters and her/their husband(s). In half that number they are linked patrilaterally – parents sharing a household with son(s) and his/their wife/wives. A few households contain a couple and both daughter(s) and sons and their spouses, while in several the core couples are linked collaterally – a pair of sisters and their husbands; a pair of brothers and their wives; and in one case a brother and sister and their spouses. Moreover, joint living is found at all levels of the community; three-fifths of these domestic units could be classified as poor or very poor, and their dwelling space as inadequate or sub-standard.[4]

While no particular household type is or has been fetishized, most Anglo-Indians hold up as their ideal the 'close family'. According to Anthony, '[f]amily ties have always been strong in the Community' (1969: 361), and I was to hear variations of this statement on many occasions during each of my visits to Madras. Not infrequently, the Anglo-Indian close family is contrasted with the 'individuality' of life in the West. A close family implies, firstly, that unmarried children remain with their parents. People often stress the fact that Anglo-Indian children, unlike young people in the West, would never leave the parental home before marriage. This means that they also submit to the authority of parents and – for those in work – that their earnings are contributed to a common pool, to be disposed of according to parental wishes. In turn, the latter accept responsibility for their children's education, employment and, as we have seen, their marriages (even if these obligations cannot always be fulfilled). The obverse of this dependency is that, in turn, children take responsibility for parents when the latter are no longer in a position to care for themselves (see below).

Secondly, it means, as a prominent member of the Madras community phrased it, that even after marriage siblings 'like to move together'. In other words, even with the establishment of their own separate households they should continue to interact and remain involved with one another. In most cases relations do remain extremely close and are continually reinforced by visiting and mutual attendance at weddings, birthday celebrations, religious rites, and so forth. Their children grow up together and, where they reside, as they often do, in the same neighbourhoods, are in and out of each other's houses. On one occasion, while I was visiting the hut house of a woman in a slum neighbourhood in the north of the city, she complained that her cousin [MZS], who lives a few doors away, had just left with a good part of the evening meal she was preparing for herself and three children. When I asked her why she had given it to him, she replied, 'When my cousin comes to ask, if I got, how I'll say "no"? That would be bad manners.' Occasionally, one sibling will 'adopt' the child(ren) of another if the parents have died or become incapacitated. Moreover, as we noted in Chapter 5 (see also Chapter 7), there is a significant rate of cousin marriage in the community, thus reinforcing already close consanguineous bonds.

These ties can be severely tested when siblings no longer living together find themselves in quite different economic positions. The outcomes are too varied to indicate a consistent pattern, but depend on a variety of circumstances. In some cases relations grow estranged when an upwardly mobile sibling, or one aspiring to better things, begins to move in different circles. At one birthday party attended by any number of aunts, uncles and cousins of the birthday boy I innocently queried the absence of one particular aunt and was informed, as much by gesture and expression as by verbal comment, that she considers herself a cut above her sisters and brothers and so increasingly absents herself – or nowadays is deliberately excluded – from most such family gatherings.

Where there are stark differences in their economic circumstances the expectation is that the one more favourably placed will help the other. In some cases, a brother or sister who has separated and subsequently fallen on hard times may be absorbed (along with spouse and children) into the household of a better-off sibling. When this kind of help is refused it can cause real offence. A homeless widow found it difficult to understand why her elder sister (also widowed) did not invite her to share her residence. 'I'd like to be with her, but she doesn't want to keep me. What to do? Selfish nature, she doesn't want to share.' In most cases when aid is given, it takes a monetary form. In some families the provision of assistance is assumed as a bounden obligation. Thus, the head and only earning member in a struggling household containing six school-age children, looks on his elder brother, comparatively well-to-do and with only a small household of his own to support, as the family guardian. 'He gives me Rs 100 every month; he makes it a duty to give.'

In other families, however, the demands may be resisted. Thus, in one sibling group of three brothers and three sisters, only one brother has managed to emerge from the family's background of dire poverty. He has a regular, well-paying job, his wife also earns a good salary, and when I met them they had just moved with their three teenage children into their own flat. When I asked whether one comparatively successful sibling is expected to help those less fortunate, the husband replied:

> We should help out a little. When you're a little better and somebody's a little down. If we have ten we can give them one. Or we can try and get them a job. With that they can manage.

His wife added, somewhat more pointedly:

> He's doing it, for years. He helps them [sisters and brothers]. Then again, they should try to move up. But if they don't want to work. . . So, most of the time we cannot help. If they come and worry [bother] us, we [tell them we] have our own families also. My own sisters and brothers are all middle [class]. We don't go to each other [for help].

Later, when I spoke to one of her husband's younger brothers, I was told:

> If he comes to [the neighbourhood] he comes and sees us. Four months [ago] I saw him. He doesn't help me or my brother, and he doesn't help my sisters. He used to help us before he got married; after getting children he doesn't help us.

When siblings go abroad the presumption is that they will aid those left behind, indeed are assumed to be in a much stronger position to do so. And, as we saw in Chapter 5, while there are exceptions, those overseas frequently assist their siblings in Madras to emigrate or support them in other ways, thereby continually demonstrating and reiterating the strength of such ties.

Finally, the notion of a 'close family' implies that these kinds of moral bonds should extend beyond the parent-child or sibling unit to a wider circle of relatives. Although Anglo-Indians are constitutionally defined and define themselves in terms of descent in the male line from a European male progenitor (Anthony 1969: 5), this does not demarcate a patrilineal kin group which, in 'classical' lineage systems, would impose an obligation of solidarity on its members (Goody 1983: 11). While continuing to insist on descent in the male line as a *sine qua non* of Anglo-Indianness, they rather stress bilateral kin ties of the kind implied in the notion of kindred, which exists not corporately or permanently, but only in relation to each individual or sibling unit (Ibid.). The precise delineation of the sphere of kinship within which close ties and moral obligations obtain depends, therefore, on family biography.

Most commonly, affective ties are created in childhood, within the domestic group, and retained long after dispersal. It is by no means unusual for grandparents (and especially grandmothers) to play a dominant role in 'parenting' their grandchildren. Perhaps one in ten of the households for which I have genealogical data contains or contained such a bond.[5] Until perhaps fifty years ago the most common reason for such an occurrence would have been the premature death of the mother. In recent times, though death and debilitating ill-health are still significant factors, the reasons for grandparental involvement are more varied. They range from a strained or broken marriage, to an inability to support the children financially, to a drink- or drug-related domestic environment. Sometimes, grandparents are said to have formed a special bond with a particular grandchild, and specifically ask to be allowed to raise him or her, a request which 'should not be refused'. Most commonly, however, because the mother of young children is more likely than ever before to be in full-time employment she can only keep her job if her own or her husband's mother assumes virtually full-time care of the children. In the majority of instances it is her own mother who does so. I was told by a woman who had, as a child, lived with her grandmother (MM), that when her mother, who had been working abroad, returned to Madras to 'reclaim' her, she had refused to go. 'I knew only my grandmother.'

While a few people who were raised by indulgent grandparents expressed some regret not only that they were separated much of the time from their parents but that, as one man phrased it, 'there was noone to tell me what to do or not to do', most developed warm and lasting bonds of affection with the grandparents who 'parented' them. A woman whose children have now grown up recalled:

> When I went out to work my mother was there to look after my babies . . . my children were more fond of her than of me because she nursed them from small, fondled and cuddled them. They called her 'mummy', she was a mother [to them].

Similarly, aunts (both paternal and, more frequently, maternal) – even great aunts – can play a significant role in the upbringing of Anglo-Indian children. Sometimes she assumes this responsibility following the death of the child's own mother, and if there is no resident grandparent able to do so. Occasionally, for reasons already noted, an aunt undertakes the parenting role while the child's mother is still alive. Thus, when I met an elderly, frail widow living on her own in a small thatched hut, she was being cared for on a daily basis by a niece whom she had brought up (along with her own six children) when the niece's own mother went to live with another man. And this is how one elderly unmarried woman explained how she had come to raise her niece and great nephew:

> I raised B. [her brother's daughter] from the hospital. Both parents were working and doing shift duties. My sister-in-law was a nurse, she had to sleep in [the hospital]. She came and left the baby with my mother and me. So until that girl finished high school she was with us. Then she got married and got a son, and he came here. He was here till he finished high school. Even today when B. comes to visit her mother next door she will come and stay with me. I'm the mother she knows. Her son comes here also.

These are not isolated instances, and the affective links formed with such relatives usually endure long after children have grown up, married, and separated from their natal domestic groups. They continue to be regarded as part of the close families (or intimate kindreds) of those individuals who were the recipients of their beneficence. Indeed, the most caustic remarks are reserved for people who had been cared for as children by indulgent aunts, grandparents or other kinsfolk and who, when adults themselves, 'forget' or refuse to reciprocate their kindnesses. The neglect or denial of such kinship obligations are not easily forgiven.

Boarding Schools and Families

The idealization of close, extended families must be seen against a background of the placement of large numbers of Anglo-Indian children in boarding schools both during the colonial and postcolonial periods. From the late eighteenth century Madras had male and female military orphan asylums (for the children of Protestant officers and soldiers), and by the beginning of the next century civil orphanages 'sprang up in imitation and partly in protest' (Arnold 1979: 107–8). Not to be outdone, a Catholic Military Orphanage and a civil institution, under the Capuchins, were opened in the 1840s (See *The Madras Catholic Expositor* Vol. VII,

1851 and Vol. XI, 1852), and in the course of the century a number of other Catholic orphanages were established in Madras. By the end of the colonial period there were five principal orphanage-cum-boarding institutions in the city (four Catholic and one Protestant) catering for some 1,000 Anglo-Indian children.[6] From the early years of the twentieth century several other, mainly Protestant, institutions in the Nilgiri Hills gave places to perhaps a further 100 Anglo-Indian children from Madras.[7] All these boarding institutions for Anglo-Indians were attached to day schools attended by mainly fee-paying children from a variety of backgrounds, both Anglo-Indian and non-Anglo-Indian. Although these figures are only approximations, they suggest that as many as 15 to 20 per cent of school-age Anglo-Indian children in Madras would have been in boarding institutions around the time of Independence. Among the domestic groups for which I have information there are forty-three people (belonging to thirty-one households) who had spent part of their childhood as boarders.

The great majority of children were accepted in these schools because of family hardship.[8] F.E. Penny suggests that some were admitted 'that they might be saved from the contamination of their wretched home' (1908: 208), although it is unclear if the contamination from which they were meant to be rescued was material or moral. The children were (a) genuine orphans, without parents or other relatives to care for them; (b) children who had lost a parent – usually the father – through death or marital breakdown and whose remaining parent was unable to support them at home; (c) children with both parents living but where there was insufficient income to meet the costs of education; and so forth.

Less frequently than poverty or orphanhood, parental (especially fathers') occupations made boarding an attractive proposition. Since, as we have seen, so many Anglo-Indians relied on railway employment during the colonial era and for a time after Independence, families frequently found themselves posted to railway centres or colonies far from their permanent home. One woman recalled how every transfer meant a change of school for her and her sisters. 'So once and for all mom put us up in the boarding.' In some of the larger stations there were railway schools, but in smaller ones adequate facilities did not always exist. Here is how one ex-railway employee explained it:

> The bigger colonies had a higher standard [school], up to ninth or tenth. But we were in a small one – P[. . .] – and it only had up to the fifth standard. After that parents had to send children to school outside [the colony]. If you were in a colony close to a big city the children could reach their school

easily, but a place like P[. . .] was too far from anything. So our parents put us three boys in boarding, St Patrick's. From all the railway colonies children were sent to Madras. The Christian institutions really helped the Anglo-Indian railway workers. Most had boarding for these children.

Other Anglo-Indian parents who worked in non-railway but transferable occupations also sometimes sent children to boarding school. ('I went to St Bede's boarding because dad was in the lighthouse, so he wasn't here to keep an eye on me.')

Since Independence, and especially during the past few decades, rising costs have forced several of these schools either to abandon their boarding sections or reduce the number of places they provide. Moreover, because international aid and charitable agencies no longer favour boarding education, their 'sponsorships', which have enabled a number of these institutions to survive financially, are gradually being withdrawn. I would estimate that the numbers of Anglo-Indian children in Madras who are able to board have nearly halved during the last quarter of a century. These places are therefore acknowledged to be harder to obtain. Moreover, the option of placing children in these institutions to circumvent the disruptions of middle-class parental occupational transfers is no longer available.[9] The principals of these institutions insist that only genuine orphans, i.e. children who have lost one or both parent(s), or children from households in dire straits are admitted. In the domestic units for which I have information there are currently twenty-eight children in orphanages, and the seventeen households to which they belong are indeed among the most impoverished. The increased concentration of children from the very poorest domestic units has meant, firstly, that scholastic achievements in these institutions have suffered: 'nowadays the examination results of children in boarding are atrocious', was the kind of remark I heard on countless occasions. Secondly, there is undoubtedly a greater stigma associated with these institutions now than in the past.

Those who attended boarding schools before Independence and shortly thereafter – and who are now in their mature years – on the whole have very favourable memories; indeed, I do not recall anyone voicing any criticism. Those from poor or 'broken' homes realize that had they not been sent to such an institution they would very probably not have attended school for more than a few years if at all. They often remember with affection particular members of staff and the (few) former boarding pupils who managed to escape from backgrounds of poverty to become successful members of the community sometimes attribute their earliest motivation to the positive influences of these teachers.

Apart from the educational experience, people speak of the time spent at boarding school as 'glorious', 'carefree', 'beautiful', 'days to be cherished'. Some link it to specific personal accomplishments. Thus, one woman (despite having an Indian Christian mother, and currently living in a wholly Tamil-speaking neighbourhood) attributes her fluent English to her time in St George's (Madras). Others ascribe their (Western) musical interests and abilities to participation in their school's orchestra, and the immediate forebears of several Anglo-Indians I know had been members of the pre-Independence Madras Governor's band.[10] Also, like the English public and grammar schools on which they were modelled (see Chapter 2), most such institutions stressed games. *The Anglo-Indian* for 28 January 1918, in its annual report on the Civil Orphan Asylum (later St George's School and Orphanage) noted that the school 'maintains its reputation for sports'. As a result, many young Anglo-Indians became accomplished sportsmen and sportswomen during their school days, and in their reminiscences they frequently mention the sports they played. ('At St Bede's I was very good at hockey, and later represented Madras. I took to sports'; 'When I was at St Patrick's football was my game'; 'I was at St George's Homes (Nilgiris) for seven years and became a boxing champion.')[11]

Others remember these institutions for their more general ambience. Many recall the 'nice food', not surprising considering the backgrounds from which the majority came, and the contrast with what was available at home – if there was a home to return to – during vacation periods. One impoverished couple whose two children are currently in boarding school remarked that 'problems arise when there are vacations and the kids are home and have to be fed'. Some people report that they never left the school, even during holidays, since there was nowhere to go, or because their families were too poor to feed them.

Others make specific and laudatory mention of the orphanages' meticulous timetabling. 'Everything was organized,' I was told on numerous occasions: children were expected to rise, wash, attend classes, eat, study, do homework and attend church services at set times. Such disciplinary regimes were meant to inculcate a sense of order and self-control, and contrasted with the often unstructured domestic settings from which they had come. There were punitive procedures as well. For one former boarding school pupil, now a prominent figure in the community

Punishment was fair, but public. Children were occasionally beaten, but not excessively. There was also public praise for good deeds, and an attempt to instill moral values in children.

Thus, while the orphanage disrupted family life for many Anglo-Indian children, for others it provided a surrogate family. While it may be something of an exaggeration to claim, as does F.E. Penny (1908: 206) that 'inmates learned to love each other as though they belonged to the same family', it is nonetheless the case that bonds formed in these institutions could be very close. Moreover, some appear to last well beyond the time at school. I know several people in Madras who turn to former boarding schoolmates for help in times of need before calling on relatives. A middle-aged man who had spent eight years at St George's School (Madras), was, when I met him, separated from his wife, and without a regular job or place to live. He explained how he managed to survive from day to day:

I got some friends who help me monthly. T.M. gives me some money. He was in the same school, St George's, as a boarder. Just senior to me. And I got another friend near Mount Rd, C.I. who also studied in that same school, one of my classmates. He's a businessman. He helps me every month. Whenever I go there I get my lunch, and Rs 50–100. 'Come again next month', he'll say. I got another friend in [a newspaper]. I go and meet him every end of the month, he gives me Rs 100. [He is] also a classmate from St George's. I only go to my classmates.

Failed Families

The Discourse of Decline

If, for many Anglo-Indian children, orphanage institutions were and continue to be a substitute for family life, for others recourse to 'boarding' was and still can be indicative of family failure. One man, who was orphaned at the age of four and raised for several years until her death by his grandmother (MM), was bitter that 'other relatives', instead of caring for him, placed him in an orphanage. Though imprecisely defined at its outer reaches, the notion of a 'close family', as we have seen and as this instance further demonstrates, serves as an exemplar against which the behaviour of individuals and domestic units can be measured. For some, however, it is an ideal no longer realized. On any number of occasions I was to hear comments about the breakdown of the family. This popular assessment echoes the views of professionals as well as community leaders and intellectuals. The (Anglo-Indian) director of a research institute on the family outlined what she saw as the problem of contemporary Anglo-Indian families:

Young people today are isolated and insulated. [Extended] family togetherness is being minimized. Their own [nuclear] family is their immediate concern. People want more [consumer goods] therefore they work extra hours, are less at home. Maybe it's modernization, Westernization, globalization. We see that values, lifestyles, behaviour patterns have changed.

The idealized close family is conceived, like the 'traditional' Hindu joint family (and especially its middle-class version), as 'free from conflict and existing outside of the contingencies of time and space' (Cohen 1998: 93). Its collapse, moreover, symbolizes the community's deterioration, much as the assumed decline of the joint family has become a trope for what is seen as the moral decay of Indian society more generally. Such formulaic lamentations, by associating decline with modernity, deny the very real tensions which have characterized Anglo-Indian family life for some time, and still do so. I have already noted above some of the ways in which individuals may fall short of the expectations of appropriate kinship behaviour. In what follows I examine the popular discourse on affines which attributes to them some of the blame for failures in achieving the archetypal close family, and highlights a structural fault-line within the extended kin unit.

The Enmity of Affines

In the absence of status distinctions between Anglo-Indian wife-takers and wife-givers, as found in Hindu (and, to an extent, Indian Christian) affinity, there are no clear guidelines as to 'proper' behaviour between such relatives. Many if not most Anglo-Indians seem to get along perfectly well with their in-laws. One woman I knew was fond of quoting her late husband's strictures to 'love your in-laws better than your own'. Indeed, several households, when I visited them, had the focal couple's two sets of in-laws residing with them, and a number of others reported that they had previously done so for a time. But most Anglo-Indians acknowledge that there are often tensions between them, leading to a curtailment of their relations. One man who had with his wife chosen to live in an old people's home to escape, in his words, the 'quarrels', 'friction' and '[hostile] looks' which he believes characterize and are a consequence of affinal ties, insisted that 'in so many families people don't like their in-laws to come to the house. They don't like them to come and talk to their own sons, or daughters, or whatever it is. Like that it goes.'

Not infrequently, the reasons for this presumed enmity are attributed to a refusal to share scarce resources. Thus, while few Anglo-Indians would suggest that it is a daughter's duty to support or even assist her parents after marriage ('we cannot demand from a daughter'), in practice many do depend on her for help (see below), and when this is not forthcoming, might blame it on the conflicting claims of in-laws. In one instance, a couple who had relied on their eldest daughter's income before her marriage, found life increasingly difficult after she married and went to live with her husband.

> She'll say to us 'this is what I can give, but I must ask my husband'. Because she depends on [is answerable to] her husband. He'll say 'what [are] you telling your mother and father? I've got my own mother and father [to help]. Tell them to go away.' What to do?

More frequently, however, it is the daughter-in-law or her parents who are seen as the main reason for a son's refusal to acknowledge what are deemed his filial/financial obligations.

> I have a son in the military. Four years since I had a letter from him. He was the best of the children. . . He used to give me Rs 300–400 [each month]. The minute he married he has forgotten me. His wife is a nice thing, but he's got a bad mother-in-law.

Complaints, moreover, are phrased not only or primarily in terms of financial privation but of the alienation of a son's love. Since married sons generally live apart from their parents – either uxorilocally or neolocally – the latter interpret any diminution in his attentions as a loss of affection, and as the fault of either his wife or in-laws. Thus, for one woman resident in an old people's home, her son's infrequent visiting was attributable only to his wife's negative influence. 'She won't send him to see his own mother.' Similarly, the failure of a son living abroad to return for his father's funeral was understood by his mother as the malign doings of her daughter-in-law: 'His hands are tied because of his wife.' In yet another instance, a woman was quite distraught because relations between her and her son had effectively been severed:

> O. is not talking to me, because of some ill feeling. Listening to his wife. She doesn't like the idea of us coming to see the son. She thinks that if we come there we might take him away from her. She used to show a cold shoulder to us whenever we went. So we stopped going.

Such feelings are not confined to situations where the son has left the parental home. In one fairly well-to-do joint household, where an elderly couple share their large dwelling with several married daughters and a son, I was told by his mother that the latter had 'of late strayed off from us'.

> Now he doesn't care a hang about us. Sometimes it happens. I think it's due to the wife only, what else can it be? She doesn't like the son to do anything much for us. You see, maybe there is a bit of jealousy there. Very often it happens among Anglo-Indians.

In this discourse there are also frequent references to the 'Hindu community', as if to confirm the universality of conflict in the mother-in-law/daughter-in-law tie. In the course of a conversation with several Anglo-Indians about these affinal links they referred to the many radio plays on All India Radio which feature such discord. 'All these quarrels . . . the mother-in-law takes up [sides with] the son and the son starts quarrelling with his wife, or the son and his wife are against his mother. So many stories.'

Indeed, the mother-in-law/daughter-in-law relationship is a prime site for charges of 'conjuring' (sorcery), especially (but not exclusively) within the poorest sections of the Anglo-Indian community. The daughter-in-law is said to fear that her mother-in-law may, as one man phrased it, 'do something' – or cause something to be done – which will turn her son against his wife and in favour of herself. One elderly woman, whose relations with her son and his wife had turned sour soon after their marriage, believed herself to be the recipient of such accusations.

> [The daughter-in-law's] nature is not good. She doesn't want me to come there. Some girls are like that. They talk all rubbish. They say we are doing conjuring, magic. She will talk about me like that. She says if I come I'll do this, do that [to her husband]; such nonsense.

Conversely, a married daughter's ties to her parents are deemed not only to be close, but to be responsible for the estrangement of the husband from his parents. Some daughters and their husbands, as we have seen, reside in joint households with her parents after marriage, while others share a 'supplemented nuclear' domestic unit with (usually) her widowed mother. But even where a daughter resides either virilocally or (more commonly) in a neolocal household, there is an expectation that she will retain close ties with her natal home. Most would agree with the comment by one woman that, unlike 'Indians', 'Anglos won't tell the girl not to go to her mother's house; won't separate the mother and daughter.' The contrast with the restrictions on a married daughter's freedom of contact with her parents' household among Indians – Hindus or even Christians – is frequently stressed. Moreover, for Anglo-Indian women married out of the Anglo-Indian fold these constraints are lived experiences. One couple, though complimentary about their Indian Christian son-in-law, complained that they had 'no chance of getting into her house . . . spend a month or even one or two days; that we can't do because she has her parents-in-law there'.

In another instance the parents of an out-married daughter admitted the subterfuge practiced to maintain contact:

> Our son-in-law [a Hindu] looks after [takes good care of] his wife. But he does not send her to this house and all. Now she comes to see us without her mother-in-law knowing. She says she's going to market, and comes to us on the way. We also can't go to their house.

Affines – and in particular in-laws – are thus often seen as the source of various tensions within the family and responsible for its failure to realize a paradigmatic closeness.

Family and Workplace

The contemporary Anglo-Indian family has to be understood, at least in part, in the context of the changing position of men and women in the economy generally and the employment market in particular. Anglo-Indian women, as we saw in Chapter 2, did not enter the workplace in any numbers until the latter part of the nineteenth century. By the second quarter of the twentieth century their participation – though still limited – had risen noticeably due, in no small measure, to the growing exclusion of Anglo-Indian men from the labour market. The introduction in the 1920s of the Montagu-Chelmsford Reforms and increasing 'Indianization' of those public services in which they had played a vital role, alongside the higher educational standards demanded of entrants, meant that Anglo-Indian males were steadily displaced from their 'traditional' employment spheres (railways, telegraphs, customs, etc.). In the post-Independence period, an intensely competitive labour market for skilled and unskilled workers has further eroded the position of what were once stable artisan households; nowadays many of their men are jobless or without secure employment.

Partly to fill the financial gap created by male job insecurity, and partly to take advantage of new opportunities becoming available in Madras, Anglo-Indian women entered the workforce in growing numbers. The labour histories of three generations of women belonging to families about which I have information illustrates the trend towards greater female participation in the labour market. Women alive during the early part of this century (the mothers of people now in their sixties and seventies), with rare exceptions – a few nurses, teachers, domestic servants – did not work outside the home. In the succeeding generation of women currently in these same age groups, who left school during the years immediately prior to or just following Independence, a greater number, though still a minority, did work, at least for a time. Those from the lowest income families did not have the education or training to obtain skilled, secure employment: they were to be found in occupations such as needleworking, domestic service, teaching (without training) in private schools or giving home tuitions, which required only minimal literacy. In somewhat better-off families women in paid employment tended to work only for a brief time before marriage (in jobs requiring moderate skills and literacy such as secretaries, typists, telephone operators, school teachers or shop assistants). Truncated working careers were often attributed by former employees to the fact that some of the largest employers of Anglo-Indian women, like Binny's (who hired secretaries) or Spencer's department store (who hired shop assistants), compelled them to leave their jobs at marriage or when they became pregnant (see Chapter 2, Note 13). A few noted the difficulties for wives of taking regular employment when so many husbands were in transferable occupations. But the general tenor of their remarks was that 'in those days' married women of this class were not expected or even permitted to work by their husbands. The kind of remark made by one elderly man, a former railway employee, is not untypical:

> Once we got married I did not allow my wife to work at all. I told her that it is better she stays at home and looks after the house and children. Even with one of us working we were able to manage a family quite well.

The situation could change if the woman lost her husband, or if he lost his job, or became unable to work himself, or if his income was insufficient for the household. A woman, married in the 1930s, made this comment:

> There were few women who worked then. Our husbands didn't want us to work, and we were contented with their pay, so we stayed at home. As the days were going on, and the times a little harder, they had to send their wives out to work.

While it is difficult to say with any confidence if a larger proportion of women entered the labour market from the lower reaches of Anglo-Indian society than from its middle and upper echelons, what is certain is that 'in those days' many fewer from all levels worked outside the home than have been doing so for the past several decades. In the current generation of adult daughters most work both before and after marriage. Indeed, nowadays, as I noted in Chapter 2, the majority of households at the lower end of the Anglo-Indian socio-economic hierarchy, and many in the artisan class, are more likely to rely on regular earnings from female members in employment than they are on income from males. According to Sharma (1989: 44), unmarried daughters who go out to work in other Indian urban communities are sometimes viewed as more 'reliable' contributors to the household budget than sons. Anglo-Indian women, whether or not they are married, are certainly so regarded.

Nowadays, as I also mentioned earlier (see Chapter 2), women without education or skills seek various kinds of menial work – for example, as domestics – while those with basic literacy can find occasional work as untrained teachers or providing after-school tuitions. At the opposite end of the continuum, women with advanced (university) qualifications are increasingly employed as civil servants, college lecturers, bank officers, computer specialists, and the like. The majority, with high school certificates and some additional training, continue to work in the 'trad-itional' Anglo-Indian occupations – secretaries, schoolteachers, telephone operators, etc. – but are also found in new employment areas such as travel and tourism. Several young women in the sample households have managed to find work in offices and hotels in the Gulf, where they earn high salaries. Thus, the unmarried third daughter in an artisan class family was, when I first met them in 1996, completing a computer course. When I visited again in 1999, she had just returned from spending several years working in a hotel in Dubai. With her earnings she is financing her younger sister on the same computer course, has paid the greater part of the wedding expenses of a recently married brother, and plans to do the same for two other siblings. Her own marriage plans, she insists, are on hold. 'Family comes first.'

Family Narratives

Without more detailed knowledge of Anglo-Indian families in the past it is difficult to be very clear about how they have been transformed in response to these developments in the workplace. At the lower end of the class spectrum family narratives suggest little change, frequently pointing to a continuity of privation from one generation to the next, or even an intensification of hardship.[12] A smaller number of their children, as we have noted, are in 'orphanages' now than in the past, which, for these families, means that many fewer receive what are seen as the benefits of institutional care, i.e. education, regular nourishment, a disciplined environment, etc. Far from being an attempt by 'irresponsible' parents to shift the burdens of caring for children on to these charitable institutions – as one recurrent elitist image of the indigent Anglo-Indian household suggests – it might better be regarded as a genuine concern on the part of parents for the welfare of their children, and perhaps somewhat paradoxically, as an endorsement of the educational, moral and spiritual aims of these institutions, to which the parents feel themselves unable to attend. It is (and was) well understood by parents and other members of their family that children who are not offered places in 'boarding' will probably find it difficult if not impossible to emerge from the poverty and associated lifestyle in which they are embedded.

The widespread depiction of the impoverished family usually attributes its condition in part to the tendency of the Anglo-Indian husband either to abandon his wife and children or to drink away the household's resources, or both. A number of persons outside the community who have occasion to interact on a regular basis with Anglo-Indians – clergy or teachers, for example – often represent family life among the Anglo-Indian poor as beset with difficulties because of husbands' wayward habits. The (Indian Christian) priest of a congregation in which Anglo-Indians still form a substantial element remarked that 'the moral side is sometimes very poor. A lot of problems in [these] families. [Husband] leaving the wife, living with another's wife'. The head teacher of an Anglo-Indian school, also an Indian Christian, had a similar opinion: 'At our preparatory school we have so many Anglo-Indian [mothers/wives] bringing their children to us and saying they have been deserted by the husband. I don't say it is the rule, but it seems to be the majority of the poor people.'

Such an image is held not only by those 'looking in' at the community, but by many within it as well. A prominent community leader expressed anger at Anglo-Indian men who, even when unemployed and dependent on working wives, 'feel they can do whatever they want. We have umpteen cases of [husbands] picking up somebody else and just deserting the wife and children. It's a real problem.'

During the late colonial period Anglo-Indian women were not infrequently deserted by men who had come out to India with the British armed forces (e.g. during both world wars), and had left precipitously when they were transferred to other parts of the country or repatriated to the UK. (In some cases these partners were killed in wartime action.) There are perhaps a dozen women belonging to the households I know who had formed attachments with – in a few cases married – and had children by such men. Most were serious, stable relationships, although a few were only fleeting. One woman, who had met the father of her son at a dance during the Second World War, commented wryly that 'he was a good tap dancer. He tapped me and buggered off.'

But most desertions of Anglo-Indian women prior to Independence and since were/are by their Anglo-Indian husbands. What seems clear from family histories is that the numbers of marriages broken in this way have increased in each of the last several generations, and there are today numerous extended families – perhaps one in six about which I have genealogical details – which contain the remnants of a collapsed marriage. (To put this figure in some perspective, however, it still represents only a tiny proportion of the total number of marriages in these families.) In about a quarter of the cases women had initiated the split, either by leaving the household themselves – usually to live with another man – or insisting that an idle, wayward or violent husband abandon the unit. Since many men live uxorilocally women are often in a position to make such a demand and are usually supported by parents or other members of their households. In the overwhelming majority of cases it is – as it was in the past – the husband who leaves his wife for another woman. On one occasion I inadvertently triggered an argument between a woman and her daughter-in-law when the former, to the consternation of the latter, revealed that her husband had left her for a woman living in the same street, and had a daughter by her. 'He was a Protestant and I was a Catholic, and he made me change my religion because he said when we die we'll be separated. Then he took off with another woman.' The daughter-in-law grew angry and snapped at her mother-in-law: 'Why that story now? That was thirty years ago! His [second] wife's daughter is here [nearby], that dark thing.' I had to apologize to both women for raising the subject.[13]

Since a majority of Anglo-Indians in Madras are Roman Catholics few such rifts end in divorce or even formal annulment. Most 'secondary' relationships are therefore various forms of cohabitation. As a result of such separations a number of households I knew contained only adult women and their unmarried children or grandchildren. In one, a widow in her sixties (whose father had abandoned her mother) lived with a daughter whose husband had left her, and the latter's now adult but unmarried daughter. Also in the house were two young daughters of the widow's eldest son. He had left his wife to live with another woman, after which his wife returned to her natal home.

While the usual assumption is that desertion is a feature of unions at the lower end of the socio-economic hierarchy, it is by no means unheard of within the middle and upper ranks. About a fifth of the cases occurred among somewhat better-off families, although virtually every one involved the husband leaving his wife, and not the other way round. Since at this economic level there is also likely to be some property or assets, desertion can have financial repercussions. When I met her in early 1999, a woman whose husband had left her many years before and had recently died, was attempting to claim a widow's rights to his pension from the railways.

> My husband never remarried, though he had a mistress, and I never did [remarry]. Neither are we divorced or legally separated. He was [employed] on the railways, so was getting a tidy amount as a pension. Having borne him six children, I think I'm entitled to the [widow's] benefit.

Even more frequently than desertion, family failures are attributed to an Anglo-Indian male penchant for drink. The husband in a poverty-stricken household, if he has not deserted his wife and children, is portrayed as an inveterate drinker. Sometimes the two are seen to go together. As one clergyman put it: 'They abandon the partner easily. Usually it is the man's fault because of drinking.' Within the community itself, and especially among the better-off, it is not the habit itself which is singled out for censure – Anglo-Indians (men and women) of all social levels freely admit to enjoying a 'peg' – as its devastating impact on the poorest households. While very occasionally a woman might acquire a reputation for excessive drinking, it is overwhelmingly the men who are thought to waste scarce resources by 'drinking away' the family's money ('They get some money, they go directly to the arrack shop'). Even if they are working the assumption is that they don't bring the greater part of their salaries home, but spend it on themselves. Anglo-Indian charities are wary of giving help to impoverished males, since it is assumed that any assistance will be diverted to drink and away from the family.

Contemporary attitudes to drink can be traced to a long-standing concern about the alcohol-related disorderly behaviour of poor whites – Europeans and Anglo-Indians – during the colonial period. *The Anglo-Indian*, in its August 1926 issue, carried an article by B.P. Norton, a prominent member of the Madras community, in which he wrote that 'most men who are addicted to "alcohol" are the poor fellows who can ill afford it.' Dr H.W.B. Moreno, a national leader, is quoted as asserting that of the average income of Anglo-Indians between a quarter and a half is spent on drink (Weston 1939: 151).

To suggest that his predilection for drink is part of a stereotypical portrait of the Anglo-Indian male is not to trivialize or underestimate the real difficulties experienced by many households, and in particular economically marginal domestic units, in which one or more of the men have serious drinking problems. The figure of a father who was compelled to leave his job, who sold the family house, diverted money away from his children's education, even brought about the decline into poverty of a previously comfortably-off family because of drink is a recurring one in Anglo-Indian household histories. Several people related that their fathers had 'died of drink' and one woman who never married gave as her reason that she saw how her mother had suffered a husband who drank and subsequently she did not 'trust Anglo-Indian boys'. Another woman whose only daughter had contracted polio as a baby suggested that the child's father was to blame. 'He made a promise to Our Lady that [after having three sons] if he gets a daughter he'll stop drinking. He broke his promise. Her arm [which is partially paralyzed] is like this because of him.'[14]

While the current drinking habits of husbands and sons are occasionally referred to jokingly as 'snip and sip' – snip the carton and sip the contents – many families continue to relate tales of misery, poverty, illness and violence. According to one elderly couple their son-in-law's drinking has blighted not only their daughter's life but their own. This is how the woman described it:

Her [daughter's] husband is a drunkard. She didn't know that when she married him. Such a different man when he's sober. At work they must know. Some day he'll get kicked out. In the evening he drinks and shouts . . . a boxing match, causing scenes . . . [If] she comes to this house he too comes here – twelve o'clock, two o'clock [in the morning]. Makes a big noise. Now they have to shift about, [because] the landlord doesn't want them causing a nuisance. Here houses are close together, no? Neighbours complain. We are telling her to do something. Take some action. She says 'he's my husband'. It's the biggest problem in our life.

I was occasionally to hear from men themselves about their own habituation. A few excused their indulgence in terms of the heavy manual work they were engaged in. 'We have to have it for our tough work. It gives us a little rest and we won't know [feel] the tiredness.' Those without a father, or with an addicted one, might blame their habit on the absence of a male parent to keep them 'on the rails', as one man put it. But the majority – along with members of their families – are more likely to place the blame on 'bad company'. Friends, neighbours or workmates are said to encourage the habit and since Anglo-Indians are 'sociable types', I was told, they succumb to these temptations. A few, however, make no attempt to excuse their habit. One man, whom I met while he was in a queue for a monthly 'pension' at his parish church, had been employed for many years as chief engine tester for a major vehicle assembly plant, but had had to leave his job: 'To be frank with you, it was my fault, because at that time I used to be taking a little alcohol, and it put me off. I went off my head.'

The belief is widespread that, if anything, and notwithstanding the 'drying out' or rehabilitation schemes which are increasingly available, the problem is even more acute among the current generation of youth. Certain neighbourhoods, containing households whose young men are without regular employment, are sometimes said to be, as one man put it, 'very bad for drinking'. Recently, attention has also turned to drug abuse among young Anglo-Indian males. Although not yet nearly as widespread, the advent of hard drugs has introduced a new 'moral panic' in the community. Since many people from the same circles as are disproportionately affected by alcohol seem to be involved, this can only exacerbate an already serious set of problems for the poorest Anglo-Indians.

The drink habit, I need hardly add, is not confined to Anglo-Indians. De Wit found that many of the Indian men in the two Madras slum settlements he studied were 'hopeless alcohol addicts. They drank daily, several times per day and spent much of their income . . . on arrack and bottled drink' (1993: 133; see also Vera-Sanso 2000: 123, 130 Note 6). De Wit rightly points out that alcoholism in India has received too little attention to date, despite its devastating impact on the urban poor (Ibid.: 279).[15] Moreover, while drinking is seen primarily as the scourge of households at the lower end of the Anglo-Indian class spectrum, men in more affluent domestic units are sometimes also known for their habit and do not escape censure. When I was discussing Anglo-Indian families with a woman who was a kind of counsellor in her church, she pointed to a nearby well-appointed house and asked me if I had met its principal occupants. When I said I had, she commented that I probably had not realized that the husband drinks. I told her I had had no idea. 'He drinks. Squandered all his money. That's the inside story. Outwardly, it's fine. Inside, there is no happiness.'

But while the everyday failings of its individual members have all along affected at least some better-off Anglo-Indian families, their narratives as a rule tend to underline the contrast between solid, patriarchal domestic domains in a previous generation with the more disharmonious structures of the present. In the past if there was paternal insecurity among the poor, at least artisan-class fathers were in steady jobs and able (if only just adequately) to support large numbers of offspring and other dependants. While children belonging to impoverished households were either placed in boarding institutions or became enveloped in local slum environments, without control or guidance, offspring of the middle and upper echelons were brought up within a stable family setting. The male head of household was a stern but fair disciplinarian, there was a very strong sense of religion, and girls especially were firmly controlled in their movements. Non-working mothers were charged with 'checking' (correcting) the children's behaviour, overseeing their school work, and running the household on a day-to-day basis. These same narratives, however, stress the collapse of patriarchal authority consequent on the growing uncertainties surrounding male livelihoods alongside the attainments of women in the workplace and increasing household reliance on female earnings. Hence, though emphasizing different family trajectories, discourses at various levels of the class hierarchy coincide in attributing, on the one side, family failures to the deficiencies of Anglo-Indian males, and, on the other, whatever stability and success it enjoys in the present to its women.

Despite the fact that greater numbers of men than ever before are going to university, entering the professions, becoming successful businessmen, finding lucrative work abroad (e.g. the Gulf) or in other parts of India, as well as achieving positions of responsibility in the community, disabilities associated with males belonging to the most disadvantaged sections of the community are now presented as typifying all Anglo-Indian males. In numerous contexts he is chastised for his work-shy ways, unreliability as a husband and father, fecklessness, and drink habits. A prominent (female) Anglo-Indian leader, who represents the community in various public contexts, insists that 'Anglo-Indian men are just not strong enough . . . more in this community than in others.'

This is by no means an exclusively female discourse, but one shared by men. A successful businessman observes that 'maturity hasn't come into these boys', so even if they are intelligent 'they don't use it because they have a mother, or a sister, or, after marriage, a wife who works hard for them, so they don't have to bother'. An (Anglo-Indian) church elder, who spends much of his free time visiting poor Anglo-Indian families in his parish, has a similar comment: 'the woman goes out, works, gets the money, and feeds the children; the man takes it easy'. This contemporary intra-community portrayal of Anglo-Indian women provides a sharp contrast with the largely negative images of these same women by the colonial British and, to some extent, by other Indians since Independence (see Caplan 2000; Schermerhorn 1978: 229–31).

Women in the Family

The Anglo-Indian woman is thus seen to contrast starkly with her male counterpart. Measured against his work-shy ways, she is assiduous and industrious; against his seeming juvenility, she is mature and dependable; against his profligate drinking, she is sober and stable. While she may share his predisposition for a carefree, fun-loving existence when still young, she very soon assumes the responsibilities placed on her by the family – since he is unable or unwilling to do so.

Women are portrayed as the stalwarts – the 'backbone' – of the contemporary Anglo-Indian family. A prominent (male) leader of one of the main Anglo-Indian Associations suggested that it might be part of Anglo-India's 'cultural heritage' that its women aspire to greater achievements than men, by which he meant not simply superior performance in school or in the workplace but a willingness to take responsibility for the family. In this respect, women are sometimes described as 'strong', their strength supporting a fragile kin unit, threatened by poverty and the untrustworthiness of its men. Since, from the late nineteenth century, so many Anglo-Indian men were employed on the railways and in other public services, which required them to spend lengthy periods of time away from home, much of the burden of orchestrating and overseeing the everyday activities and welfare – physical, moral and spiritual – of the family usually fell to its women. One elderly man, whose father had been a driver on the railways, noted how 'everybody in the house accepted the old lady [his mother] as its head, and listened to her. She looked after everyone. We all remember her as the hero.' Thus, even before entering the workplace in any numbers themselves, Anglo-Indian women from all sectors of the community were regarded as anchoring the domestic unit.

This is still the situation in most of the 'sample' domestic groups. Indeed, a substantial number of them (fifty-seven or 28.5 per cent) may be said to be 'headed' by women. While this is an ambiguous term, in this context it suggests that a woman is the principal (or sole) income earner, or at least controls the budget, and generally is deferred to in decisions which concern the unit. Approximately one in four artisan class or elite households and one in three among the poor are, in these senses, headed by women.[16]

The centrality of women in the family was and continues to be demonstrated in their crucial roles not only as its protectors (and more recently providers), but as principal carers for widowed or ageing parents. There is general agreement in the Anglo-Indian community that parents, and especially those unable to manage on their own, should be looked after by their children. Most people see this as a reciprocal process: 'It is because of our parents that we come into this world; they looked after us, in return we should look after them.' Alternatively, 'I worked very hard for my children, so they are repaying.' Others might stress duty to or feeling for parents: one woman, referring to her bedridden mother, commented, 'she contributed such a lot, that's why we think it is our duty to do what is necessary. The feeling is there too, not just duty.' Still others might acknowledge the fear of local disapproval as an incentive. As one woman who, along with her sisters, had cared for her own mother and father until their deaths, remarked:

> Here, if we don't give our parents a place in our home, people will say, 'see how uncared they are, why can't [s/he] give them a room?' That's how they're gossiping. And if you put your mother and father into a Home [for the aged], people will say, 'the children are making a living, how can they do such a thing?' It's a shame.

While there are occasional voices bemoaning the disregard of these obligations by the present generation, most would insist that Anglo-Indians do not behave towards their parents as do people in the West. The view is widespread that in 'foreign places' when parents get old they are put into a Home. By contrast Anglo-Indians 'look after their parents very well'.

But if there is wide acceptance of filial obligations within the community, there is no clear rule as to whether these lie with sons or daughters. The 'traditional' stress in the wider (Hindu) society – and Anglo-Indians frequently draw attention to it – is on the responsibility of sons for their elderly parents, and the complementary notion that daughters are free of this duty. Recent studies have confirmed that most aged Indians are still supported by married sons in a domestic setting (Vatuk 1991). By contrast, Anglo-Indian parents are more likely to reside with daughters than with sons, and this is widely acknowledged to be a practice going back at least several generations. Moreover, where Anglo-Indian parents/mothers reside with their daughters, the practice is not regarded as somehow disreputable, as it seems to be in the wider south Indian society. Thus, Vera-Sanso reports that mothers staying with married daughters prefer to regard themselves as 'paying guests' or 'temporary self-supporting' additions to the family. This, she suggests, 'serves to safeguard the reputation and masculinity of the son-in-law' (1999: 586). Several women I knew had eschewed marriage altogether because of filial obligations. One told me: 'I had to think of what will happen if my mother doesn't get on with [her son-in-law]. Everybody praises me that I gave up everything for my mother. But I don't deserve this praise.'

Matrifocal domestic arrangements vary. In some instances the daughter remains in the parental home after marriage, and her husband comes to live uxorilocally. In other instances parents join a married daughter when they are no longer able to manage on their own. Not uncommonly, parent and daughter become co-resident when one is either widowed or deserted. Other changes of circumstances within a family – a new job, sudden financial downturn, removal to another house or relocation to a different part of the city, emigration, the birth of grandchildren or their new schooling requirements, etc. – may also necessitate a rethinking of living arrangements.

In approximately one-quarter of the 200 households for which I have genealogical information, the core lineal relationship is that between parent(s) and a married daughter; in only half that number the elder(s) reside(s) with a married son. Where there are several daughters, no particular one is expected to assume the responsibility, since this will depend on circumstances prevailing at a given time, although parents occasionally admit to having a favourite. ('I was very close to her, she was my youngest. Usually the mother is very attached to her youngest.') Sometimes daughters agree to take turns caring for elderly parents, or at least come to some arrangement to share the financial burden along with their brothers.[17]

Since the overwhelming majority of Anglo-Indian elderly – some three quarters – are women, the likelihood is that the core relationship in a household will be between a widow and her married daughter, whether or not the latter is in a stable marriage and whether or not she has a living brother able to help assume the burden of care. Even when married daughters live separately they tend, whenever possible, to keep in regular contact with parents. I knew of one case where a daughter was spending every week-end with her mother, another where food was cooked for and sent over to a handicapped mother a few blocks away each evening, and a third where an elderly woman was provided for, in turn, by several daughters, all of them in straightened circumstances themselves. One told me 'Mommy's [three daughters] all give [her] food. If we got [food] in this house we'll call her. If we haven't we'll keep quiet. My sisters will also call and give.' In this way, even elderly people on their own are seldom completely isolated from family, since they can rely on daughters or other close female relatives to take some interest in their well-being.

Daughters are not only more likely than sons to bear the burden of caring for elderly parents but for other needy relatives as well, matrilateral and patrilateral. Some of the households I knew included the focal female's sister, her widowed or maiden aunt (maternal and paternal), her father's brother, and in one case, her deceased husband's mentally retarded brother.

Anglo-Indians explain this tendency for daughters to assume the responsibility for parents or other elderly kin in several ways. One suggestion is that women have a caring 'instinct', or at the very least have imbibed such behaviour from the example of their own mothers. In any event girls have more 'feeling' for or 'affection' towards their parents, hence are more willing to help them. Another is that, for their part, parents themselves prefer to be with daughters than with daughters-in-law, since with the former they 'have more freedom'. A more contemporary rationalization for this situation is that many women are in a better economic position and hence able to afford the financial burden, but this overlooks the many instances where this is emphatically not the case.

The obverse of these explanations is that, after marriage, sons 'forget' their parents, 'take no notice' of or no longer 'bother' about them. 'Till they get married,' commented one woman, 'they are very loving [of their parents]. Then all the love goes.' Numerous people cited the aphorism: 'A daughter is a daughter all her life; a son is a son till he finds a wife,' and attributed the son's neglect of his parents to the influence of his spouse. ('They listen to what their wives say,' or 'the son's wife only is responsible.') Just as affines, and especially the daughter-in-law, is seen as threatening the 'close family' (see above), so she is seen as liable for her husband's failure to assume responsibility for his parents.

Many sons do, in fact, play an important role in the care of parents. Some are the main support, others contribute willingly – financially or otherwise – when required. I recall a near destitute widow praising her son for his efforts to make her living arrangements more agreeable.

> He is a good son. He bought me a fan for my room, and a cot; before I was sleeping on a mat on the floor. And he gives me Rs100 a month. If my daughter-in-law complains he tells her he can get 101 wives, but not another mother.

There are a substantial number of households in which parents reside with sons even though they have daughters. And I was present on several occasions when a son, resident elsewhere, was visiting his parents' home, having brought some small but much-needed gift of food, money or household item. But the recurrent image of the Anglo-Indian son is that he lacks his sister's emotional attachment to their parents. Moreover, being under his wife's thumb, he is much less likely than his sister to accept the responsibilities of caring for them. Married daughters are also more likely than sons voluntarily to remain behind with ageing parents if the latter do not qualify for migration or (as sometimes happens) are not inclined to abandon their lifelong homes in India (see Chapter 5).

While there are striking exceptions, the mother-daughter bond among Anglo-Indians and, as already noted, that between sisters, between nieces and aunts, and between grandchildren and especially their mothers' parents are very close and durable. In 1996, when I was with several members of a hard-pressed family who were discussing the Friend-in-Need Society, a home for indigent elderly members of the Madras community, I asked a 76-year-old widow if she would consider applying for one of its scarce places. Her response was adamant:

> Oh no! You see, here I'm with the family, and [pointing at her widowed daughter] she's a help to me to do anything. This morning I got chest pain. So she rubbed me with balm. I like to be here with her.

By the time I returned to visit the family again in early 1999 the elderly woman had died. We talked about her for a time and her daughter remarked:

> She died here; she was seventy-seven. She only had me. J. [her own daughter] and myself, we did everything for her. [What we did] boys won't do. I won't go into FINS [the old age home] myself [because] I got my daughter. Only girls love the mother. I don't know why. Everywhere you go, every family, they talk about the boys. But as soon as these boys get married they forget. All the love goes. We should have only girls, and be happy.

Conclusion

The colonial encounter, which brought together two quite distinct kinship traditions, fashioned in the resultant Anglo-Indian community a creolized, if somewhat distinctive domestic regime. This chapter has attempted to identify some of its salient features in both the contemporary and colonial periods – as far as the latter is accessible to us. It has also identified internal class-based differences, along with certain significant influences shaping its transformation over time.

Notwithstanding the rhetoric emphasizing their British provenance, occasionally underlined by the idolization of Western nuclear forms of household and family, it is apparent that Anglo-Indian kinship organization is (and probably has been for some time) much influenced by ideologies and practices in the surrounding Indian society, though undoubtedly more so now than in the colonial past. Their idealized 'close family' reflects the high valuation placed in India generally on the extended family (although it is just as imprecisely defined). It emphasizes sibling solidarity and mutual support both before and after separation, the durability of ties between parents and married children, and the obligation to care for elderly relatives, especially those with whom links have been close in the past. As Joshi and Krishna write of the ideal Hindu-Indian family (quoting one of their informants), 'dependence and interdependence are far more valued than autonomy and separation' (1998: 179–80). Moreover, as already noted in Chapter 5, there is growing evidence of a developing critique, especially within more affluent sections of the community, of the Western domestic regime which is seen to compare unfavourably with their own. The family abroad, even that in which their own relatives are enveloped, is now perceived by many Anglo-Indians who travel abroad or hear reports from kin overseas as, among other things, insular, undisciplined and irreligious, and as lacking the coherence of their own close family in India.

Poverty within the Anglo-Indian community has had a profound effect on its domestic domain. Various late-colonial employment policies and postcolonial developments in the workplace have resulted in increased levels of hardship within certain segments of the community, adversely affecting its men in particular. Their increasing economic insecurity, alongside higher levels of marital desertion, drink and (nowadays) drugs, have had a devastating impact on many households, underlining here, as elsewhere, the adverse effects of unemployment and other economic problems on family stability (see Wilson and Neckerman 1986: 252). At the same time, extended household practices may be seen to have important benefits for the poor, as a mechanism both for supporting the most vulnerable members of the group and pooling limited economic resources (Taylor et al. 1990: 997). Moreover, from the turn of the nineteenth century large numbers of poor Anglo-Indian children – and some from the artisan class – were in boarding schools and orphanages and, to this day, these institutions are sometimes perceived either as surrogate families or as inimical to the very concept of close family.

Some years ago Vatuk (1971) noted the trend towards greater interaction among matrilateral kin in urban India, notwithstanding the persistence of patrifocal ideologies in the wider society. Among Anglo-Indians, who have been largely urban-based since their emergence as a community, this 'matrilateral asymmetry' is a long-standing one. Women have for some time been acknowledged as the mainstay of the household, a status related in some respects to the peripatetic nature of male occupations during the colonial era. Nonetheless, the virtual exclusion of women from the workplace, the low pay of the few in work, and the comparatively secure employment position of men in all but the poorest sectors of the community until earlier last century buttressed the patriarchal character of the Anglo-Indian household. What seems to have occurred since is that, on the one hand, women's central domestic role has been reinforced by their enhanced economic position and, on the other, the already close relationships among married women and their (mainly female) kin have become more pronounced, solidary and efficacious in light of the reduced economic role played by Anglo-Indian men. These developments support the view that family structure and the economic situations of men and women are inextricably linked (Taylor et al. 1990: 1008; Zinn 1989: 857), but challenge the notion that the centrality of women in the family is somehow 'responsible' for household poverty (see Bane 1986: 209; McLanahan 1985: 873; Wilson and Neckerman 1986: 256).

Discourses within the community highlight the contrast between the accomplished woman and what is presented as the stereotypically incompetent Anglo-Indian male.[18] This rhetoric of gender distinctions must be seen in the context of colonial and postcolonial economic and political developments – in India and worldwide – which have, for the past three-quarters of a century, had the effect of encouraging women into the work force and excluding certain categories of men.

Anglo-Indian families and their associated values and practices form one part of a complex cultural field within which this population is located. The next chapter continues this discussion, focusing explicitly on those features of Anglo-Indian society which many of its members (and those who interact regularly with them) specify as exemplifying its 'culture'.

Notes

1. In a survey of Anglo-Indians in Calcutta in 1957 the investigators found an average of 4.3 persons per household (see Anglo-Indian Survey Committee 1959).

2. Bhattacharya (1968) reports that of the households he studied in Bombay, 70 per cent were nuclear. In the remaining cases 'some near relation of wife or husband were found living with them' (Ibid: 166). He thus implies that the remaining households were 'supplemented nuclear'.

3. Uberoi refers to some recent longitudinal studies which suggest that, if anything, the 'prevalence of joint families may . . . be increasing rather than declining' (1993: 387). In any event, as Wadley and Derr point out, until relatively recently the environment was such that the joint family was demographically 'implausible' (1993: 415).

4. While it is possible that more domestic units would be jointly constituted if dwellings were more spacious, there is no simple correlation between size of house and household composition. There are joint units where space is at a premium, and alternatively, nuclear groups living in commodious homes.

5. The phenomenon of grandparents parenting grandchildren has recently been discussed by Jendrek (1993). Research in the USA suggests that this is likely to occur more frequently in black families than in white ones (Ibid.: 610; Taylor et al. 1990: 998).

6. These were, for Protestants, the co-educational Civil Orphan Asylums, soon to be renamed the St George's School and Orphanage, and, for Catholic boys, St Patrick's (which had grown out of the East Indian Orphanage) and St Bede's, while St Ursula's and St Francis Xavier catered for girls.

7. Arnold suggests that by 1905 there were some sixty European schools and orphanages along the southern slopes of the Himalayas with about 5,400 pupils (1979: 109). The principal institutions in the Nilgiris providing places for Anglo-Indian children from Madras were St George's (subsequently Laidlaw Memorial) Homes (for boys) and Mountain Home School (for girls).

8. The introduction of certain colonial family laws also led to the institutionalization of many Anglo-Indian children.

9. In any case, the situation hardly arises, since very few Anglo-Indians are currently in transferable public service employment.

10. The bands of several schools were often called on to provide entertainment at special celebratory events in the Anglo-Indian calendar.

11. Anglo-Indians were for many years in the forefront of national sport, especially hockey, boxing and athletics. In 1928 ten members of the fourteen-man Indian hockey team which won the Olympics were Anglo-Indians. The women shone in hockey and athletics (Anthony 1969: Chapter X).

12. According to a survey of the Anglo-Indian community in Calcutta in the 1950s, the 'general opinion' was that the condition of the population had deteriorated in the twenty-year period before the survey.

13. Although some men leave their wives to cohabit with Indian women, most seem to end up with other Anglo-Indian women.

14. Writing about the mixed-race or Coloured population of South Africa, Lewis notes how alcoholism among the poor 'formed the most visible and humiliating indicator of their community's poverty and degradation' (1987: 14).

15. There is no evidence to suggest that periodic changes in the laws governing the sale of alcohol (including periods of prohibition) have had a fundamental impact on the level of consumption. These laws have, of course, affected the kinds of product sold, their availability and price.

16. It is difficult to compare these figures with those given by researchers in the USA since it is not always clear how they use the term 'female-headed' (e.g. Bane 1986; Wilson and Neckerman 1986). De Wit, who found that 18 to 19 per cent of households in the two Madras slums he studied were 'women-headed', appears to mean that they were 'single parent' households (1993: 278).

17. While some elderly parents may remain with only one child, others may spend some time with several in turn. For example, a widow with seven children had, after her husband died, lived with a daughter for two years, then with a son for a year, then another daughter for two years, and when I met her had recently rejoined the same son.

18. There is a certain similarity here with gender distinctions within the Parsi community. Parsi men are now deemed soft and apathetic, no longer physically vigorous, while the women are seen as powerful and successful. This is a discourse which Luhrmann argues is related to a sense of community decline and perceived loss of status from colonial times, when Parsis were, in Luhrmann's words, 'the most English-identified, westernized community on the subcontinent' (1996: 84). Her explanation that 'a shift in power relations can cause a dramatic reversal in symbolic self-description' (Ibid.: 349) would certainly have some application to the Anglo-Indian case.

The Practice of Culture

Our English makes our identity. Also we dress like the British: in those days you'd never catch an Anglo-Indian wearing a *lungi* or a sari. When we were young we had a prayer before meals and ate at table, like Englishmen. Then we have dances, ballroom dancing, and we play whist, housie. We have a good time . . . a couple of 'pegs' and some good food. But since so many have gone away things have changed.

Strictly speaking what is our culture, except that we speak in English? Everything else – the clothes we wear, the food we eat, the way we eat it – is not very different from general Indian culture any more. . . And what festivals do we mark? We celebrate Christmas and have parties [but] this is common to all Christians.

The Anglo-Indians who live in poverty have lost their identity, merged into their surroundings. Sometimes they can't even talk English. Their dress, movements, behaviour, associations are totally different.

Introduction

In chapter 5 I suggested that since Independence many Anglo-Indians, and especially those within the artisan class, may be portrayed as 'out-focussed'. This is evidenced not only in the substantial resources and energies directed towards the goal of settling abroad, but also in con-temporary rhetorics reiterating earlier colonial themes that this community, by virtue of blood and culture, somehow belongs to and in the West. The obverse is that such Anglo-Indians eschew Indian lifeways and institutions as unsuited to a European-descended population. Yet these same Anglo-Indians – along with others (both well-to-do and poor) who do not participate in the discourse of emigration – engage in a set of cultural practices which may be seen to contribute to what Appadurai (1995) has termed the 'production of locality'. Thus, as we saw in the previous chapter, while many people might insist that Anglo-Indian families follow European or British models, they are to a greater or lesser extent influenced by values of domesticity found in their immediate surroundings. In other words, certain kinds of recurrent or everyday activities engender a sense of shared identification with a parochial group, shape much of its social life, and occasion an 'ideology of situated community' (Ibid.: 213). In this chapter I consider an additional cluster of practices which, while perceived as distinguishing Anglo-Indians from others amongst whom they live, at the same time locates them in the urban Indian environment.

Emblematic Lifeways

When specifically asked what cultural habits distinguish them from other groups, Anglo-Indians themselves tend to mention several which they regard as 'emblematic' (Thomas 1992: 215) of the Anglo-Indian way of life: these are related to their religious, language, dress, food, and marriage practices. I have at several points in the book noted that Anglo-Indians are devout Christians, the majority – at least in south India – Roman Catholics. Virtually all Catholic homes – and some Protestant ones as well – feature an altar with a picture of the Sacred Heart, which is 'enthroned' annually, and serves as the focus of domestic ritual activity. Mills notes that 'the religious picture, crucifix, or other symbol of religious attachment, is an Anglo-Indian given in India' (n.d.). Yet most portrayals of this community, both in colonial times and since, seem to omit this crucial religious element. Nonetheless, while Anglo-Indians frequently distinguish themselves from Indian Christians by claiming that the latter were 'converts' while they were born Christian, the everyday exercise of their religious faith is no different. The chapter therefore omits further discussion of Anglo-Indian religious behaviour.

Furthermore, since I have already touched (in earlier chapters) on the importance of English as a defining component of Anglo-Indian identity claims I will not elaborate on this feature here either. However, it is worth recalling that despite their diverse origins, by the end of the first quarter of the nineteenth century English had become the language in which Anglo-Indians communicated with one another. They claimed English as their first language, and on these grounds denied (and still deny) an Anglo-Indian identity to other groups of mixed-race origin descended from European male forebears, but who speak an Indian language.[1] Anglo-Indian leaders and intellectuals sometimes dismiss the idea of a community monopoly on English, acknowledging that (especially elite) members of other groups use it with equal if not greater facility, although they might point out that the latter have acquired this ability more recently than themselves. A few might even insist that their own command is still superior: theirs is, as one woman put it, 'the King's English'. Yet almost without exception, Anglo-Indians, whatever their views on the matter, will point out that their own English contains idioms which distinguish it from other varieties of English spoken in south India.

Among the most poverty-stricken, least educated section of the community, who live in some of the poorest residential areas of Madras, many everyday interactions among neighbours (and, where Anglo-Indians have married partners from outside the community, among family members as well) are conducted in Tamil. Here Anglo-Indian residents speak (and have the opportunity to speak) little English. In the course of a long conversation (in English) with an Anglo-Indian woman in a single-room 'hut house' in north Madras, we were briefly interrupted by the arrival of her Anglo-Indian sister-in-law and neighbour. They proceeded to talk to one another in a mixture of Tamil and English, and when I pointed this out after the visitor had left, my hostess shrugged and said: 'Tamil comes easier; I speak to my children in Tamil although they also know a little English.'

One point I want to underline therefore is that cultural practices, even those which are deemed by its members to define the community, are differentially clustered within the population. Another is that in the face of essentialist claims that characteristic beliefs and observances circumscribe and set off the Anglo-Indian population (the 'one people, one culture' view), we have to acknowledge that cultural boundaries are no less porous than social ones, now as in the past. We find a heterogeneity of cultural practices across as well as within the lines dividing the constituent groups which comprise the urban social order. Finally, while such a creolist image characterizes the contemporary no less than the colonial cultural world inhabited by the Anglo-Indians of Madras, it is important not to assume that even the most cherished and 'traditional' of lifeways are unchanging. In this chapter I will examine the manner in which Anglo-Indian cultural practices – related to dress, food and marriage – have developed in response to and alongside circumstances in the wider environment.

Depicting Anglo-Indian Lifeways

Before examining the trio of emblematic practices identified by Anglo-Indians themselves as constituting their 'culture', it may be instructive to note some general perceptions of Anglo-Indian lifeways held by those who interact on a regular basis with persons in the community but are not themselves members of it – teachers in the schools Anglo-Indians attend and clergy in the churches to which they belong. Several main themes recur in their comments. Teachers, especially, remark on the 'temperament' of Anglo-Indian children as compared with that of their Tamil fellow pupils. The former are consistently described as more open, outgoing, affectionate, friendly and communicative, whereas the latter are deemed much more reticent or reserved. Several teachers to whom I spoke referred to the contrasting responses to (physical) punishments as a way of illustrating differences of temperament. One commented:

> If you give [an Anglo-Indian boy] a punishment he'll say 'you hit me so hard', then half an hour later he'll forget. The other [Tamil] boys won't look at you for two weeks. They are inner hurt . . . but not Anglo-Indian boys, very friendly and open.

While I was with one head teacher two groups, one of Anglo-Indian children, and another of Tamil children, came to his office and indeed, the differences in their manner of relating to him were striking. The former crawled on his lap, examined the contents of his desk (and my tape recorder), and answered his questions confidently. The latter kept their distance, adopted a demeanour of respect, and responded to queries in barely audible monosyllables. These qualities were occasionally associated by teachers with the differential scholastic abilities of their pupils, with Anglo-Indian children being regarded as unable to perform adequately in school precisely because of their somewhat 'uninhibited' approach to life. According to one: 'They are easily distracted, flighty. It's like they're sitting on hot coals. So they have to be kept still and made to study.'

Another principal theme in these assessments is what most clergy claiming familiarity with Anglo-Indians describe as their 'enjoyment of life'. Anglo-Indians 'celebrate properly'. They mark birthdays, first communions, festivals, weddings and anniversaries, but they also contrive to entertain themselves and each other without an ostensible reason. And the feature of these celebrations most remarked on is the dancing that ensues. Anglo-Indians, says D'Cruz, are seen as a 'dancing, jiving community' (1999: 2). According to one clergyman, 'only Anglo-Indians have gatherings, socials, where they dance. Other communities in India don't have this tradition.' The fact that these dances follow the Western custom in bringing men and women into bodily contact ensures that it is a practice which most Indians (Christians included) do not emulate and serves as one marker of their cultural separation.[2] One man who was employed in the Telegraphs for many years recalled that

There were two big Balls in Madras – the Medical Ball and the Telegraph Ball. By invitation only. All the young ladies used to bother us for tickets. Very selective. The Telegraph Ball was run by the Telegraph Recreation Club, and was held at the Banqueting Hall during [the] Christmas period. Our PMG [Postmaster General] used to attend. But it faded out in the 1960s.

Nowadays the main dances for the Madras Anglo-Indian population take place around Christmas and New Year when the All-India Anglo-Indian Association and one or more prominent members of the community organize major events – each attended by many hundreds of people – to raise funds for charity or other community purposes.[3] The repercussions of such dances have been felt on more than one occasion by one priest who has found himself having to conduct English-language services on New Year's eve and New Year's day:

Anglo–Indians love to dance, and especially on New Year's [eve]. The midnight service [in English] will be very sparsely attended. For the Anglo-Indians we have an earlier thanksgiving service, at 6.30 p.m. By 8 o'clock everything is over; they have to go home to get ready for the big bash. And on New Year's day nobody will be [in church]. There is no one here to give the response. I have to give my own response.

The wish to enjoy life, it is commonly asserted, means Anglo-Indians have no thought for tomorrow. If Tamils acquire money, 'they keep it, and make full use of it.' By contrast, Anglo-Indians spend theirs. 'They have no motivation to keep money for the future. They want to have a happy life, so they spend everything.' While they are hospitable and generous to a fault, 'always willing to share what they have', their 'happy go lucky' attitude is a contributory factor in their poverty. According to one clergyman

if Tamilians are poor you can see their poverty. But when we see Anglo-Indians, wearing nice clothes and eating good food, we think they are rich. Only when we see them in their homes, we realize the truth.

Such evaluations are usually expressed with affection and sympathy, unlike the generally harsh judgements of some contemporary Indian writers and journalists.

Moreover, the image of a 'pleasure complex' (Orans 1965), constructed by those outside the Anglo-Indian fold who have occasion to interact with and observe Anglo-Indians in their schools and churches, is not discursively challenged by members of the community themselves. On the contrary, on numerous occasions I was to hear comments of an identical kind from Anglo-Indians. Thus, 'Anglo-Indian culture,' I was told by one man, 'is in our feet.'[4] Others point to the Anglo-Indian love of parties, entertainments, and social life. Time and again I was to hear comments such as this: 'We live for today, enjoy ourselves, like to be generous, and share what we have. What makes us different is that we're very sociable. Our culture is like that.'

I turn now to the set of three cultural practices or 'culture signs' (Sahlins 1999: 414–15) – omitting language and religion – which Anglo-Indians themselves suggest identifies them as a distinct community.

Dress: Changing Gear

In her study of clothes and identity in India, Tarlo (1996) argues that 'the problem of what to wear' is not and should not be regarded as a trivial matter, but has important social, cultural and political implications. Most Anglo-Indians I met in Madras would agree: they see their modes of dress as crucial indicators of group affiliation. During the colonial period, they say, their forefathers never wore 'Indian' dress – *dhoti* or *veshti* (a kind of sarong) and *kurta* or *jhubba* (long collarless shirt) with sandals on their feet. Anglo-Indian men would have been regarded as improperly attired unless wearing trousers, shirt, jacket and tie, and shoes, 'like the British'. More formal occasions called for Western suits. I was frequently told that because they sought to maintain high standards of dress, Anglo-Indians were referred to respectfully by other Indians as *chata-karar* (shirt people). How many lived up to these idealized notions is impossible to say, but the example of the Europeans in their midst would undoubtedly have provided a model which at least the middle and upper socio-economic levels of the community could seek to emulate. Moreover, the British encouraged certain dress conventions in the workplace. One man recalled having been required to wear a *sola topi* or pith helmet, along with shorts, 'half-sleeved' shirt and socks as part of his uniform at the government office where he was employed: 'all government servants used to wear special clothes, including the pith hat'. Indeed, because it was so widely adopted by Anglo-Indians, they were sometimes called *topi-karar* (topi people). This icon of British authority, which became ubiquitous from the mid-nineteenth century (Cohn 1989: 327) was, according to Caro and Jordan, worn 'with even greater zeal' by Anglo-Indians than by the English themselves, 'as a badge of the European identity that they preferred to emphasize' (1984: 234, 241; also Tarlo 1996: 30). The British, for their part, lost no opportunity to deride these attempts at close association by telling jokes about Anglo-Indians wearing the *topi* at inappropriate times and places (Caro and Jordan 1984: 241). Indeed, ridicule was a favourite British device to maintain sartorial and social distinctiveness (see Chapter 3).

What remains unclear is the extent to which Anglo-Indian men within the ranks of the poor sought or were able to emulate European dress. Certainly, in the schools and orphanages catering for this class of children the clothing they were issued underlined the quasi-European ambience in which they were educated (see Chapter 2). The dress regulations at the Madras Male Orphan Asylum, for example, stipulated that boys should normally wear a 'shirt and long drawers', which would be supplemented by 'sleeved waistcoat with leather cap' on Sundays and holidays (Bell 1812: 100). But comments by school authorities and Anglo-Indian leaders on the cultural, not to say moral impoverishment of Anglo-Indians living alongside and sharing the habits of the 'Indian' poor in the city's slum neighborhoods suggest that such Anglo-Indians probably had little choice but to adopt the latters' dress conventions outside these institutional settings.[5]

Dress practices among the majority of the urban male population have changed during the past five decades or so. Many successful, Western-educated Indian males adopted European styles (other than pith helmets) in the latter part of the nineteenth century (see Cohn 1989: 334; Tarlo 1996: 320).[6] Those within the middle reaches of society probably only took to 'Western' modes on a large scale after Independence, with the increasing spread to India of selected European fashions. Nowadays, at work and in other everyday contexts there is little to distinguish Anglo-Indian from other Indian males of similar class – the majority dress equally in light trousers, shirts and sandals (see also Gaikwad 1967: 135). Yet many artisan-class Anglo-Indians continue to insist on a clear difference in their respective attire, and in doing so usually revert to the stereotype of the Indian villager or of his urban slum-dweller counterpart as a foil for themselves. One young man, when asked if his 'Indian' friends dress any differently from himself, exclaimed, 'I always tell them "you should wear a *veshti* [sarong] and a *jubba* [long collarless shirt], that's your dress; you're wearing our dress!"'.

Some sartorial customs have remained much the same. Thus, at the weddings of all but the poorest Anglo-Indians the men still tend to wear Western suits and ties. For the community's major annual dances, as well, Anglo-Indian men are expected to wear suits, and apart from regarding this convention as a way of 'maintaining standards', people also insist that it is a way of keeping young non-Anglo-Indians from gate-crashing these events.

Nonetheless, I was often to hear from artisan-class Anglo-Indians that 'standards have dropped since the British left'. This implies, for one thing, that among the poorest members of the community men are as likely to wear Indian-style clothes as those more commonly associated with Anglo-Indians. Although, as already suggested, this is probably not a practice which has only emerged since Independence, it is certainly one which can now be readily observed. Since they marry with, live and work alongside the poor of other communities, who by and large wear 'Indian' garments, most such Anglo-Indians feel no need to signify a separate identity from that of relatives, friends, neighbours and workmates in their surroundings. For another, although not yet common, it is by no means unusual for Anglo-Indian men of any class to wear some kinds of Indian dress at home, such as a *veshti*. On a number of occasions when visiting Anglo-Indian homes I was asked to wait while my host changed into something he considered more appropriate (i.e. 'Western' dress) in which to receive a guest.

Finally, there is a feeling that not only have young men belonging to the Indian middle and upper classes abandoned traditional dress in favour of Western-inspired modes, but that they have overtaken Anglo-Indians in the fashion stakes. Today, they are the main customers in the shops offering expensive designer clothes and labels whether made in India or abroad. Referring to his 'Indian' acquaintances, an Anglo-Indian artisan-class male commented:

> they learned to dress from the Anglo-Indians. But nowadays they make fun of us. We don't know how to dress, they tell us. I say 'What do you mean by saying that?' I suppose they mean Anglo-Indians don't dress so neat. Not enough money.

The public dress of Anglo-Indian national and regional leaders also draws occasional comment from local people, and can be employed as a weapon in political contestation within the Anglo-Indian fold. Thus, one prominent member of the All-India Anglo-Indian Association in Madras pointed out with some pride that the late Frank Anthony, for many years one of the two representatives of the community in the Lok Sabha, only ever wore a 'full [Western] suit' to parliament, while several other prominent figures in the same Association who were appointed members of state legislatures dress(ed) similarly when they attend(ed) their regional assemblies. By contrast, opponents – including principals of the Southern India Association – are said to have appeared (or to appear) on public political occasions in 'Indian' dress, whether 'Nehru jacket', *jubba, dhoti,* or even 'safari suit'. Such practices are condemned not only as misguided attempts to curry favour with political parties, and thereby secure their own nominations to central and state assemblies, but as an unwelcome statement, in the language of clothing, that Anglo-Indians should no longer seek to distinguish themselves from the rest of Indian society. With the appointment of several women to represent the community in national and state legislatures the matter of their dress on public occasions also draws comment from politically sensitive members of the Anglo-Indian fold.

Where female dress is concerned, the distinction between Anglo-Indians and Indians has all along been more evident than among the men. Quite apart from the disdain with which the colonial rulers treated Anglo-Indian women's adoption of Western dress (see Chapter 3), the fact is that it probably served to distance them from rather than identify them with British women. This sartorial choice obviously distinguished Anglo-Indian women clearly from the vast majority of Indian women who throughout the period of British rule retained their 'traditional' clothing preferences (Tarlo 1996: 320). Indeed, the European frock came to be seen by the Indian middle class and nationalist leaders as immodest and thus unworthy of Indian women: one symbol of the ruling power which should and could be rejected.

Today a significant number of Anglo-Indian women persist in wearing frocks, and keeping their hair short, another feature of their distinctiveness. For many it is as much a matter of age and routine as a wish to communicate difference. Those born during colonial rule claim to find it difficult to change the dress habits of a lifetime. Time and again I was to hear comments of this kind from elderly women: 'I was born in the British reign, so from the time I am born to this day I wear only dresses.' 'I've always had this Western dress. I won't change my rig now.' 'I'm an old lady. I can't change now.' Even for some younger women, the frock is a mark of continuity with the past. ('I never saw my mother or grandmother in anything but a dress, and I'm most comfortable in this attire.') For others it is very much a matter of resolutely asserting their identity in the face of increasing pressures within the wider society to adopt the sari. One woman, a senior secretary in a large, Brahmin-owned firm, wore her dress as a badge of defiance.

> I'm an Anglo-Indian and it's my dress, I like it. When I put on my dress to go [to work], not every day, but maybe once a month, they come up to me: 'you know you're working for an Indian company?' 'Yeah, I know, this is my dress, my costume.' They smile and walk away. They don't like it so much. If I want to wear it every day I can, but then I got to answer a lot of questions. Sarcastic comments.

Most Anglo-Indian women acknowledge that significant changes in dress modes have been occurring during the past several decades. It is not uncommon, when entering an Anglo-Indian household, to find the older generation wearing the time-honoured, calf-length, short-sleeved, fitted frocks, while the younger women are in *shalwar-kamiz/churidar* set (matching baggy trousers and long shirts popular among the young of all communities) or a sari. The adoption of the sari is attributed to several factors.

For one thing, the very poor find saris less costly, since they can easily be bought on credit, whereas dress materials must be purchased outright, are moreover expensive, and require a further outlay for tailoring. For another, dress codes at work may require women to wear a sari. Whereas those who worked as secretaries, typists or telephonists for major British-owned firms during the colonial period and for some years after Independence remember offices full of 'Anglo-Indian women wearing dresses', nowadays many female employees in large Indian companies claim that they are encouraged if not compelled to wear a sari. ('In Indian Airlines it's compulsory.') Third, some younger Anglo-Indian women insist that they feel more 'at ease' when wearing a sari, that it is more 'graceful', or 'decent'.

The latter comment relates to a further justification for its growing adoption: the hostility felt by many members of the Indian public towards the European/Anglo-Indian frock – deemed immodest if not vulgar – which was muted by the colonial presence, has become more openly manifest since the withdrawal of the British. I was told by several people, including one who works for a theatrical casting company, that in Indian films 'the vamp always wears a dress, and has a name like Judy or Lily, so [the audience] knows she's an Anglo-Indian'. Any number of Anglo-Indian women report being teased and even abused in public places if they wear dresses which expose their legs. Not untypical was the comment by one middle-aged woman: 'These people harass and tease us. They pass remarks because our arms and legs are bare.' Another reported that 'if a lady comes on a bus in a dress the men will not give a seat, but if a sari comes in they will'. The most unpleasant experiences are reported by those who live in or visit slum neighbourhoods. Several quoted impertinent rhymes recited by children. In the words of one:

> If we walk into a slum area with a dress on they criticize a lot, scream at you, and call out names, and make you feel terrible. They laugh at you, and make fun, say dirty things, which embarrasses you a lot.

Thus, among the poorest Anglo-Indians, resident in slum colonies, the sari is now quite commonly worn, and I would imagine was more in evidence in colonial days as well. Since they interact principally with Tamilians, as neighbours, workmates, and occasionally as domestic partners, they – like Anglo-Indian men in similar circumstances – adopt the everyday cultural practices of their surroundings, including the mode of apparel. I was told by several Anglo-Indian women married to Tamilians that they had stopped wearing frocks from the time they went to live with their husbands – in one case over twenty-seven years ago. Marital breakdown, however, can lead to a deliberate change of clothing. An Anglo-Indian woman whose 'Indian' husband had deserted her was adamant that her daughter would wear only frocks. 'I don't want her to wear saris. She must be an Anglo-Indian!'

Among the well-to-do, where many women are likely to have married out of the community, and to work and mix socially with non-Anglo-Indians of similar high status, there is also a tendency to adopt the sari as the primary mode of dress for most formal occasions, while *tika* (or *pottu* in Tamil) on the forehead, and flowers in the hair – once regarded as the preserve of Hindu women – are increasingly worn as well. In this context, the sari serves to communicate their self-definition as both cosmopolitan and Indian. As a successful female academic explained:

> When you move in circles that are not exclusively or even primarily Anglo-Indian, where people don't wear your kind of dress, you have to adapt. Personally, I'm comfortable wearing a sari or anything that is traditionally Indian.

At the same time, they are as likely to wear slacks as *churidar* sets or dresses in informal settings. Younger women from such families follow the styles of their school or university peers, and are increasingly influenced by designs emerging from Delhi, Europe or North America.

For women in the Anglo-Indian artisan class – whose fashion contexts are more localized and more restricted – clothing choices have also expanded. Many alternate styles between work (sari) and home or church (frock, *churidar*, suit, etc). As one woman, wearing a frock when we met, told me: 'I sometimes wear a sari, sometimes a frock. When I feel that a place is not good to wear a frock, I wear a sari.' Moreover, a number of external influences are beginning to impinge on their dress sense. Relatives visiting from abroad present new fashion ideas while film and television offer others. An Anglo-Indian tailor in Perambur, who caters to many customers from within the Madras community, mentioned that she regularly watched several popular television serials, such as *Santa Barbara* and *The Bold and the Beautiful*, because she was often asked to copy items of clothing worn by the main characters. Moreover, she commented, 'castes' i.e. non-Anglo-Indians are also becoming more clothes conscious, and many of her younger customers for current fashions are from outside the Anglo-Indian fold.

Food: Custards and Curries

Culinary habits constitute another key ingredient of Anglo-Indian cultural self-identity. Food, I was often told, 'is a way of distinguishing an Anglo-Indian'. Here too, an idealized image of difference is constructed. Some Anglo-Indians insist that the comparison is between their own 'traditional English fare', eaten at four daily meals (breakfast, lunch, afternoon tea and dinner) and the typical south Indian diet eaten at two main – morning and evening – meals (see also Younger 1987: 38). Moreover, Indians take their food from a banana leaf with their fingers, while seated on a floor-mat. The Anglo-Indian, by comparison, dines at table, from proper plates and with cutlery. Most people, however, draw the contrast not only in terms of dining etiquette but of food preferences: the 'Indian', they would say, is a vegetarian, while the Anglo-Indian eats meat. As one man phrased it:

> They have rice, *sambar* [a south Indian curry], or *rasam* ['pepper water' or soup]. In our case we like to eat meat: chicken, bacon, ham, beef. For them meat is horrible.

One woman seemed to take a mischievous delight in taunting her Hindu fellow employees during the meal break by bringing her meat dishes to the workplace:

> They have that curd rice, and pickles, or maybe plantain. They take it daily. Every day, 220 people are having tiffin in the office: 219 are having that curd rice. That's their way of eating. I have mine. Meat.

Indeed, when Anglo-Indians use the word 'meat' without qualification, they are generally referring to beef. Since it is rarely eaten by Indian Christians (and never – openly – by caste Hindus), beef virtually becomes a metonym for Anglo-Indian culinary identity. Despite their claim that this penchant for beef is the reason they are frequently refused housing by Hindu landlords, and the fact that the only other sections of Indian society who eat this food are Muslims and outcastes, the idea of giving it up seems never to be considered by Anglo-Indians of whatever class. An Anglo-Indian medical doctor who treats many members of the community attributed some of their health problems to diet. 'Most are beef-eaters, but if you tell an Anglo-Indian patient to lay off beef – maybe because of atherosclerosis or angina – he'll say, "what, doc, how can I live?"'

Many Anglo-Indians are insistent that they have their own distinctive cuisine, in terms of both particular dishes and a unique cooking style (see also Brown 1998). When asked what preparations were typically Anglo-Indian, most people would mention 'ball curry' (made with minced beef), which is accompanied by coconut rice and a hot relish made of red chillies, onions, lime juice and sugar – variously termed 'devil's', 'hell's flame', or 'mother-in-law's' chutney. They would also list a special fish curry as well as a variety of (usually meat) 'roasts' and 'fries' as peculiar to Anglo-Indians.[7]

While a handful deny any real difference between Indian and Anglo-Indian culinary styles (save in certain ingredients used), the great majority insist that Anglo-Indian dishes have a special character, although there is little agreement on how it can be defined. The most precise explanation I heard came from an elderly woman who suggested that

> Anglo-Indians use a lot of coconut in their dishes. And we have the habit of whatever spices are used, they are fried, and then we put in the meat or vegetable. Tamils grind their dal and spices together, but don't fry them. They cook their spices with their vegetables and then season. So we get two different flavours.

While some might formulate the distinction in other ways, few would deny the contrast. One man, whose household includes his Tamil wife and Anglo-Indian mother, claimed to experience the difference first hand. 'I like to eat mommy's cooking. Very tasty. She makes meat, meat fry, meat curry.' Then, pointing at his wife and laughing, 'she makes *appalam* and *sambar* only'. Similarly, several people I knew had moved from a highly regarded Catholic home for the elderly to the Anglo-Indian Friend-in-Need Society (FINS), deemed to be much less well-appointed, because, they explained, the former served Indian food – since it housed people of various ethnic groups – while the latter offered a more satisfying (and familiar) Anglo-Indian menu.[8]

But the picture we get by examining Anglo-Indian eating behaviour through time is more complex than that given simply by perceptions of culinary differences between Anglo-Indians and 'the rest', whatever the validity of such assertions. In the institutions established for the Anglo-Indian poor (and 'orphans') in Madras by the British, the menu was largely 'Indian' though certain meals might have been meant to remind them of their European ancestry. Thus, at the beginning of the nineteenth century the Madras Male Orphan Asylum offered rice and curry and pepper water every day of the week save Sundays when the children were given roast mutton, a vegetable, and bread. By the middle of the century at the Female Asylum, the only 'European' food served was bread or buns in the morning (with coffee) and bread (with tea) for Sunday supper.[9]

But for those outside an institutional setting, food practices depended, and still depend, as we might expect, very much on income and class position. The evidence we have suggests that, while the British were in India, well-to-do Anglo-Indians ate a varied diet, but one which included a number of English dishes. By the mid-nineteenth century there appears to have been no discernible Portuguese or other continental European influence on Anglo-Indian cooking in Madras, or at least none that is acknowledged. The notion of 'Western' or 'European' food, therefore, implies only that identified with the British. For one thing, these were the preferred foods of the dominant Europeans in colonial society, with whom Anglo-Indians claimed association. For another, through such food choices Anglo-Indian elites differentiated themselves from those lower down the socio-economic scale in their own community, since most people on low or even average incomes would have found many of the branded foods which went into this cuisine beyond their means. By the early part of this century Madras newspapers were carrying advertisements promoting any number of food items imported from abroad or manufactured in India under foreign licence, and these were undoubtedly considered among the most up-to-date in culinary fashions. In its advice to mothers on the best way to feed their young children *The Anglo-Indian* in January 1929 suggested Western fare exclusively: Quaker oats with honey or golden syrup for the morning; mutton broth with toast and custard pudding for lunch; and for supper, coddled eggs with bread and butter, milk jelly (made with Coignet's Crystaline gelatine powder) and a small cup of Glaxo or Ovaltine.

Nowadays, elderly Anglo-Indians from well-off families generally recall eating a much more Western diet while their parents were still alive (and before the British left India).

When my parents were alive we had only a European diet. In the morning porridge oats, toast, eggs and coffee. In the evening a roast, soup, cutlets, maybe sandwiches, cauliflower cheese, or a bake. We used to have a pudding, but we stopped it because of my father's diabetes.

The heavy bias towards British foods is attributed to the fact that, on the one hand, the ingredients of the diet were available locally in shops catering for English tastes. One elderly Anglo-Indian, who had worked before the Second World War in Spencer's department store, which served mainly a European clientele, recalled that 'we used to get foreign things only . . . butterscotch almonds, marshmallows, cheese. . .'. On the other hand, well-to-do families often employed Indian cooks who had learned to prepare Western foods.

> All the cooks in those days, and I remember in our own home, they prepared food in Western style. They were non-Anglo-Indians who were trained to cook Western food. Our old male cook used to make all the best dishes. But that breed is dying out. I doubt if there are still any of them in service.

While the menu of even the most affluent family would have included some 'Indian' dishes, the general consensus is that since Independence more and more have been incorporated in their diet. Thus, according to a woman in her eighties, 'when I was young we ate mainly eggs, bread and jam for breakfast. We didn't know about *idli* (south Indian steamed rice cakes) and *dosai* (rice-flour pancakes); they are a comparatively recent addition.' With more Indian foods, I was told, has also come a tendency to eat with the fingers instead of with knives and forks. One man thought that the 'bread and butter Anglo-Indians' might still be found in other cities like Calcutta and Bangalore, but not Madras.

> These people would still maintain their cutlery [along with] their English breakfast. At one time we lived like that. In my father's house I didn't know how to use my hands. But now in Madras we've settled down to Indian ways. The Madrassi is the country cousin.

Nowadays, the higher up the scale, the wider the choice of diet, and the greater the likelihood that 'typical' English dishes will still be indulged, though even then not exclusively. In most of the well-to-do families I met where people report a mixture of Western and Indian dishes, the most common tendency is for the former to be eaten in the morning (porridge, eggs, bread)[10] and the latter at noon and in the evening, although at least one of the 'Indian' preparations usually includes meat, and very probably beef. Occasionally, however, I would encounter Anglo-Indians who claimed to reject virtually all non-Western dishes. One quite affluent couple outlined their preferences (and their pretensions) as follows (the wife is speaking):

In the morning we like to have toast, butter, cheese, eggs, bacon or sausages. Not that I don't eat *idli* or *dosai*, but not in the morning. . . I don't like curd rice, although my husband does; he has it at the office with the other managers. I'm not a lover of rice. At lunch, I like a little soup. And we don't eat pungent food. Indian food is very pungent. For dinner, we might have some bread and soup, or what they call chapatis, with a side dish, and a dessert, maybe custard. Continental. We do make rice, because we also have servants to feed, but we eat only a little ourselves.

Since the social circles of affluent, cosmopolitan Anglo-Indians are, as I have pointed out, increasingly likely to include people of different ethnic backgrounds, culinary compromises have to be agreed. When such gatherings occur dishes which might cause offence are eschewed, and a wide enough variety of morally neutral foods, catering to disparate tastes and sensibilities, is offered. Moreover, there is now growing evidence of significant changes occurring in the eating practices of urban dwellers at this class level more generally. First, there is a greater interest in and access to the culinary traditions of other Indian regions. Second, this is accompanied by an increase in 'eating out', providing exposure to a range of popular regional and international dishes (e.g. pizzas) not previously encountered in south India. Third, recent structural adjustments have resulted in many more branded, processed and instant foods – many imported from abroad – being available in 'supermarkets' sprouting up around Madras. And finally, encouraged by an explosion of cookery books (see Appadurai 1988) and women's magazines, these various trends and developments are leading to increased culinary 'innovation' in the home. Indian upper and upper-middle-class women are experimenting not only with baking cakes, but with a whole range of unfamiliar dishes culled from diverse sources (P. Caplan 1985). The upshot is a much more cosmopolitan culinary ambience among the city's elites which, at least in certain contexts, transcends previous food barriers.

At the same time, the eating practices of the poor, who rely for their subsidized supply of staples on government 'fair price' ration shops, differ little from the wider category of disadvantaged Indians.[11] Those able to afford fairly regular meals will likely have *idli* and coffee or tea in the morning, rice and curry at mid-day, and a meat dish in the evening (fry or curry) with rice or just pickle. For the very poor, whose incomes are uncertain, meals are irregular. ('Sometimes we cook and sometimes we don't cook.') A few purchase *idli* in the morning from local women who make and sell them in the neighbourhood – it is cheaper than making them at home. Others report that after morning coffee or tea they go without food all day, cooking only in the evening:

At eight-nine o'clock we cook. Whatever we got. Sometimes plain rice with pickles. With four annas (twenty-five peysa) we buy pickle. If we got money we make curry – like drumstick or aubergine. Maybe fry. Best is meat.

De Wit found that in the Madras slums he studied the main part of 'daily spendable income' was spent on food, leaving little over for 'shelter' (1993: 157; 245). For Anglo-Indians at this class level, priorities are reversed. Of the resources available food takes second place to rent. I was often told that while meals can be foregone, the rent – and so a roof over their heads – cannot (Caplan 1996).

During the Christmas season considerable emphasis is placed on providing festive food for the poor. Anglo-Indian associations and charities, as well as a few individual philanthropists invite some of the community's most disadvantaged members to enjoy special meals at which they are served 'Christmas fare' – usually centred on chicken biryani. Several organizations also raise substantial funds to provide 'hampers', containing a variety of ingredients to enable the recipients to prepare a proper Christmas meal. A woman involved in one such hamper scheme explained:

We rate Christmas as a special day in India, especially Madras. With the hamper the family will have some special food for Christmas. So once [in] the year we would like the [poor] Anglo-Indian children to have a real good, substantial meal, like all other Anglo-Indians have. We give them pork, chicken, rice, bread, fruit, vegetables, a cake. . .

Christmas thus enables community leaders and philanthropists to reiterate the association of particular food practices with the sense of being Anglo-Indian, at the same time insisting on the inclusiveness of the community.

Religion, language, dress and food behaviour are nominated by Anglo-Indians as key ingredients in defining their cultural identity although, as we have seen, there are in practice significant divergences within the community itself as well as overlaps with usages found in the wider Indian society. The celebration of marriage is another which, while seldom specifically designated as such, can be seen to draw together a range of beliefs and activities – in these diverse arenas – which underline the particularity of Anglo-Indian lifeways while at the same time situating the community firmly in its locality.

Making and Celebrating Marriages

In Chapter 3 I focused on the widespread practice among Anglo-Indians since colonial times of establishing unions – formal and informal – outside the community. But however substantial their numbers, the fact remains that only a minority of people participate in such conjugal arrangements. The majority marry – and probably have done since at least the early nineteenth century – within the community, with others, that is, whom they identify and who identify themselves, as Anglo-Indians. Thus, Emma Roberts insisted that while young Anglo-Indian women at the orphan schools in Calcutta could aspire to marriages with Europeans, their brothers – 'the greater number [of whom] only qualified to fill the lower order of clerkships' – were 'less ambitious', content to 'match with those of their own condition' (1835 (III): 97–8). But even the Anglo-Indian men whose condition was more elevated – such as those in Madras who, according to Major Bevan, attained 'wealth, rank, and respectability', or were, by the 1830s, significant figures in the uncovenanted civil service – would have had no option but to seek marriage partners from within Anglo-India (Bevan 1839: 20; Hawes 1996: 48).

While 'endogamous' marriages occur now, as in the past, at all levels of Anglo-Indian society, they are mainly concentrated in the middle ranks of the community.[12] In the remainder of the chapter I examine how these marriages are organized and celebrated, and note certain changes which appear to be taking place.

Studies of marriage in India have long focused on the vital importance of mate selection for the protection of a family's caste and lineage status, the maintenance of its economic and social capital, the guarantee of its future welfare, and the maximization of its children's potential. The choice of connubial partners, in other words, is too important an activity to be left to the individuals concerned. To the extent that such considerations have not diminished through the years and are no less critical in contemporary India, 'arranged marriages' are still very much the norm. In her Introduction to a recent reader on family, kinship and marriage in India, Uberoi remarks that '[w]hatever the other changes in Indian society, matchmaking still remains the prerogative of family elders, not of the two persons involved' (1993: 36). This observation would apply as much to Indian Christians as to Hindus (Caplan 1987).

However, the few studies conducted among Anglo-Indians in the post-Independence period argue for a view of marriage as based on free choice. Writing about the community in Lucknow, Gupta insists that 'it is only "romantic love" that brings men and women into marriage. . . [T]here is an absence of arranged marriages' (1968: 39–40). Referring to Anglo-Indians in Bombay, Bhattacharya maintains that they 'follow the western style of selection of mates' (1968: 166). Sen, too, has more recently contended that '[in Calcutta] arranged marriage is out of the question', indeed is 'looked down upon', so that 'selection of the life's partner is considered an affair of the persons concerned' (1988: 243). For Madras, Brennan has similarly commented that 'marriages are not generally arranged' (1979: 200). These assertions thus imply a stark disjunction between Anglo-Indian and other Indian systems of matrimony. To pose such a simple dichotomy, however, ignores the considerable variation within each 'system', the overlap between them, and the possibility for changes in each.

There is wide agreement, bordering on stereotype, both within and outside the community, that young Anglo-Indians (and especially women) differ from other Indians in having a great deal of freedom to meet members of the opposite sex (Gist 1967: 15; Schermerhorn 1973: 75–6; Younger 1987: 140–3). Anglo-Indian girls were among the first females in India to attend school, and numerous marriages in Madras have resulted and still result from friendships which began during schooldays ('We fell in love in school. We knew each other for many years'). Then, large numbers of Anglo-Indian women in cities like Madras have been going out to work since the second quarter of the twentieth century – as nurses, secretaries, teachers and, during both world wars, as members of the armed forces – and this has meant opportunities to establish relationships in the workplace leading eventually to marriage ('We were both working in the Telegraphs and we used to meet; that's how I came to know her'). Others report meeting their future spouses in the often crowded tenements and neighbourhoods inhabited by Anglo-Indians belonging to the artisan class ('He lived upstairs, so I used to see him and talk to him nearly every day'), or in the railway colonies in which many of them spent at least part of the lives ('My father was on the railways, and so was hers. I was sixteen and had just started as a fireman when I met her'). Still others met their future spouses at one of the dances which, as we have seen, are a feature of Anglo-Indian social gatherings ('I met my wife when I was best man at a wedding and she was a guest. I asked her to dance'), or in church ('The first time I saw him was when he stepped on my foot at the altar rail').

In this latter connection it has to be noted that, although marriages between Roman Catholics and Protestants did preoccupy the East India Company's representatives in seventeenth- and eighteenth-century Madras, denominational differences have seldom been a bar to marriage since. While most Anglo-Indians in Madras marry with co-religionists, there are numerous instances of Catholics marrying Protestants, a phenomenon reported for other parts of Anglo-India as well (Bhattacharya 1968: 166 on Bombay; Gupta 1968: 52 on Lucknow; Sen 1988: 248 on Calcutta). A small minority of Anglo-Indians, who have in recent years affiliated to evangelical churches, now tend to practice a more exclusive marriage policy, seeking to confine their unions to within circles whose members share a similar religious commitment (as 'true believers').

Apart from the public contexts in which Anglo-Indians can meet prospective partners, there is also the private arena of the family in which bonds are created which can lead to marriage. I encountered numerous instances of two brothers marrying sisters (and one of three brothers married to three sisters), of brother and sister marrying siblings of the opposite sex, and unions of cross or parallel cousins. Moreover, distant relatives come together during family visits, celebrations, funerals, and the like, at which time potential spouses are met. Finally, in a small community like that in Madras it is relatively easy to locate others – particularly others of similar status – in a finite network of relations and friends. Despite the range of opportunities available for encountering potential marriage partners, most in fact ensure that people meet others of similar background and circumstances. The idea that Anglo-Indian youth, even when they select their own partners, have a completely free choice about whom they shall marry is therefore much exaggerated.

Studies of Anglo-Indian marriage have almost certainly underestimated the parental role in these matters. Their part is evident from the moment courtship begins.[13] This can extend for a lengthy period – between one and five years – giving time, I was told, for reflection (women tend to marry in their early to mid-twenties, men in their mid-twenties to early thirties), for the families and the couple to get to know one another better, and for savings to be accumulated.[14]

The principal agents of control are the young woman's parents. A number of married women I spoke to recollected the careful surveillance exercised by their parents (especially fathers) during their courtship. One woman, now in her sixties, whose father had held a post on the railways, recalled:

> When my [future] husband wanted to take me to a picture, he had to take permission from daddy. 'Can I take her to a picture?' 'What picture?' Mommy and daddy must see [know] which picture before they send us. 'Yes, you can take her, but on one condition. You take the other two [her brother and sister] as well.' They won't send me alone with him.

Another related that she had met her husband at an Independence Ball in the Port Trust. 'I was with my friends and my brother, of course.' When I asked her why 'of course', she replied: 'Because my brother was from my family. My parents were very strict. They would not let us [she and her friends] go alone, unless we went with someone responsible or trustworthy, like family members.'

Thus, while young men are comparatively unrestricted by their own parents, their freedom is constrained by the young woman's guardians. One former mechanic, now retired, remembers how, when he was courting, his visits to his fiancée's home were strictly regulated. 'I could sit in the house until eight o'clock, then her mother would shout, "come on, come on, it's eight o'clock". And I had to leave'. While the degree and intensity of superintendence has diminished in recent times, I was on a number of occasions told about and witness to the supervision exercised by parents and future parents-in-law over the courting couple, and the equanimity with which such control is accepted. For example, the parents of a young woman, recently engaged, whose fiancé was working in another city, forbade her to go to dances in his absence, since they deemed it inappropriate, a view with which she concurred.

Most of the many people with whom I discussed issues surrounding marriage would maintain that young Anglo-Indians choose their own partners. But they would also insist on the need for parents to be satisfied with the choice, and with the intended spouse's family. One couple, whose two daughters were happily married, insisted that they had not 'interfered' when their daughters' male friends had come to visit, but when the girls eventually announced their intention to marry, they had asked to meet the boys' parents. 'It's just confirmation,' they added.

An even more active parental involvement was asserted by many people. One woman used the term 'planned marriage' when referring to those which are initiated by the couple, but which parents must approve and then go on to organize. One retired railway driver recalled: 'When we wanted to marry my parents should approach her parents. If they say "yes", everything goes. If "no", it means no go. Most of us follow our parents' advice.'

His sister, who was present at the same discussion, added:

We always wait for the blessings of our parents. Their choice comes first, secondly ours. [If someone comes to ask for a girl] they ask for her opinion. Suppose she doesn't want to marry the man, then her parents won't force her. The parents express their wish, then the children have their say. The Indians have no choice about it. Luckily, his [her husband's] parents liked me very much and my parents liked him.

In most cases a young couple's wish to marry is conveyed by one or both of the pair to their parents and future in-laws, but there are also numerous instances of hopeful bridegrooms announcing their intentions first to the girl's father. One former head teacher in a girl's school recounted how she and her husband had been playmates in a railway colony, and later were in the church choir together. He would come and visit her house and called her father 'Uncle E. . .'. He proposed the marriage to her father, who suggested he ask her first. 'So then he asked me.'

Usually, approaches to prospective parents-in-law are delivered verbally, but I was also told by several people that they had made or received written 'applications'. One man, now in his eighties, recalled that when his son indicated that he had met a girl he wished to marry, 'I did not go, but made an application. I wrote to her father: "permit your daughter to marry my son", like that I wrote. Then they called us to lunch.' I was even told that in the past some Anglo-Indians used specifically designed application forms. One elderly couple insisted that his proposal had been made to her father on

> Letter paper, with all lace work. In that [the boy] wrote to [her father] 'Dear Mr F. . . [her maiden name]. I am applying for the hand of your daughter, D. . ., because I have fallen in love with her.' Then within a certain number of days we had to reply, on the same type of paper. 'I have pleasure in handing over my daughter.' [Her father] sent that letter to the boy, not to his father.

In a small minority of cases, Anglo-Indian marriages are arranged by elders. At the age of thirty-one Ronnie, a clerk in a transport company, was still unmarried, and his father's brothers decided to 'settle this fellow'. 'They searched for a girl for me. I went with my parents to see the girl, and we engaged. It was [an] arranged marriage. That was in 1968.'

For Nora, who was in the WAC (India) during the Second World War, the memory of her arranged marriage was still painful after nearly fifty years: 'My parents got me married. I didn't want to marry him. I didn't like him, that's the honest truth.' When I asked Mr and Mrs M. how they had come to meet and marry, he replied, 'it was a love marriage', at which point she interjected: 'Why should I voluntarily marry an old man [there is an eighteen-year age difference]?' It was, she insisted, arranged by their respective elder brothers.

What seems clear is that despite the strong emphasis on young Anglo-Indians being free to select their own marriage partners, an ideology articulated at all levels of the society (and echoed in the sociological and anthropological literature), the experiences of a substantial number of people suggest that parents or other close senior relatives exercise a significant influence on the outcomes, and have done so for some time. They commonly employ the phrase 'I got my son/daughter/children married', indicating acceptance of some measure of responsibility for their unions. Moreover, there is evidence that, if anything, this tendency is increasing. There arc several reasons why this should be so.

First of all, as already noted in Chapter 5, there has been a large exodus of Anglo-Indians to the West since Independence, so that there are now substantial settlements of Anglo-Indians abroad, whose origins are in south India, and many of whom still have relatives in the city. They – or their children – therefore represent a fund of potential marriage partners, and hold out to young men and women in Madras the possibility of emigrating as spouses. But it is mainly through family elders that overseas contacts are maintained, and possible matches mooted.

Second, there has of late been a growing feeling within the more successful sections of the community that Anglo-Indians must seek more and more to identify themselves as Indians (rather than, as in the past, as British or Europeans). Part of this process is a growing sensitivity to the negative constructions placed on what are assumed by people outside the community to be unregulated Anglo-Indian marriages, and the accompanying stereotypes of Anglo-Indians (and women in particular) as immodest, shameless and indelicate. Anglo-Indians are also perfectly aware that within the wider society 'arranged marriages' are the cultural norm and an indicator of status and respectability. Indeed, as I have noted, Anglo-Indians themselves portray 'Indian marriage' stereotypically, as entirely the province of the elders, in which the prospective partners continue to have absolutely no say. The assumption, therefore, is that the greater the control over marriage, the higher the regard in which respectable Anglo-Indian families will be held.

Third, those members of the community who have been able to take advantage of new economic opportunities available in the past several decades, and whose circumstances have improved accordingly, have increasingly tended to invest in property, particularly housing. As we saw in Chapter 2 during much of the colonial period and into the early post-Independence era Anglo-Indians neither had the wherewithal nor felt the need to own their own houses. But recent developments have encouraged those who can afford it to become property owners. This new property-owning class, though still small, takes an increasing interest and role in the marriages of their children, although paradoxically, it is from this very section of the community that many young women tend to marry 'out', sometimes without benefit of parental involvement.

Fourth, and finally, an increasingly competitive wedding scene coupled with spiralling costs have encouraged if not compelled wider involvement in these unions. Nowadays, the partners themselves, if they are well employed, will contribute a portion – even the greater portion – of the costs, but in most cases parents accept responsibility for organizing and funding the weddings of their children, with expenses generally shared equally between the two sides.

During the late colonial period – if not earlier – affluent and prominent families spent prodigiously on their weddings, even while Anglo-Indian leaders (and some European 'well-wishers') were urging members of the community to reduce their expenditure. *The Anglo-Indian* would occasionally report the marriages of offspring of the Association's office-holders, note the many guests in attendance, and the generous hospitality offered. An (unattributed) article in the *Madras Mail* in July 1926 accusing Anglo-Indians of extravagance prompted a discussion in the pages of *The Anglo-Indian*. One letter from 'a Parent' agreed that the opinion expressed in the *Mail* was 'correctly applicable to those in the lower walks of life', but hardly fair as regards 'respectable Anglo-Indians'. With tongue-in-cheek, and in a clear reference to current debates about the political status of the community, the correspondent went on to point out that 'after all we are statutory Indians' and 'did you ever hear of an Indian who [would] spare money or pains [on] his daughter's wedding?' (July 1926).

Artisan-class weddings were, as we might expect, more modest. Several people now in their latter years recalled that when they were married (forty to fifty years ago) the custom was to have a morning wedding, followed by a lunch. Members of the succeeding generation, married perhaps thirty to forty years ago, remembered a somewhat later wedding, with 'high tea' served afterwards. The guests ('not the 500–700 you have now') stayed for a 'little dancing' and a snack and left soon after. By all accounts, Anglo-Indian weddings have become more elaborate and expensive during the past few decades. The church ceremony takes place in the late afternoon and is followed by a reception which features a dinner and dance lasting well into the early hours. Judging by the weddings I have attended, the videos of them I have seen, and the reports I have heard, they tend to follow a fairly standard pattern. Below I note several key features of an artisan-class Madras wedding which encapsulate the complex mix of practices that constitute contemporary Anglo-Indian 'culture'.

Anglo-Indian brides wear white bridal dresses. The tailor quoted earlier, who specializes in these garments, had this to say:

Tamilians don't wear bridal gowns, but Anglo-Indians are very particular about them. They use satin, lace, net, and beaded embroidery. They want a good dress for that one day, for that occasion, and pay a lot for the materials and the tailoring.

In addition, great care is taken over the style and colour of the dresses and shoes to be worn by the bridesmaids and flower girls. Women in the family and many female guests have dresses or suits made for the occasion. It is not thought proper to appear in saris or other items of Indian clothing for an artisan-class Anglo-Indian wedding, even if these are worn in other contexts throughout the year.

The bridegroom and his 'best men' are attired in dark suits, black shoes, white (usually dress) shirts, bow ties and white gloves. Male guests wear suits and ties; indeed, I felt most inappropriately dressed when I showed up at one wedding in a 'safari suit', which would have been a quite acceptable dress for an 'Indian' wedding.

The wedding rite follows the format current in the host church (usually the bride's), but features the couple exchanging rings (a recent innovation) or, as in the past, the bridegroom placing a ring on the bride's finger, not a *tali* around her neck, as would occur in an Indian Christian wedding. After the church ceremony guests make their way to the reception, usually held in a large nearby hall.[15] Families able to afford the costs – sometimes children or other close relatives working abroad send a contribution for this purpose – may hold it in one of the city's better hotels, and invite political or film celebrities whose attendance marks their prominence within the wider society. But most people make do with the church's own facilities, at which anything between 300–800 guests can be accommodated.[16]

The reception itself includes several key elements, and a 'master of ceremonies' – usually an older relative or friend of one side or both – is expected to ensure that everything proceeds as expected. The arrival of the bride and bridegroom is soon followed by their circumambulation and cutting of the (three-tier) wedding cake. A toast (in 'wine') to the couple is then proposed by (usually) a senior relative of the bridegroom; the cake and wine are distributed and the guests join in the toast.[17] These aspects of Anglo-Indian weddings have apparently begun to attract some attention within Indian Christian circles. I was told by a priest whose congregation includes both Anglo-Indians and Indians that some of the latter now want a wedding cake and wine. 'They see the Anglo-Indians cutting the wedding cake, and taking wine, so they want to do the same. I have seen two or three families [doing this]. I said, "But this is not our

Tamil culture." They said, "Father, what they are doing we are also doing."
It isn't traditional!'

The bridegroom's response to the toast is expected to pay tribute to
his own and to his bride's relatives, since the marriage is regarded not
simply as a union of two individuals but of two families. Indeed, much
of the activity during the reception involves the renewing of ties among
family members and friends who may not have seen each other for some
time, and the creation of new bonds among others who have not yet met.
I recall being taken aback by the fact that Anglo-Indians, when meeting
old friends and family members, kiss on both cheeks, a custom I have
not seen practiced by any other community in India.[18]

With the bridegroom's speech the 'formal' part of the proceedings is
concluded and the dancing can begin, led off by the couple.[19] Indeed,
when planning a wedding reception, one of the first tasks is to arrange
for a band, since during the wedding season (December and January) the
better ones are in great demand. Though the (Western) music played has
changed with the times, the inclusion of couple dancing, as we have seen,
is a long-standing feature of these wedding celebrations.

Finally, no wedding is complete until the guests are fed, and while the
dancing goes on people are directed in sequence to the dining area.
Whereas at one time, I was told, wedding guests would have been offered
a light snack – sandwiches and cakes, or perhaps a cold buffet – nowadays
a 'full meal' has to be served, usually chicken or mutton biryani.
According to one man who has organized and attended numerous Anglo-
Indian weddings over the years, this change is the result of influences
from outside the community. 'People see Indian weddings, where the
main thing is food, so it has gradually come into this [Anglo-Indian]
society as well.' He might have mentioned that the menu has become
more 'Indianized' as well.

Conclusion

In examining certain emblematic lifeways of Anglo-Indians we encounter
a complicated cultural field. At the level of rhetoric the portrayal of their
usages, especially within the artisan class, is meant to demonstrate a clear
distinction between themselves and other Indians. Culture, after all, 'is a
particularistic claim – one that requires other cultures with other identities'
(Fardon 1995: 11). Each is stereotyped as following a largely unchanging
set of behaviours rooted in the past: thus, Anglo-Indian habits of dress,
food and marriage – to say nothing of language and religion – derive
from their European (mainly British) forebears; those of Indians are

enveloped in their own (mainly Hindu) traditions. Such a portrayal homogenizes and flattens an immense diversity of tradition and behaviour. When we examine what Anglo-Indians themselves identify as specific cultural markers, we note both differences in practices within the community as well as significant overlaps with non-Anglo-Indian groups in the urban milieu. Throughout the extent of the Anglo-Indian fold, cultural elements whose provenance might be regarded as distinct are brought together in a creative synthesis.

One aspect of this cultural complexity is highlighted when we examine the question of transformations in key Anglo-Indian practices since Independence. Where changes are acknowledged to have occurred, evaluations are somewhat contradictory: for some, they mean a decline in standards (from eating with cutlery to eating with fingers); for others an improvement (from dresses which invite abuse to saris which are both acceptable and elegant). Furthermore, both represent the changes as a movement from 'Western' to 'Indian', but this is to oversimplify the process we have been examining. For one thing, the notion of a meta-morphosis from one assumed homogeneous cultural state to another takes no account of the diversity or potential for transformation and innovation in each. Indian dress and food habits (to say nothing of marriage observances) have not been static over the years. Most recently, new technologies and the influx of consumer goods from abroad (from the West but also the Far East and elsewhere) have brought dramatic trans-formations in consumption patterns. For another, the changes which are occurring are not invariably or inevitably moving in one direction. With alterations in their circumstances – for better or worse – many Anglo-Indian families abandon certain of their 'Indian' ways of eating or dressing or celebrating marriages and adopt what they think of as 'Western' modes. Others take the opposite path; still others choose to retain certain of their long-standing habits in the face of changes all around them.

Hence, gender and age – not to mention personal predilection – are bound to affect individual behaviour. Even more crucially, class location is an important influence on the practice of culture: people in the middle ranks clothe and feed themselves and celebrate their marriages in somewhat different ways from those at both ends of the socio-economic spectrum. Anglo-Indian lifeways may be placed along a continuum, from cosmopolitan (or British, when referring specifically to colonial times) at one end, to 'local Tamilian' at the other. Affluent Anglo-Indians increasingly share the urbane lifestyles current among India's rich. I was often to hear remarks like that made by one wealthy professional man: 'Anglo-Indian culture is not very different from the general Indian culture any more, if it ever was, but part and parcel of it.'

Moreover, the cultural practices of the poor are said to have become more attuned to those similarly located within the wider society. For some prominent Anglo-Indians the latter tendency represents a 'loss of culture'. Brennan, referring to Madras some two decades ago, reports Anglo-Indian leaders then as saying that the poor 'are losing their identity . . . no shoes . . . no furniture . . . speaking Tamil' (1979: 108). Similar comments continue to be made today. In the words of one man:

> A lot of the poor have drifted. I see some of the children and grandchildren of people well known to me [and they are] completely Indianized. Poverty has taken its toll.

Brennan argues that the adoption of Indian practices is a last resort, when the poor can no longer support the expensive 'British-derived' culture of the Anglo-Indian. But they nonetheless 'have in mind the acceptable Anglo-Indian style of life' even if they cannot aspire to it (1979: 108–10, 133). While there is some truth in the claim that certain quintessential Anglo-Indian usages are comparatively expensive (frocks are said to be dearer than saris, a non-vegetarian diet dearer than a vegetarian one, etc.), such an approach derives from the position that culture is bounded, coherent and detachable, a commodity-like entity which, since it comes with a cost, only some can afford to practice. But with such a model of understanding how can we account for the kinds of cultural transformations accurring among affluent Anglo-Indians, who certainly have the cash for culture? More generally, it does not allow for the kinds of negotiation with 'mainstream' lifeways which occur at all levels of Anglo-Indian society, and most of all at both ends of the class spectrum where, for different reasons, cultural practices are in greatest flux. My own preference would be for an approach which distinguishes between but incorporates both a mode of self-representation through reifications of certain features of culture, and the empirical complexity of the cultural domain – untidy, porous, creolized, and so on. Only through such a lens can we appreciate Anglo-Indian insistence on a unique cultural identity (rooted in the West via the colonial British), alongside cultural practices which situate the community firmly in contemporary India.

Notes

1. Unlike in other areas of the colonized world, a creole language did not emerge in this Indian setting.

2. In the early part of 1919 several articles appeared in the press about the number of dances held in Madras and there were also letters complaining at the large attendance of Anglo-Indians at these. *The Anglo-Indian* of 28 June commented that 'judging from these letters there are some people in [the city] who think that Anglo-Indians are too fond of dancing and spend too much of their time and money at local dancing halls'. There are no longer any dance halls in the city.

3. These are usually held at the Railway Institute in Perambur and the main recreation hall at Binny's, both venues capable of holding large numbers.

4. In a recently published Anglo-Indian cookbook, the Anglo-Indian author writes of the 'carefree lifestyle and devil-may-care attitude that has allowed [Anglo-Indians] to flout convention, and for the most part live happily beyond their means'. See Book Review, STOPA Newsletter (Perth, Australia) May 1999. I am grateful to Christopher Hawes for sending me a copy of the Newsletter.

5. Stoler suggests that in the East Indies many poor Europeans and Indo-Europeans adopted styles that 'indicated not a failed version of European culture but an outright rejection of it' (1997: 210).

6. Tarlo suggests this was done to 'dissociate themselves from the uneducated Indian majority while at the same time associating themselves with the ruling British élite' (1996: 320).

7. As a vegetarian I was unable to taste most of these dishes, but I attended a number of Anglo-Indian functions where they were served. I did eat, and enjoyed, the chutney in question.

8. The weekly menu at the FINS features a host of mainly non-vegetarian dishes which would be familiar to most Anglo-Indians: fries, meat curries, stews, eggs, etc.

9. Arnold suggests that in some orphanages the diet 'was as ambiguous as their social position: boiled beef, carrots and potatoes one day, curry, dal and rice the next' (1979: 111).

10. Gaikwad found that 'only upper class and some middle class people . . . are accustomed to the English type of breakfast. In these families it consists of porridge, toast and butter, eggs and coffee' (1967: 131).

11. 'To the urban poor daily cooking and eating depends directly upon government rationing, fair-pricing shops, and subsidized food' (Khare 1986: 290).

12. By 'endogamy' here I imply a tendency rather than any rule prescribing marriage within the community.

13. The term 'courtship' is not used by Anglo-Indians in Madras, who tend to employ phrases like 'we were caught up together' or 'we made friends'.

14. Gupta records a courtship period of between one and two years among the Anglo-Indians in Lucknow (1968: 54). He also notes the late marriage age (between thirty-one and forty-five) of men (Ibid.: 35).

15. Nowadays many Anglo-Indians adorn both church and reception hall, not only with flowers, but with decorations based on a theme chosen by the couple. One Anglo-Indian interior designer in Madras specializes in 'thermacole' (polystyrene) decorations for weddings and other festive occasions.

16. For marriages in Perambur (which area contains the largest concentration of Anglo-Indians in the city) the favourite venue is the spacious Railway Institute.

17. Usually a relative or neighbour with a reputation for making good wine is asked to do so for a wedding. Some people charge for this service, others do it as a favour. Since it is only made several weeks before the wedding it has virtually no alcoholic content.

18. It would be interesting to know how this custom originated. I doubt very much it would have been much in evidence among the British in colonial India.

19. Dancing is unlikely to be included if the family is strongly evangelical, but otherwise it features equally in Protestant and Catholic artisan-class marriage celebrations.

Conclusion

I think the problem with most of us is that we don't know clearly what our ancestry is. Frankly, I don't care. I never doubted that I am an Anglo-Indian.

I remember a function at the [. . .] railway colony in 1949 – two years after Independence. And at the end instead of the national anthem the band played 'God Save the King'! Can you imagine that?

It's ridiculous to say that most Anglo-Indians look on England as home. They think we sit and yearn for England. But it's just not true, this is our home!

The study of colonialism, argues Pels, 'erases the boundaries between the post-colonial present and the colonial past' (1997: 163). I would also suggest that our understanding of each can only be augmented by examining them as a continuous political field and by means of detailed, historicized ethnographic investigation. This study of Anglo-India suggests that the line separating the colonial past from the postcolonial present cannot be precisely demarcated, that neither can be conceptualized as an undifferentiated entity, and, moreover, that the transition from one to the other is characterized by both continuities and disjunctions. This book may be read, therefore, as part of an ongoing conversation about the complex relationship between the colonial and the postcolonial in diverse settings.

As descendants of the initial offspring of unions involving European men and local women, Anglo-Indians are quintessentially the children of colonialism. And like similar métis populations in the colonized world, they were seen by their British rulers at times as potential enemies and at others as allies in their imperial adventure, alternately preferred and promoted or discriminated against and victimized. While Anglo-India's relations with the colonial power were anything but straightforward, Anglo-Indian chroniclers tend to represent these links as a fairly uncomplicated series of epochs characterized as either propitious or unfavourable for the community. Thus, the period up to the end of the eighteenth century is portrayed as their 'halcyon days'. At that point the colonial rulers introduced a series of punitive orders which effectively excluded members of this mixed-race group from virtually all but the most humble military and civil appointments. These measures, it is generally agreed, resulted in 'days of turmoil and adversity' which lasted until the outbreak of the Sepoy rebellion, when Anglo-Indians again gained the rulers' favour and were given preferred access to certain strategic areas of employment, such as the railways and telegraphs. This inaugurated a new 'period of prosperity and contentment' which lasted through the first decades of the twentieth century. At that time the colonial authorities initiated reforms giving Indians a greater say in government and encouraging Indianization in many spheres of the economy. These are seen to have impacted negatively on Anglo-Indians, driving many out of employment, and leaving 'the community as a whole . . . demoralised and discouraged' (Weston 1939: 100–9; see also Stark 1936 for a similar chronology).

Contemporary ethno-chroniclers and commentators on Anglo-India's postcolonial circumstances provide varied perspectives. They tend to portray the past fifty years as an heroic battle to prevent further community decline by struggling to retain long-standing community privileges in employment and political representation against the predations of the Indian state, which is not invariably supportive of minority interests (see Anthony 1969). More informally, those belonging to the artisan class, faced with a daily struggle to maintain a precarious livelihood in the face of intense competition, regard the end of colonial rule (and of Anglo-Indians' privileged status vis à vis other Indians) as the beginning of the downturn in Anglo-Indian fortunes. For their part, the current leadership – mainly in the context of internal political contestation – also portrays the postcolonial period as one of continual deterioration, due not so much to the state as to the activities of rivals in the community. Only the educated well-to-do present a more upbeat view of Anglo-India's contemporary situation. Their exegesis not infrequently focuses specifically on the lifting of the pre-Independence ceiling on advancement, and the ending of social exclusion imposed by colonial elites, as prime factors in the transformation of the community's fortunes.

The growth of 'scientific racism' in early nineteenth century Europe saw the 'hybrid' become a trope for moral failure and degeneration. In *Purity and Danger* (1966) Douglas contends that those phenomena which do not fit into the ordered and discrete categories of a culture – the anomalous or interstitial – are regarded as polluting or forbidden (see also Leach 1964). Douglas's theory as it applies to hybrids is somewhat mitigated by the absence of an historical dimension, since attitudes to mixed-race populations obviously changed over time (as in Europe) and in varied contexts. The British in India, who at first included Anglo-Indians in their colonial project, from the early nineteenth century excluded and demeaned them by virtue of their métis status. Branded with any number of degrading epithets, Anglo-Indians became figures of contempt and ridicule. In both life and fiction Anglo-Indians were frequently portrayed in disparaging stereotypes, many of which focused on women, regarded as the principal mimics of European mores and seducers of their men.

However, Anglo-Indians did not invariably accept these depictions nor acquiesce in such prescribed statuses. Standing astride the ordered social and cultural categories set in place by the colonial authorities, they were inclined to challenge their validity. Through refusing official census designations and asserting alternative modes of belonging, marrying out and even 'disappearing' back into the surrounding Indian society, they demonstrated the fragility and permeability of colonial racial and ethnic boundaries.

Further, while the colonial powers indulged in what Jean and John Comaroff call 'body work', through which they sought to impose themselves upon the everyday lives of their subjects, this was frequently resisted and subverted by the very persons whose habits they sought to 'retune' (1992: 41–2). In areas such as language, dress and cuisine Anglo-Indians evolved practices which defied ready assignment to clearly bounded spheres and classes, underlining the fragility of the categorical edifice on which British colonial rule was predicated. Thus, perhaps more so than any other single colonial population, Anglo-Indians served as both a factor in and a potent reminder of the fluidity of the urban social environment during the British period. Their ambiguous positioning focuses attention on the theoretical importance of this or any other métis group, however demographically insignificant they might be.

Notwithstanding the existence of a hybridized social field, those who spoke for and about Anglo-India proclaimed not a rhetoric of mixture, but one of purity in the sense of an insistence on unequivocal association to the dominant European group. Encouraged, no doubt, by their special privileges in employment and education (in comparison to other Indians), their common language and Christian faith, and their inadvertent align-ment with the political project of colonial rule, Anglo-Indians stressed, in the idioms of blood and culture, their affiliations with the British. At the same time, partly to defend what advantages they enjoyed and in pursuance of greater benefits, they early on exhibited considerable self-awareness and consciousness of community despite their disparate origins. Goodrich argues that only when the British began to set their own interests apart from those of Eurasians, and allocate to them an identity 'as a class' did the latter begin to conceive of themselves as constituting a group apart from the European community in India (1952: 6). While she makes a strong case, it fails to attribute any agency to the Anglo-Indians, rendering them entirely the subjects of British will, neglecting the complex ways in which the former negotiated the diversity of possible modes of belonging.

Postcolonial Anglo-India reveals a more disparate set of discourses about affiliation. Indeed, from the end of the first quarter of the twentieth century, when it became apparent that British rule in India was drawing to a close, increasing voices were heard within the community urging alliance with the nationalist project. In the contemporary setting, Anglo-Indian elites, though encompassed within the multi-ethnic, multi-religious, cosmopolitan and increasingly globalized ambience of the affluent, insist on a strong connection with India. At the other end of the spectrum, among the most disadvantaged, enveloped in the surroundings of the poor, a variety of credentials are enunciated, as alternative forms of association become possible. It is principally within the middle ranks of Anglo-India, where economic uncertainties and 'downward mobility' have been most acutely felt, that claims to a European affinity continue to be declared.

Gillis, echoing the views of any number of social scientists, argues that nowadays 'everyone claims a right to their own identity . . . [it] has taken on the status of a sacred object, an "ultimate concern"' (1994: 2). But it is important not to assume that 'the intensive practice of identity', as Friedman (1990: 312) phrases it, is a monopoly of the postcolonial world, even if it has become more ubiquitous since the withdrawal of colonial regimes. The practice of identity is and has always been 'situated in a specific social context' (Friedman 1997: 88). In the postcolonial present, no more nor less than in the colonial past, it must be understood against the background of particular historical circumstances, and with regard to the social position and interests of those who 'orient themselves in relation to a larger reality which they define in defining themselves' (Ibid.). The movement from a uniform enunciation of alignment through-out much of the British period to more fragmented expressions as Independence loomed should be noted. These disparate affirmations of belonging in late colonial and especially contemporary Madras (and India more generally) can better be understood if both evolving political circumstances and the matter of class location are taken into account. O'Hanlon and Washbrook are undoubtedly right to point out that class identities are 'so often played down or screened off' in histories (and, I would add, ethnographies) of India (1992: 165).

Placement in the social and economic spectrum is also significant when considering the matter of emigration. The poorest, who have neither the skills nor the wherewithal to leave the country, entertain no serious hopes of leaving India. The well-to-do, many of whom, despite having family overseas and spending time abroad themselves, resist emigration, and increasingly offer a critique of European lifeways, which are compared unfavourably with those of India. The majority of those who have gone away belong to the artisan class, and it is within this segment of the Madras community that the hopes and fantasies of emigration remain alive. Indeed, most of them believe that, of India's numerous communities, Anglo-Indians are singularly qualified by language, kinship, religion and culture to live in the West. Their continuing affirmations of European identity are therefore not unrelated to the aim of settling overseas.

A great deal of current scholarly attention is devoted to the ethnographic and methodological implications for anthropology of transnational movements of migrants, who increasingly live their lives across and beyond national borders (Appadurai 1991; Clifford 1992; Gupta and Ferguson 1992). Anglo-Indians, to be sure, are now widely dispersed around the globe, and we await the ethnographers who will enlighten us about the transnational circuits and networks they create, and reveal the processes through which they 'reterritorialize their practices as well as their identities' (Basch et al. 1993: 34). The focus here, however, has been on the implications of emigration for the sending society, and especially that section most involved in the exodus. The yearning for abroad has created a 'spirit' of emigration among them, and has come to colour much of their lives. It can encourage new educational and occupational skills, influence the selection of marriage partners, reveal family strains and promote new solidarities. Thus, while population movements from the 'Third' to the 'First' world must be understood in the wider context of European withdrawal from former colonies alongside subsequent Euro-American capitalist developments, it is important to appreciate and analyze the local impacts of these global trends.

The social environment of postcolonial Anglo-India remains fluid, despite the withdrawal of the British and the ending of Anglo-Indian privileges in employment. Notwithstanding the continued existence of opposition within the wider society to matrimonial alliances which violate the confines of caste, from both ends of the Anglo-Indian class spectrum, marital 'crossings' continue to occur. Nowadays they tend to involve women from better-off families seeking or being sought out by well-to-do partners mainly, but not only, within the Indian Christian community, and men from the poorest sectors – denied connubium within their own group – entering unions with similarly impoverished, low-caste women outside the Anglo-Indian fold. Thus new hybridities and identities are added to an increasingly polyglot urban environment, one moreover which the offspring of these unions have learned to negotiate with some skill. The porosity of Anglo-Indian boundaries now as in the colonial past helps to explain why community leaders, unlike both their British and Indian counterparts, do not – and never did – attempt to defend community frontiers in the language of women's bodies.

In the literature on inter-group marriage (focused mainly on Western societies) the consensus seems to be that unions of this kind involve many more persons from dominant or upper classes than from groups lower down the social scale (Spickard 1989: 348–9). Similarly, Mines has argued that in Madras not only have cross-caste marriages increased in recent times, but that this is largely an 'upper-middle-class' phenomenon (1998: 228). His view is that this entails a new recognition of 'personal choice' and of the 'role of individual decision-making' in the formation of social relations (Ibid.: 246). The Anglo-Indian experience suggests that 'mixed' domestic partnerships need not necessarily be confined to the better-off, and moreover, apart from the exercise of individual will, must be understood in a broader historical, social and demographic context.

Just as colonial projects were not all of a kind, so each produced its own form of métissage. In her study of Europeans and Eurasians in the Dutch East Indies, Taylor traces – among other things – the emergence and decline of mestizo society in Batavia. In the Epilogue she concludes that, with the departure of the Europeans, the Eurasian claim to a special status 'was severed', and mestizo society 'as a separate entity could not endure. It disappeared' (1983: 174). The end of the Raj, by contrast, which led to the withdrawal of the British from India, and so the removal of the principal socio-cultural reference point for many Anglo-Indians, did not result in the disappearance of the Anglo-Indian community. On the contrary, it has endured into the postcolonial period, shaped indelibly by its colonial legacy, but also transformed by new global circumstances – such as large-scale migratory movements, as we have seen – and more local influences following Independence. This became evident through the examination, in the final chapters of the book, of Anglo-Indian cultural practices.

In the domestic sphere, the predominant rhetoric within the group – echoed by many of the social scientists who have written about the community – insists that Anglo-Indian consanguineal forms are Western-derived. As such, the argument goes, they differ markedly from those found in the surrounding society. Yet, we find that Anglo-Indians value kinship regimes which, by and large, are favoured widely in south India. While a majority belong to nuclear-based households (simple, supplemented, or sub-nuclear) – as do most other Indians – they idolize the 'close' family. Among other things, this implies that siblings continue to support each other even after they have formed their own domestic units, that children maintain close ties with parents throughout their lives, and that they acknowledge the obligation to assist elderly relatives. These and similar expectations serve as a measure against which certain kinds of behaviour – refusal of aid, denial of care – can be deemed a failure of kinship obligations and morally condemned. Abdications of responsibility are also seen as an inevitable accompaniment of the European domestic regime, and form the core of critiques directed increasingly at Western families, including those of Anglo-Indians settled abroad.

Moral censure is frequently directed at the Anglo-Indian poor, and particularly at males of this class. They were especially affected by the 'Indianization' policies introduced by the colonial authorities and more recently by transformations in the workplace in the wake of late capitalist developments. Significant degrees of insecurity and hardship have had a serious impact on their ability to maintain a family; increasing instances of marital desertion, drink and, of late, drug abuse are regarded as evidence of the Anglo-Indian male's inability to fufill his proper role in the household. Such evaluations help to explain the refusal of so many Anglo-Indian women from poorer households to marry men of their own class.

The women, by contrast, are now seen as the backbone of the family. Because male occupations during the colonial period required a fair degree of mobility, Anglo-Indian women have historically had a stabilizing influence in the domestic sphere. With their own increasing entry into the workforce from the early part of the twentieth century, and especially during and following the Second World War, coupled with the gradual exclusion of poorly skilled males, the women added to their role as family guardians that of its providers, as well. In a significant proportion of contemporary Anglo-Indian domestic units it is women rather than men who are the economic mainstay. Moreover, the expectation is that married or widowed daughters rather than sons will live with and care for elderly parents, or other senior relatives, and that is indeed what tends to happen in most cases. This contrasts with practices in the surrounding ('Hindu') society, where it is sons who are obliged to provide support for elderly parents and who, by and large, do so. Unfortunately, information on

Anglo-Indian household composition in the late nineteenth and early twentieth centuries is not yet available, so it is not possible to compare contemporary regimes with those obtaining during the high colonial period. What seems evident is that to arrive at a better understanding of Anglo-Indian domestic patterns – both present and past – we have not only to consider ideal forms, but the extent to which they are capable of being realized in the context of both changing political circumstances and specific economic locations (see also Vera-Sanso 1999: 591). Moreover, developments in global capitalism traceable to the early twentieth century and continuing into the present have had a profound impact on local labour markets, and ultimately on Anglo-Indian gender constructs and contrasts.

The influence on Anglo-Indian families of the colonial orphanages and boarding schools in which many children spent at least part of their early lives is a topic requiring much further study. For some commentators these institutions, in taking children away from their closest relatives, and inculcating values at odds with those of the surroundings out of which they were drawn, can be regarded as having been a pernicious influence on the Anglo-Indian family and its idealization. For others, including most former 'inmates' of boarding establishments, in the context of poverty and/or family dislocation occasioned by peripatetic employments, these institutions acted as surrogate families, offered a welcome structure, reasonably comfortable circumstances, and a strict moral, religious and civic upbringing for the children. Such evaluations continue to be heard among those – mainly from the very poorest families – who have experienced these establishments themselves, and/or seek to place their children in them. Contemporary educational thinking in the West now abjures such kinds of institionalization, and the withdrawal of overseas sponsorship is largely responsible for their decreasing availability.

Turning to other cultural practices, I noted that before Independence Anglo-Indians tended to proclaim a British cultural heritage, and were frequently encouraged in this conviction by both the Euro-colonial authorities and members of the wider Indian population who viewed them as at one with the colonizers. Both the fictional literature and personal chronicles of the Raj written mainly by Europeans in India reinforced this view by insisting that Anglo-Indians aped Western habits, even if the results were often a distortion or travesty of the original. While postcolonial Anglo-Indian self-identifications are more disparate, those within the middle ranks, more so than in other sections of the community, still insist on their Western cultural lineage. Such a claim, moreover, is commonly advanced in the social science literature dealing with Anglo-Indians. Thus Cottrell reiterates Gaikwad's (1967) contention that post-Independence Anglo-Indians are a culturally homogeneous group, cut off from mainstream Indian society, and that their lifestyles 'continue to follow the British' (1979: 356). The notion that the Anglo-Indian way of life is 'characteristically European' (Gist 1972: 40), 'essentially western' (Younger 1987: 36) or that Anglo-Indians are 'almost totally western in culture' (Brennan 1979: 5), and have for generations 'maintained European standards of dress, diet, family life' (Schermerhorn 1978: 213) is more an echo of (artisan-class) Anglo-Indian self-depictions than a description of the heterogeneity of everyday lifeways.

On the one hand, these assertions neglect the fact that 'the British' in India were by no means all of a kind and, moreover, that the 'culture' of the British (or other Westerners) in colonial India was not itself a simple transplantation of the European 'original'. Rather, this was, as has been argued for the East Indies, a 'medley of borrowed forms' (Taylor 1983: 68), 'homespun creations' which acquired new political meanings in the setting of colonial society (Stoler 1989: 136–7). Thus, the model against which many Anglo-Indians measured and still measure their own cultural practices was already, by the early nineteenth century, a parochial cultural hybrid.

On the other hand, an examination of contemporary cultural observances reveals a complex picture. What we find is a mélange fed by distinctive 'cultural streams' – European, Indian, 'global' or what-have-you – yet producing a set of practices which often defy ready apportionment to one source or another, though influenced in different measure by each. The urban cultural milieu in which Anglo-Indians are situated is therefore best viewed as creolized in several senses. For one thing, while all cultures 'evolve historically through unreflective borrowings, mimetic appropriations, exchanges and inventions' (Werbner 1997: 4–5), a population which is recognized as having arisen from several cultural springs invites interest for the way in which it combines these diverse elements.

For another, a creolist image allows a conception of culture which, against prevailing claims of homogeneity, grants the possibility that a variety of circumstances, not least social or economic location, can have a profound influence on cultural practices *within* a self-identified population. Anglo-India is a culturally rich and diverse domain, and for the anthropolgist to represent it otherwise seems to me to impoverish both the community and the analysis.

Then again, such a creolist approach stresses the notion of a continuum, thereby acknowledging mutual influence and overlap between cultural groups. But while eschewing a view of cultures as bounded and coherent, it does not deny the possibility that people may define their own culture and that of others in absolutist, essentialist terms (Friedman 1992: 852; Thomas 1994: 188). Anglo-Indians, as we have seen, despite their disparate ancestry and hybridized lifeways, were adamant in proclaiming an unequivocal sense of cultural belonging during the colonial era. They came to expound a rhetoric of purity every bit as vigorously as the British rulers, but the outcomes were of course different in each case. As the dominant power, the British were able to erect barriers to distinguish and defend an untarnished image of self as culturally pristine, and at the same time designate the Anglo-Indian other – against the latter's own self-identification – as hybrid. Thus, in the colonial context certain populations, like the Anglo-Indians, were destined to remain what Glissant (1989: 141) refers to as a 'composite people' – those without the power to deny successfully their creolist culture, or to have their claims to a chaste pedigree accepted. Here, the anthropological focus shifts from the specific elements of a culture to the political significance with which attestations of cultural difference or affinity may be endowed (see also Stolcke 1995: 12).

In contemporary Anglo-India not only are certain values and usages associated with different sections of the community, but each presents somewhat disparate discourses of belonging. In such circumstances it is pointless to imply homogeneity of cultural practices or to see them primarily as assertions of ethnic identity. The recognition of diversity invites more complex readings of 'culture'. In the debate accompanying Brumann's defence of the notion, Hannerz suggests a 'reformed conception', which might explore boundedness and mixing, internal variation, integration and coherence, and change and stability over time (Brumann 1999; Hannerz 1999: S19). This latter theme brings me to my final observation regarding a creolist perspective: that it allows for, even implies, the idea of change.

As historical circumstances alter, as colonialism gives way to post-colonial conditions, some cultural practices may persist, others may be reshaped, assume new meanings, or give way to alternative habits and beliefs. Since Independence, Anglo-Indian lifeways, though perceived by many as timeless and distinctive, have been profoundly touched by the dual magnets of globalization and Westernization. Even more so, they have been increasingly influenced by cultural practices in their local surroundings. Thus, by situating these modifications in the context of an evolving political milieu – colonial and postcolonial – we can better understand the multiple mechanisms of cultural production and transformation.

Bibliography

Abel, E. (1988), *The Anglo-Indian Community: Survival in India*, Delhi: Chanakya Publications.

Abu-Lughod, L. (1991), 'Writing against Culture', in R. Fox (ed.), *Recapturing Anthropology: Working in the Present*, Santa Fe: School of American Research Press.

Ahmad, A. (1995), 'The Politics of Literary Postcoloniality', *Race and Class*, 36: 1–20.

Amselle, J-L. (1998), *Mestizo Logics: Anthropology of Identity in Africa and Elsewhere*, Stanford: Stanford University Press.

Anderson, B. (1983), *Imagined Communities: Reflections on the Origin and Spread of Nationalism*, London: Verso.

Anderson, Sir G. (1939), 'Anglo-Indian Education', *The Asiatic Review*, 35: 71–96.

Anglo-Indian Survey Committee (1959), *Pilot Survey of Socio-economic Conditions of the Anglo-Indian Community 1957–58*, Calcutta: The authors.

Anon. (1821), *A Visit to Madras, being a Sketch of the Local and Characteristic Peculiarities of that Presidency in the Year 1811*, London: Sir Richard Phillips & Co.

Anon. (1908 [1789]), *Hartly House Calcutta: a Novel of the Days of Warren Hastings*, Calcutta: Thacker, Spink & Co.

Anthony, F. (1969), *Britain's Betrayal in India: the Story of the Anglo-Indian Community*, Bombay: Allied Publishers.

Appadurai, A. (1988), 'How to make a National Cuisine: Cookbooks in Contemporary India', *Comparative Studies in Society and History*, 30: 3–24.

—— (1991), 'Notes and Queries for a Transnational Anthropology', in R. Fox (ed.), *Recapturing Anthropology: Working in the Present*, Santa Fe: School of American Research Press.

—— (1993), 'Number in the Colonial Imagination', in C.A. Breckenridge and P. Van der Veer (eds), *Orientalism and the Postcolonial Predicament: Perspectives on South Asia*, Philadelphia: University of Pennsylvania Press.

—— (1995), 'The Production of Locality', in R. Fardon (ed.), *Counterworks: Managing the Diversity of Knowledge*, London: Routledge.

Appleyard, R. (1989), 'International Migration and Developing Countries', in R. Appleyard (ed.) *The Impact of International Migration on Developing Countries*, Paris: Development Centre of the Organisation for Economic Co-operation and Development.

Arnold, D. (1979), 'European Orphans and Vagrants in India in the Nineteenth Century', *Journal of Imperial and Commonwealth History,* 7: 104–27.

—— (1980), 'Industrial Violence in Colonial India', *Comparative Studies in Society and History*, 22: 234–55.

—— (1983), 'White Colonization and Labour in Nineteenth-century India', *Journal of Imperial and Commonwealth History*, 11: 133–58.

—— (1985), 'Bureaucratic Recruitment and Subordination in Colonial India: the Madras Constabulary, 1859–1947', in R. Guha (ed.), *Subaltern Studies IV: Writings on South Asian History and Society*, Delhi: OUP.

Bailey, F.G. (1957), *Caste and the Economic Frontier*, Manchester: University Press.

Baines, J.A. (1893), *Census of India 1891 General Report*, London: Government of India.

Ballhatchet, K. (1980), *Race, Sex and Class under the Raj: Imperial Attitudes and Policies and their Critics, 1793–1905*, London: Weidenfeld and Nicolson.

Bane, M.J. (1986), 'Household Composition and Poverty', in S.H. Danziger and D.H. Weinberg (eds), *Fighting Poverty: What Works and What Doesn't*, Cambridge, Mass.: Harvard University Press.

Barr, P. (1976), *The Memsahibs: the Women of Victorian India,* London: Secker and Warburg.

—— (1989), *The Dust in the Balance: British Women in India 1905–1945*, London: Hamish Hamilton.

Basch, L., Schiller, N.G. and Blanc, C.S. (1993), *Nations Unbound: Transnational Projects, Postcolonial Predicaments, and Deterritorialized Nation-states*, Amsterdam: Gordon and Breach.

Bayer, J.M. (1986), *A Sociolinguistic Investigation of the English Spoken by the Anglo-Indians in Mysore City*, Manasagangotri, Mysore: Central Institute of Indian Languages.

Bayly, S. (1995), 'Caste and "Race" in the Colonial Ethnography of India', in P. Robb (ed.), *The Concept of Race in South Asia*, Delhi: OUP.

Bear, L.G. (1994), 'Miscegenations of Modernity: Constructing European Respectability and Race in the Indian Railway Colony, 1857–1931', *Women's History Review*, 3: 531–48.

—— (1998), 'Traveling Modernity: Capitalism, Community and Nation in the Colonial Governance of the Indian Railways', PhD, University of Michigan.

Bell, Rev. A. (1812), *The Report of the Military Male Orphan Asylum at Madras*, London: John Murray.

Berger, M.T. (1988), 'Imperialism and Sexual Exploitation: a Response to Ronald Hyam's "Empire and Sexual Opportunity"', *Journal of Imperial and Commonwealth History*, 17: 83–9.

Béteille, A. (1965), *Caste, Class and Power: Changing Patterns of Stratification in a Tanjore Village*, Berkeley: University of California Press.

Bevan, Major H. (1839), *Thirty Years in India: or, a Soldier's Reminiscences of Native and European Life in the Presidencies, from 1808 to 1838*. (Two vols) London: Pelham Richardson, Cornhill.

Bhabha, H. (1992), 'Comment on J. Clifford's "Traveling Cultures"', in L. Grossberg, C. Nelson and P.A. Freichler (eds), *Cultural Studies*, New York: Routledge.

—— (1994), *The Location of Culture*, London: Routledge.

Bharucha, N.E. (1994), 'The Writings of the Unconventional Memsahibs: a Subaltern View of the Raj', in V. Nabar and N.E. Bharucha (eds), *Postcolonial Perspectives on the Raj and its Literature*, Bombay: University of Bombay.

Bhattacharya, D.K. (1968), 'The Anglo-Indians in Bombay: an Introduction to their Socio-economic and Cultural Life', *Race*, 10: 163–72.

Bickerton, D. (1975), *Dynamics of a Creole System*, Cambridge: University Press.

Biddiss, M.D. (1976), 'The Politics of Anatomy: Dr Robert Knox and Victorian Racism', *Proceedings of the Royal Society of Medicine*, 69: 245–50.

Bower, J.A.H. (1939), *Ambition Mocked our Useful Toil: Autobiographical Sketches and Musings on Anglo-Indian Problems*, Madras: The author (xeroxed).

Boxer, C.R. (1963), *Race Relations in the Portuguese Colonial Empire 1415–1825*, Oxford: Clarendon Press.

Brass, P.R. (1994 [1990]), *The Politics of India since Independence*, The New Cambridge History of India (2nd Ed), Cambridge: University Press.

Breckenridge, C.A. and Van der Veer, P. (1993), 'Orientalism and the Postcolonial Predicament', in C.A. Breckenridge and P. Van der Veer (eds), *Orientalism and the Postcolonial Predicament: Perspectives on South Asia*, Philadelphia: University of Pennsylvania Press.

Breger, R. and Hill, R. (1998), 'Introducing Mixed Marriages', in R. Breger and R. Hill (eds), *Cross-cultural Marriage: Identity and Choice*, Oxford: Berg.

Breman, J. (ed.) (1990), *Imperial Monkey Business: Racial Supremacy in Social Darwinist Theory and Colonial Practice*, Casa Monographs 3, Amsterdam: VU University Press.

Bremner, D.S. (1903), *Higginbotham's Guide to the City of Madras*, Madras: Higginbotham.

Brennan, N.L. (1979), 'The Anglo-Indians of Madras: an Ethnic Minority in Transition', PhD Thesis, Syracuse University.

Brown, J. (1994), *Modern India: the Origins of an Asian Democracy*, Oxford: University Press.

Brown, P. (1998), *Anglo-Indian Food and Customs*, Delhi: Penguin.

Brumann, C. (1999), 'Writing for Culture: Why a Successful Concept Should not be Discarded', *Current Anthropology*, 40: S1-S13 (and comments S13-S27).

Busia, A.P.A. (1986), 'Miscegenation as Metonymy: Sexuality and Power in the Colonial Novel', *Ethnic and Racial Studies*, 9: 360–72.

Caplan, L. (1984), 'Bridegroom Price in Urban India: Class, Caste and "Dowry Evil" among Christians in Madras', *Man*, 19: 216–33.

—— (1987), *Class and Culture in Urban India: Fundamentalism in a Christian Community*, Oxford: Clarendon.

—— (1989), *Religion and Power: Essays on the Christian Community in Madras*, Madras: Christian Literature Society.

—— (1998), 'Gifting and Receiving: Anglo-Indian Charity and its Beneficiaries in Madras', *Contributions to Indian Sociology*, 32: 409–31.

—— (2000), 'Iconographies of Anglo-Indian Women: Gender Constructs and Contrasts in a Changing Society', *Modern Asian Studies*, 34: 863–92.

Caplan, P. (1985), *Class and Gender in India: Women and their Organizations in a South Indian City*, London: Tavistock.

Caro, F. de and Jordan, R.A. (1984), 'The Wrong Topi: Personal Narratives, Ritual, and the Sun Helmet as a Symbol', *Western Folklore*, 43: 233–48.

Castles, S. (1992), 'The "New" Migration and Australian Immigration Policy', in C. Inglis, S. Gunasekaran, G. Sullivan and Chung-Tong Wu (eds), *Asians in Australia: the Dynamics of Migration and Settlement*, Singapore: Institute of Southeast Asian Studies.

Chatterjee, P. (1989), 'The Nationalist Resolution of the Women's Question', in K. Sagari and S. Vaid (eds), *Recasting Women: Essays in Colonial History*, New Delhi: Kali for Women.

Bibliography

—— (1993), *The Nation and its Fragments: Colonial and Postcolonial Histories*, Princeton: University Press.

Clarke, T.G. (1878), *The Fortunes of the Anglo-Indian Race: Considered Retrospectively and Prospectively by One of Fifty Years Knowledge and Experience*. (2nd ed) Madras: Higginbotham.

Cleland, J. (1996), 'Demographic Data Collection in Less Developed Countries 1946–1996', *Population Studies,* 50: 433–50.

Clifford, J. (1992), 'Traveling Cultures', in L. Grossberg, C. Nelson and P.A. Treichler (eds), *Cultural Studies*, New York: Routledge.

Cohen, A.P. (1985), *The Symbolic Construction of Community*, London: Tavistock.

Cohen, L. (1998), *No Aging in India: Alzheimer's, the Bad Family, and Other Modern Things*, Berkeley: University of California Press.

Cohn, B.S. (1987), *An Anthropologist Among the Historians and Other Essays*, Delhi: OUP.

—— (1989), 'Cloth, Clothes, and Colonialism: India in the Nineteenth Century', in A. Weiner and J. Schneider (eds), *Cloth and Human Experience*, Washington: Smithsonian Institute.

Comaroff, J. and Comaroff, J. (1992), *Ethnography and the Historical Imagination*, Boulder: Westview.

Cooper, F. and Stoler, A.L. (eds) (1997), *Tensions of Empire: Colonial Cultures in a Bourgeois World*, Berkeley: University of California Press.

Cornish, W.R. (1874), *Report on the Census of the Madras Presidency, 1871.* Madras: Government Gazette Press.

Cottrell, A.B. (1973), 'Cross-national Marriage as an Extension of an International Life Style: a Study of Indian-Western Couples', *Journal of Marriage and the Family*, 35: 739–41.

—— (1979), 'Today's Asian-Western Couples are not Anglo-Indians', *Phylon*, 40: 351–61.

Cressey, P.F. (1935), 'The Anglo-Indians: a Disorganized Marginal Group', *Social Forces*, 14: 263–8.

Das, V. (1995), *Critical Events: an Anthropological Perspective on Contemporary India*, Delhi: OUP.

Daus, R. (1989), *Portuguese Eurasian Communities in Southeast Asia*, Singapore: Institute of Southeast Asian Studies.

D'Cruz, G. (n.d.), '"The Good Australians": Anglo-Indians and Multiculturalism'. Unpublished paper.

—— (1999), '"Representing" Anglo-Indians: a Genealogical Study', PhD thesis, University of Melbourne.

DeSouza, F. (1969), *The House of Binny*, Madras: Binny and Co.

De Wit, J. W. (1993), *Poverty, Policy and Politics in Madras Slums: Dynamics of Survival, Gender and Leadership*, Academisch Proefschrift, Amsterdam: Vrije Universiteit.

Dickey, S. (1993), 'The Politics of Adulation: Cinema and the Production of Politicians in South India', *The Journal of Asian Studies*, 52: 340–72.

—— (1995), 'Opposing Faces: Film Star Fan Clubs and the Construction of Class Identities in South India'. Unpublished paper for a workshop on 'The Consumption of Popular Culture in India'.

Dirks, N.B. (1992), 'Introduction: Colonialism and Culture', in N.B. Dirks (ed.), *Colonialism and Culture*, Ann Arbor: University of Michigan Press.

D'Monte, D.V. (1994), 'Anglo-Indians of Periamet', *Indian Express*, 22 March.

Dodwell, H. (1926), *The Nabobs of Madras*, London: Williams and Norgate.

Douglas, M. (1966), *Purity and Danger: an Analysis of Concepts of Pollution and Taboo*, London: Routledge and Kegan Paul.

—— (1970), *Natural Symbols: Explorations in Cosmology*, London: Barrie and Rockliff, The Cresset Press.

Dover, C. (1929), *Cimmerii? or Eurasians and their Future*, Calcutta: The Modern Art Press.

—— (1937), *Half-Caste*, London: Martin Secker and Warburg.

Drummond, L. (1980), 'The Cultural Continuum: a Theory of Intersystems', *Man*, 15: 352–74.

D'Souza, A.A. (1976), *Anglo-Indian Education: a Study of its Origins and Growth in Bengal up to 1960*, Delhi: OUP.

Dyson, K.K. (1978), *A Various Universe: a Study of the Journals and Memoirs of British Men and Women in the Indian Subcontinent, 1765–1856*, Delhi: OUP.

Dyson, T. and Crook, N. (1984), 'Issues in India's Demography', in T. Dyson and N. Crook (eds), *India's Demography*, Atlantic Highlands, N.J.: Humanities Press.

Eriksen, T.H. (1993), 'In Which Sense do Cultural Islands Exist?' *Social Anthropology,* 1: 133–48.

Ernst, W. (1991), *Mad Tales from the Raj: the European Insane in British India, 1800–1858*, London: Routledge.

Fardon, R. (1995), 'Introduction', in R. Fardon (ed.), *Counterworks: Managing the Diversity of Knowledge*, London: Routledge.

Featherstone, M., Hepworth, M. and Turner, B.S. (eds) (1991), *The Body: Social Process and Cultural Theory*, London: Sage.

Bibliography

Fortes, M. (1958), 'Introduction', in J. Goody (ed.), *The Developmental Cycle in Domestic Groups*, Cambridge: University Press.

Francis, W. (1902), *Census of India, 1901 (Vol XV) Madras (Part I) Report*, Madras: Government Press.

Friedman, J. (1990), 'Being in the World: Globalization and Localization', *Theory, Culture and Society*, 7: 311–28.

—— (1992), 'The Past in the Future: History and the Politics of Identity', *American Anthropologist*, 94: 837–59.

—— (1994), *Cultural Identity and Global Process*, London: Sage.

—— (1997), 'Global Crises, the Struggle for Cultural Identity and Intellectual Porkbarrelling: Cosmopolitans Versus Locals, Ethnics and Nationals in an Era of De-hegemonisation', in P. Werbner and T. Modood (eds), *Debating Cultural Hybridity: Multi-cultural Identities and the Politics of Anti-racism*, London: Zed.

Frykenberg, R.E. (n.d.), 'The Socio-political Morphology of Madras: an Historical Interpretation'. Unpublished paper.

Gaikwad, V.R. (1967), *The Anglo-Indians: a Study in the Problems and Processes Involved in Emotional and Cultural Integration*, London: Asia.

Gartrell, B. (1984), 'Colonial Wives: Villains or Victims?', in H. Callan and S. Ardener (eds) *The Incorporated Wife*, London: Croom Helm.

Ghosh, S.C. (1970), *The Social Condition of the British Community in Bengal, 1757–1800*, Leiden: Brill.

Gidney, Lt-Col H. (1925), 'The Status of the Anglo-Indian Community under the Reforms Scheme in India', *The Asiatic Review*, 21: 657–62.

—— (1934), 'The Future of the Anglo-Indian Community', *The Asiatic Review*, 30: 27–42.

Gillis, J.R. (1994), *Commemorations: the Politics of National Identity*, Princeton: University Press.

Gist, N.P. (1967), 'Conditions of Inter-group Relations: the Anglo-Indians', *International Journal of Comparative Sociology*, 8: 199–208.

—— (1972), 'The Anglo-Indians of India', in N.P. Gist and A.G. Dworkin (eds), *The Blending of Races: Marginality and Identity in World Perspective*, New York: Wiley-Interscience.

—— (1975), 'Anglo-Indian Migrants in Britain', *Plural Societies*, 6: 39–49.

—— and Dworkin, A.G. (1972), 'Introduction', in N.P. Gist and A.G. Dworkin (eds), *The Blending of Races: Marginality and Identity in World Perspective*, New York: Wiley-Interscience.

—— and Wright, R.D. (1973), *Marginality and Identity: Anglo-Indians as a Racially Mixed Minority in India*, Leiden: Brill.

Glissant, E. (1989), *Caribbean Discourse: Selected Essays* (trans) J.M. Dash, Charlottesville: University of Virginia.

Gluckman, M. (1955), *Custom and Conflict in Africa*, Oxford: Blackwell.

Goodrich, D.W. (1952), 'The Making of an Ethnic Group: the Eurasian Community in India', PhD thesis, University of California.

Goody, J. (1983), *The Development of the Family and Marriage in Europe*, Cambridge: University Press.

Graham, Very Rev J.A. (1934), 'The Education of the Anglo-Indian Child', *Journal of the Royal Society of Arts*, 23: 22–47.

Graham, M. (1812), *Journal of a Residence in India*, Edinburgh: Arnold Constable & Co, London: Longman, Hurst, Rees, Orme and Brown.

Gray, J.N. and Mearns, D.J. (1989), 'Introduction: Household and Domestic Group – Society from the Inside Out', in J.N. Gray and D.J. Mearns (eds), *Society from the Inside Out: Anthropological Perspectives on the South Asian Household*, New Delhi: Sage.

Greenberger, A.J. (1969), *The British Image of India: a Study in the Literature of Imperialism 1880–1960*, London: OUP.

Grimshaw, A.D. (1958), 'The Anglo-Indian Community: the Integration of a Marginal Group', *Journal of Asian Studies*, 18: 227–40.

Gupta, S.K. (1968), *Marriage among the Anglo-Indians*, Lucknow: Ethnographic and Folk Culture Society, UP (Uttar Pradesh).

Gupta A. and Ferguson, J. (1992), 'Beyond "Culture": Space, Identity, and the Politics of Difference', *Cultural Anthropology*, 7: 6–23.

Hall, S. (1991), 'Old and New Identities, Old and New Ethnicities', in A.D. King (ed.), *Culture, Globalization and the World-System*, Basingstoke: Macmillan.

—— (1996), 'When was "the Post-colonial"? Thinking at the Limit', in I. Chambers and L. Curtis (eds), *The Post-Colonial Question: Common Skies, Divided Horizons*, London: Routledge.

Hamilton, P. (1985), 'Editor's Foreword' to A.P. Cohen, *The Symbolic Construction of Community*, London: Tavistock.

Hannerz, U. (1987), 'The World in Creolisation', *Africa*, 57: 546–59.

—— (1992), *Cultural Complexity: Studies in the Social Organization of Meaning*, New York: Columbia University Press.

—— (1999), Comment on C. Brumann, 'Writing for Culture: Why a Successful Concept Should not be Discarded', *Current Anthropology*, 40: S18–19.

Harris, O. (1995), 'Knowing the Past: Plural Identities and the Antinomies of Loss in Highland Bolivia', in R. Fardon (ed.), *Counterworks: Managing the Diversity of Knowledge*, London: Routledge.

Hartley, D. (1938), 'Anglo-Indian Women as Nurses', *The Anglo-Indian*, December: 15–16.

Hawes, C.J. (1993), 'Eurasians in British India, 1773–1833: the Making of a Reluctant Community', PhD Thesis, University of London (SOAS).

—— (1996), *Poor Relations: the Making of a Eurasian Community in British India 1773–1833*, London: Curzon.

—— (1997), 'Indeterminate Boundaries: the Place of Eurasians in the Social and Economic Order of British India'. Unpublished paper.

Heathcote, T.A. (1974), *The Indian Army: the Garrison of British Imperial India, 1822–1922*, Vancouver: David and Charles.

Hedin, E.L. (1934), 'The Anglo-Indian Community', *American Journal of Sociology*, 40: 165–79.

Helweg, A.W. (1991), 'Indians in Australia: Theory and Methodology of the New Immigration', in S. Vertovec (ed.), *Aspects of the South Asian Diaspora*, Oxford Papers on India (Vol. 2, Pt. 2), Delhi: OUP.

Hemenway, S.I. (1975) (Vol 1), *The Novel of India: the Anglo-Indian Novel*, Calcutta: Writers Workshop.

Hull, E.C.P. (1871), *The European in India; or, Anglo-Indian's Vade-Mecum. A Handbook of Useful and Practical Information for those Proceeding to or Residing in the East Indies, etc.* London: Henry S King & Co.

Hutton, J.H. (1933), *Census of India 1931 (Vol 1) India (Part 1) Report*, Delhi: Government of India.

Hyam, R. (1986), 'Concubinage and the Colonial Service: the Crewe Circular (1909)', *Journal of Imperial and Commonwealth History*, 14: 170–86.

—— (1990), *Empire and Sexuality: the British Experience*, Manchester: University Press.

Hyma, B. (1971), 'The Rural-Urban Fringe of a Growing Metropolis: Madras, an Indian Example', PhD Thesis, University of Pittsburgh.

Ignatius, C. (1990), 'Care and Concern for the Anglo-Indian Child in School: a Report from Madras'. Unpublished paper.

Inden, R. (1990), *Imagining India*, Oxford: Basil Blackwell.

Inglis, C., Gunesekaran, S., Sullivan, G. and Wu, C-T (eds) (1992), *Asians in Australia: The Dynamics of Migration and Settlement*, Singapore: Institute of Southeast Asian Studies.

Jendrek, M.P. (1993), 'Grandparents who Parent their Grandchildren: Effects on Lifestyle', *Journal of Marriage and the Family*, 55: 609–22.

Joshi, M.S. and Krishna, M. (1998), 'English and North American Daughters-in-law in the Hindu Joint Family', in R. Breger and R. Hill (eds), *Cross-Cultural Marriage: Identity and Choice*, Oxford: Berg.

Kearney, M. (1986), 'From Invisible Hand to Visible Feet: Anthropological Studies of Migration and Development', *Annual Review of Anthropology*, 15: 331–61.

Khare, R.S. (1986), 'Hospitality, Charity and Rationing: Three Channels of Food Distribution in India', in R.S. Khare and M.S.A. Rao (eds), *Aspects of South Asian Food Systems: Food, Society, and Culture*, Durham: Carolina Academic Press.

Khilnani, S. (1998), *The Idea of India*, Harmondsworth: Penguin.

Kinkaid, D. (1938), *British Social Life in India, 1608–1937*, London: Routledge and Kegan Paul.

Kirk-Greene, A. (1986), 'Colonial Administration and Race Relations: Some Research Reflections and Directions', *Ethnic and Racial Studies*, 9: 275–87.

Klor de Alva, J.J. (1995), 'The Postcolonization of the (Latin) American Experience: a Reconsideration of "Colonialism," "Postcolonialism," and "Mestizaje"', in G. Prakash (ed.), *After Colonialism: Imperial Histories and Postcolonial Displacements*, Princeton: University Press.

Kolenda, P. (1968), 'Region, Caste and Family Structure: a Comparative Study of the Indian "Joint" Family', in M. Singer and B.S. Cohn (eds), *Structure and Change in Indian Society*, Chicago: Aldine.

Koop, J.C. (1960), *The Eurasian Population in Burma*, New Haven: Southeast Asia Studies, Yale University.

Krishna, K.B. (1939), *The Problem of Minorities: or Communal Representation in India*, London: George Allen and Unwin.

Lamb, H.B. (1955), 'The "State" and Economic Development in India', in S. Kuznets, W.E. Moore and J.J. Spengler (eds), *Economic Growth: Brazil, India, Japan*, Durham: Duke University Press.

Law, N.N. (1915), *Promotion of Learning in India: by Early European Settlers (up to about 1800 A.D.)*, London: Longmans, Green & Co.

Leach, E.R. (1964), 'Anthropological Aspects of Language: Animal Categories and Verbal Abuse', in E.H. Lenneberg (ed.), *New Directions in the Study of Language*, Boston: M.I.T. Press.

Leeuwen, M.H.D. van (1994), 'Logic of Charity: Poor Relief in Preindustrial Europe', *Journal of Interdisciplinary History*, 24: 589–613.

Lewandowski, S. (1975), 'Urban Growth and Municipal Development in the Colonial City of Madras, 1860–1900', *Journal of Asian Studies*, 34: 341–60.

—— (1980), *Migration and Ethnicity in Urban India: Kerala Migrants in the City of Madras 1870–1970*, New Delhi: Manohar.

Lewis, G. (1987), *Between the Wire and the Wall: a History of South African 'Coloured' Politics*, Cape Town: David Philip.

Bibliography

Lobo, A.I.G. (1994), 'A Comparative Study of Educational Disadvantage in India within the Anglo-Indian Community: a Historical and Contemporary Analysis', PhD Thesis, Institute of Education, London.

Loch, C.S. (1883), *How to Help Cases of Distress: a Handy Reference Book for Almoners, Almsgivers, and Others*, London: Longmans, Green & Co.

Love, H.D. (1913), *Vestiges of Old Madras* (3 Vols), London: John Murray.

Luhrmann, T.M. (1994), 'The Good Parsi: the Postcolonial "Feminization" of a Colonial Elite', *Man*, 29: 333–58.

—— (1996), *The Good Parsi: the Fate of a Colonial Elite in a Postcolonial Society*, Cambridge, Mass.: Harvard University Press.

Macmillan, M. (1984), 'Camp Followers: a Note on Wives of the Armed Services', in H. Callan and S. Ardener (eds), *The Incorporated Wife*, London: Croom Helm.

—— (1988), *Women of the Raj*, London: Thames and Hudson.

Madras Mail (1886), *References to Madras in 'The Asiatic Journal', 1829 to 1840*, Madras: *Madras Mail*.

Madras Government (1885), *Manual of the Administration of the Madras Presidency*, Vol II, Appendices, Madras: Government Press.

Maher, R. (1962), *These are the Anglo-Indians*, Calcutta: Swallow Press.

Maitland, J.C. ['A Lady'] (1843), *Letters from Madras During the Years 1836–1839*, London: John Murray.

Mandelbaum, D.G. (1970), *Society in India: Change and Continuity* (2 Vols), Berkeley: University of California Press.

Mannsaker, F.M. (1980), 'East and West: Anglo-Indian Racial Attitudes as Reflected in Popular Fiction, 1890–1914', *Victorian Studies*, 24: 33–51.

Mast, M.K. (1969), *Trade Union Movement in Indian Railways*, Meerut: Meenakshi Prakashan.

Mathur, H.N. (1955), 'Education of European and Eurasian Children in India, 1860–1884', *Indian Historical Records Commission: Proceedings of Meetings*, XXXI (Part 2): 113–20.

McClintock, A. (1993), 'The Angel of Progress: Pitfalls of the Term "Post-colonialism"', in P. Williams and L. Chrisman (eds), *Colonial Discourse and Post-colonial Theory: a Reader*, New York: Harvester.

McGilvray, D. (1982), 'Dutch Burghers and Portuguese Mechanics: Eurasian Ethnicity in Sri Lanka', *Comparative Studies in Society and History*, 24: 235–63.

McIver, L. (1883), *Imperial Census of 1881, Madras Presidency (Vol. 1) The Report*, Madras: Government Press.

McLanahan, S. (1985), 'Family Structure and the Reproduction of Poverty', *American Journal of Sociology*, 90: 873–901.

MIDS (Madras Institute of Development Studies) (1988), *Tamilnadu Economy: Performance and Issues*, Delhi: Oxford and IBH.

Mills, M.S. (n.d.), 'The Anglo-Indians – a Christian Community of India'. Paper posted on the internet (meg0399.html at www. alphalink.com.au).

Mines, M. (1994), *Public Faces, Private Voices: Community and Individuality in South India*, Berkeley: University of California Press.

—— (1998), 'Hindus at the Edge: Self-awareness Among Adult Children of Interfaith Marriages in Chennai, South India', *International Journal of Hindu Studies*, 2: 223–48.

—— and V. Gourishankar (1990), 'Leadership and Individuality in South Asia: the Case of the South Indian Big-man', *The Journal of Asian Studies*, 49:761–86.

Minto, J.R. (1974), *Graham of Kalimpong*, Edinburgh: William Blackwood.

Misra, B.B. (1961), *The Indian Middle Classes: their Growth in Modern Times*, Delhi: OUP.

Mitter, P. (1985), 'Architectural Planning and Other Building Activities of the British in Madras, Bombay and Calcutta (c. 1630 – c. 1757)', in D.K. Basu (ed.), *The Rise and Growth of the Colonial Port Cities in Asia*, Berkeley: University of California Center for South and Southeast Asia Studies.

Moktali, L. (1994), 'Neither Fish nor Flesh: Attitude towards Eurasians in Novels by Anglo-Indian Women', in V. Nabar and N.E. Bharucha (eds), *Postcolonial Perspectives on the Raj and its Literature*, Bombay: University of Bombay.

Moore, G.J. (1986a), *The Anglo-Indian Vision*, Melbourne: AE Press.

—— (1986b), *The Lotus and the Rose: an Anglo-Indian Story*, Melbourne: River Seine Publications.

Moreno, H.W.B. (1923), 'Some Anglo-Indian Terms and Origins', *Indian Historical Records Commission: Proceedings of Meetings* V: 76–82.

Munro, I. (1789), *A Narrative of the Military Operations on the Coromandel Coast* (written as a series of letters 1780–1784), London: the Author.

Muthiah, S. (1981), *Madras Discovered: a Historical Guide to Looking Around*, Madras: East-West Press.

Nabar, V. (1994), '"The Past is Before Us": the Colonial as Postcolonial', in V. Nabar and N.E. Bharucha (eds), *Postcolonial Perspectives on the Raj and its Literature*, Bombay: University of Bombay.

Naidis, M. (1963), 'British Attitudes toward the Anglo-Indians', *South Atlantic Quarterly*, 62: 407–22.

Bibliography

Naik, M.K. (1994), 'Piebald Trisanku: the Eurasian in Anglo-Indian Fiction', in V. Nabar and N.E. Bharucha (eds), *Postcolonial Perspectives on the Raj and its Literature*, Bombay: University of Bombay.

Nandy, A. (1983), *The Intimate Enemy: Loss and Recovery of Self under Colonialism*, Delhi: OUP.

Narayanan, G. (1986), *The Sahibs and the Natives: a Study of Guilt and Pride in Anglo-Indian and Indo-Anglian Novels*, Delhi: Chanakya.

Nichols, B. (1944), *Verdict on India*, London: Jonathan Cape.

Noponen, H. (1991), 'The Dynamics of Work and Survival for the Urban Poor: a Gender Analysis of Panel Data from Madras', *Development and Change*, 22: 233–60.

Nundy, A. (1900), 'The Eurasian Problem in India', *The Imperial and Asiatic Quarterly Review and Oriental and Colonial Record* (3rd Series), IX: 56–73.

O'Hanlon, R. and Washbrook, D. (1992), 'After Orientalism: Culture, Criticism, and Politics in the Third World', *Comparative Studies in Society and History*, 34: 141–67.

Orans, M. (1965), *The Santal: a Tribe in Search of a Great Tradition*, Detroit: Wayne State University Press.

Pagden, A. (1987), 'Identity Formation in Spanish America', in N. Canny and A. Pagden (eds), *Colonial Identity in the Atlantic World: 1500–1800*, Princeton: University Press.

—— and Canny, N. (1987), 'Afterword: from Identity to Independence', in N. Canny and A. Pagden (eds), *Colonial Identity in the Atlantic World: 1500–1800*, Princeton: University Press.

Park, R.E. (1930–31), 'Mentality of Racial Hybrids', *American Journal of Sociology*, 36: 534–51.

Parkin, D. (1993), 'Nemi in the Modern World: Return of the Exotic?', *Man*, 28: 79–99.

Pels, P. (1997), 'The Anthropology of Colonialism: Culture, History, and the Emergence of Western Governmentality', *Annual Review of Anthropology*, 26: 163–83.

Penny, Rev F. (1904), *The Church in Madras: Being the History of the Ecclesiastical and Missionary Action of the East India Company in the Presidency of Madras in the Seventeenth and Eighteenth Centuries* (Vol I), London: Smith, Elder & Co.

—— (1912), *The Church in Madras: Being the History of the Ecclesiastical and Missionary Action of the East India Company in the Presidency of Madras from 1805 to 1835* (Vol II), London: Smith, Elder & Co.

—— (1922), *The Church in Madras: Being the History of the Ecclesiastical and Missionary Action of the East India Company in the*

Presidency of Madras from 1835 to 1861 (Vol III), London: Smith, Elder & Co.

Penny, F.E. (1908), *On the Coromandel Coast*, London: Smith, Elder & Co.

Prakash, G. (1995), 'Introduction: After Colonialism', in G. Prakash (ed.), *After Colonialism: Imperial Histories and Postcolonial Displacements*, Princeton: University Press.

Ranger, T. (1996), 'Postscript: Colonial and Postcolonial Identities', in R. Werbner and T. Ranger (eds), *Postcolonial Identities in Africa*, London: Zed.

Ranson, C.W. (1938), *A City in Transition: Studies in the Social Life of Madras*, Madras: Christian Literature Society.

Renford, R.K. (1979), 'The Non-Official British in India, 1883–1920', PhD Thesis, University of London.

Rhoades, R.E. (1978), 'Foreign Labor and German Industrial Capitalism 1871–1978: The Evolution of a Migratory System', *American Ethnologist*, 5: 566–7.

Ricketts, J.W. (1831), *Report of Proceedings Connected with The East Indians' Petition to Parliament, Read at a Public Meeting Held at the Town Hall, Calcutta, March 28, 1831, with an Appendix*, Calcutta: Baptist Missionary Press.

Robb, P. (1995), 'Introduction', in P. Robb (ed.), *The Concept of Race in South Asia*, Delhi: OUP.

Roberts, E. (1835), *Scenes and Characteristics of Hindostan, with Sketches of Anglo-Indian Society* (3 Vols), London: Wm H. Allen.

Roberts, M., Raheem, I. and Colin-Thomé, P. (1989), *People Inbetween: the Burghers and the Middle Class in the Transformations within Sri Lanka, 1790s–1960s* (Vol 1), Ratmalana, Sri Lanka: Sarvodaya Book Publishing Services.

Roland, J.G. (1989), *Jews in British India: Identity in a Colonial Era*, Hanover: Brandeis University Press.

Rowe, W.L. (1968), 'Mobility in the Nineteenth-century Caste System', in M. Singer and B.S. Cohn (eds), *Structure and Change in Indian Society*, Chicago: Aldine.

Roy, W.T. (1974), 'Hostages to Fortune: a Socio-political Study of the Anglo-Indian Remnant in India', *Plural Societies*, 5: 55–63.

Roy, P. (1999), *Indian Traffic: Identities in Question in Colonial and Postcolonial India*, New Delhi: Vistaar Publications.

Sahlins, M. (1999), 'Two or Three Things that I Know about Culture' (Huxley Lecture 1998), *Journal of the Royal Anthropological Institute* (NS), 5: 399–421.

Sanyal, N. (1930), *Development of Indian Railways*, Calcutta: University of Calcutta.

Schermerhorn, R.A. (1973), 'Sex Roles among the Anglo-Indians', *Australian and New Zealand Journal of Sociology*, 9: 75–6.

—— (1978), *Ethnic Plurality in India*, Tucson: University of Arizona Press.

Seabrook, J. (1985), *Landscapes of Poverty*, Oxford: Basil Blackwell.

Sen, J. (1988), 'Marriage among the Catholic Anglo-Indians of Calcutta', in B.B. Goswami, J. Sarkar and D. Danda (eds), *Marriage in India (Tribes, Muslims and Anglo-Indians)*, Calcutta: Anthropological Survey of India.

Sharma, U. (1989), 'Studying the Household: Individuation and Values', in J.N. Gray and D.J. Mearns (eds), *Society from the Inside Out*, New Delhi: Sage.

Shohat, E. (1992), 'Notes on the "Post-colonial"', *Social Text* (31/32), 10: 99–113.

Silverberg, J. (ed.) (1968), *Social Mobility in the Caste System in India: an Interdisciplinary Symposium*, (Comparative Studies in Society and History, suppl. 3), The Hague: Mouton.

Skipton, H.P.K. (1912), *Our Reproach in India*, London: Mowbray & Co.

Spear, T.G.P. (1932), *The Nabobs: a Study of the Social Life of the English in Eighteenth Century India*, Oxford: Humphrey Milford.

Spencer, J. (1966), 'The Anglo-Indians and their Speech: a Socio-linguistic Essay', *Lingua*, 16: 57–70.

Spickard, P.R. (1989), *Mixed Blood: Intermarriage and Ethnic Identity in Twentieth-century America*, Madison: University of Wisconsin Press.

Srinivasachari, C.S. (1939), *History of the City of Madras: Written for the Tercentenary Celebration Committee*, Madras: P. Varadachary & Co.

Staines, J.R. (1986), *Country Born: One Man's Life in India, 1909–1947*, London: Croscombe Press.

Stark, H.A. (1932), *The Call of the Blood: or Anglo-Indians and the Sepoy Mutiny*, Rangoon: British Burma Press.

—— (1936), *Hostages to India or the Life-story of the Anglo-Indian Race*, Calcutta: the Author.

Steuart, A.F. (1913), 'Some Notes on the Position of Early Eurasians', *The Asiatic Quarterly Review* (NS), II: 93–101.

Stolcke, V. (1995), 'Talking Culture: New Boundaries, New Rhetorics of Exclusion in Europe', *Current Anthropology*, 36: 1–24.

Stoler, A.L. (1989), 'Rethinking Colonial Categories: European Communities and the Boundaries of Rule', *Comparative Studies in Society and History*, 31: 134–61.

—— (1991), 'Carnal Knowledge and Imperial Power: Gender, Race, and Morality in Colonial Asia', in M. di Leonardo (ed.), *Gender at the Crossroads of Knowledge: Feminist Anthropology in the Postmodern Era*, Berkeley: University of California Press.

—— (1995), *Race and the Education of Desire: Foucault's History of Sexuality and the Colonial Order of Things*, Durham: Duke University Press.

—— (1997), 'Sexual Affronts and Racial Frontiers', in F. Cooper and A.L. Stoler (eds), *Tensions of Empire: Colonial Cultures in a Bourgeois World*, Berkeley: University of California Press.

Stonequist, E.V. (1937), *The Marginal Man: a Study in Personality and Culture Conflict*, New York: Charles Scribner.

Stracey, E. (1981), *Odd Man In: My Years in the Indian Police*, Delhi: Vikas.

Stuart, H.A. (1893), *Census of 1891 (Vol. XIII) Madras. The Report on the Census*, Madras: Government Press.

Symonds, R. (1987), 'Eurasians under British Rule', in N.J. Allen, R.F. Gombrich, T. Raychaudhuri and G. Rizvi (eds), *Oxford University Papers on India* (Vol. 1, Pt 2), Oxford: University Press.

Tarlo, E. (1996), *Clothing Matters: Dress and Identity in India*, London: Hurst.

Taylor, R.J., Chatters, L.M., Tucker, M.B. and Lewis, E. (1990), 'Developments in Research on Black Families: a Decade Review', *Journal of Marriage and the Family*, 52: 993–1014.

Taylor, J.G. (1983), *The Social World of Batavia: European and Eurasian in Dutch Asia*, Madison: The University of Wisconsin Press.

Tharu, S. (1989), 'Tracing Savitri's Pedigree: Victorian Racism and the Image of Women in Indo-Anglian Literature', in K. Sagari and S. Vaid (eds), *Recasting Women: Essays in Colonial History*, New Delhi: Kali for Women.

Thomas, N. (1992), 'The Inversion of Tradition', *American Ethnologist*, 19: 213–32.

—— (1994), *Colonialism's Culture: Anthropology, Travel and Government*, Oxford: Polity.

Thurston. E. (1898), 'Eurasians of Madras City and Malabar', *Madras Government Museum Bulletin* II: 69–114.

Tindall, G. (1982), *City of Gold: the Biography of Bombay*, London: Temple Smith.

Tiwari, R. (1965), 'The Social and Political Significance of Anglo-Indian Schools in India', MA Thesis, Institute of Education, London.

Trouillot, M-R. (1992), 'The Caribbean Region: an Open Frontier in Anthropological Theory', *Annual Review of Anthropology*, 21: 19–42.

Bibliography

Tsing, A.L. (1993), *In the Realm of the Diamond Queen: Marginality in an Out-of-the-way Place*, Princeton: University Press.

Uberoi, P. (ed.) (1993), *Family, Kinship and Marriage in India*, Oxford in India Readings in Sociology and Social Anthropology, Delhi: OUP.

Vatuk, S. (1971), 'Trends in North Indian Kinship: the "Matrilateral Asymmetry" Thesis', *Southwestern Journal of Anthropology*, 27: 287–307.

—— (1991), 'Gerontology in India: the State of the Art', *Journal of Cross-cultural Gerontology*, 6: 259–71.

Vera-Sanso, P. (1994), 'What the Neighbours Say: Gender, Personhood and Power in Two Low-income Settlements of Madras', PhD Thesis, University of London.

—— (1999), 'Dominant Daughters-in-law and Submissive Mothers-in-law? Cooperation and Conflict in South India', *Journal of the Royal Anthropological Institute*, 5: 577–94.

—— (2000), 'Risk-talk: the Politics of Risk and its Representation', in P. Caplan (ed.), *Risk Revisited*, London: Pluto.

Wadley, S.S. and Derr, B.W. (1993), 'Karimpur Families over Sixty Years', in P. Uberoi (ed.), *Family, Kinship and Marriage in India*, Oxford in India Readings in Sociology and Social Anthropology, Delhi: OUP.

Wallace, K.E. (1935), *Brave New Anglo-India*, Calcutta: The Modern Art Press.

—— (1947 [1930]), *The Eurasian Problem*, Calcutta: Spink.

Warden, J.J. (ed.) (1915), *Problems of the Domiciled Community in Modern Light*, Madras: the Author.

Werbner, P. (1990), *The Migration Process: Capital, Gifts and Offerings among British Pakistanis*, Oxford: Berg.

—— (1997), 'Essentialising Essentialism, Essentialising Silence: Ambivalence and Multiplicity in the Constructions of Racism and Ethnicity', in P. Werbner and T. Modood (eds), *Debating Cultural Hybridity: Multi-cultural Identities and the Politics of Anti-racism*, London: Zed.

Werbner, R. (1996), 'Introduction: Multiple Identities, Plural Arenas', in R. Werbner and T. Ranger (eds), *Postcolonial Identities in Africa*, London: Zed.

Weston, C.N. (1939), *Anglo-Indian Revolutionaries of the Methodist Episcopal Church*, Bangalore: Scripture Literature Press.

Westwood, J.N. (1974), *Railways of India*, Newton Abbot: David and Charles.

Wheeler, J.T. (1861), *Madras in the Olden Time: Being a History of the Presidency from the First Foundation to the Governorship of Thomas Pitt, Grandfather of the Earl of Chatham 1639–1702 (Compiled from Official Records)*, Madras: J. Higginbotham.

—— (1878), *Early Records of British India: a History of the English Settlements in India as Told in the Government Records, the Works of Old Travellers, and Other Contemporary Documents, from the Earliest Period down to the Rise of British Power in India*, London: Trubner & Co.

White, D.L. (1991), 'From Crisis to Community Definition: the Dynamics of Eighteenth-century Parsi Philanthropy', *Modern Asian Studies*, 25: 303–20.

White, D.S. (1882), *Guide to the Eurasian and Anglo-Indian Villages Proposed to be Established in the Province of Mysore*, Madras: Eurasian and Anglo-Indian Association of Southern India.

Wilkinson, A. (1958), *A Brief History of Nursing in India and Pakistan*, Madras: Trained Nurses Association of India.

Wilkinson, T. (1976), *Two Monsoons*, London: Duckworth.

Williams, P. and Chrisman, L. (1993), 'Colonial Discourse and Post-colonial Theory: an Introduction', in P. Williams and L. Chrisman (eds), *Colonial Discourse and Post-colonial Theory: a Reader*, New York: Harvester.

Williamson, Capt. T. (1810), *The East India Vade-Mecum; or, Complete Guide to Gentlemen Intended for the Civil, Military, or Naval Service of the Hon. East India Company* (Vol I), London: Black, Parry, and Kingsbury.

Wilson, W.J. and Aponte, R. (1985), 'Urban Poverty', *Annual Review of Sociology*, 11: 231–58.

Wilson, W.J. and Neckerman, K.M. (1986), 'Poverty and Family Structure: the Widening Gap between Evidence and Public Policy Issues', in S.H. Danziger and D.H. Weinberg (eds), *Fighting Poverty: What Works and What Doesn't*, Cambridge, Mass.: Harvard University Press.

Wolpert, S. (1989), *A New History of India*, New York: OUP.

Young, R.J. (1990), *White Mythologies: Writing History and the West*. London: Routledge.

—— (1995), *Colonial Desire: Hybridity in Theory, Culture and Race*, London: Routledge.

Younger, C. (1987), *Anglo-Indians: Neglected Children of the Raj*, Delhi: B.R. Publishing Corp.

Yule, H. Col. and Burnell, A.C. (1886), *Hobson-Jobson: Being a Glossary of Anglo-Indian Colloquial Words and Phrases, and of Kindred Terms; Etymological, Historical, Geographical, and Discursive*, London: John Murray.

Zinn, M.B. (1989), 'Family, Race, and Poverty in the Eighties', *Signs*, 14: 856–74.

Archival Sources

Anglo-Indian and Domiciled European Association of Southern India, Madras.

British Library, Oriental and India Office Records.

British Library, Newspaper Library, Colindale.

Friend-in-Need Society, Madras.

Miscellaneous private papers, Madras.

School of Oriental and African Studies Library, Reserve Collections.

Author Index

Index

Index

Maitland, J.C., 64–5
Mandelbaum, D.G., 75
Mannsaker, F.M., 62, 65
Mast, M.K., 29, 88n12
Mathur, H.N., 37
McClintock, A., 10–11
McGilvray, D., 4, 24
McIver, L., 66–7, 69
McLanahan, S., 190
Mearns, D.J., 161
MIDS (Madras Institute of Development Studies), 36
Mills, M.S., 194
Mines, M., 116, 119, 228
Minto, J.R., 93, 132
Misra, B.B., 28
Mitter, P., 22
Moktali, L., 77
Moore, G.J., 77, 90n24, 131–3
Moreno, H.W.B., 106
Munro, I., 3, 18n3, 61
Muthiah, S., 22, 53n1

Nabar, V., 3
Naidis, M., 5, 61, 65
Naik, M.K., 5, 61, 65
Nandy, A., 11, 18n8, 60
Narayanan, G., 5, 65
Neckerman, K.M., 189–90
Nichols, B., 64
Noponen, H., 36
Nundy, A., 93

O'Hanlon, R., 226–7
Orans, M. 197

Pagden, A., 87n1, 98
Park, R.E., 8
Parkin, D., 9
Pels, P., 11, 223
Penny, Rev F., 22, 37, 40–1, 66, 78, 94
Penny, F.E., 25, 78, 168, 171
Prakash, G., 6

Raheem, I., 4, 24
Ranger, T., 11, 13
Ranson, C.W., 22
Renford, R.K., 7, 27, 88n9, 95, 109–10, 123n5, 125n26

Ricketts, J.W., 23–4, 53n5, 95, 97
Rhoades, R.E., 130
Robb, P., 4
Roberts, E., 62–5, 76–8, 210
Roberts, M., 4, 24
Roland, J.G., 54n7
Rowe, W.L., 75
Roy, W.T., 19n12, 56n25
Roy, P., 62

Sahlins, M., 12, 18n11, 198
Sanyal, N., 38
Schermerhorn, R.A., 184, 211, 231
Schiller, N.G., 227
Seabrook, J., 120
Sen, J., 90n24, 92, 211–12
Sharma, U., 177
Shohat, E., 10–12
Silverberg, J., 75
Skipton, H.P.K., 42
Spear, T.G.P., 5
Spencer, J., 88n6
Spickard, P.R., 18n2, 228
Srinivasachari, C.S., 22
Staines, J.R., 89n16, 99
Stark, H.A., 26, 97, 99, 223–4
Steuart, A.F., 62–3, 88n8
Stolcke, V., 14, 232
Stoler, A.L., 2, 4–5, 7, 11–12, 25–6, 51, 76, 85–6, 123n1, 221n5, 231
Stonequist, E.V., 8
Stracey, E., 100
Stuart, H.A., 67, 69
Symonds, R., 29, 32, 42

Tarlo, E., 198–9, 201, 221n6
Taylor, R.J., 35, 189–90
Taylor, J.G., 7, 17n1, 53n3, 89n17, 90n23, 228, 231
Tharu, S., 87
Thomas, N., 7, 10, 12, 194, 232
Thomé, C., 4, 24
Thurston. E., 67, 69
Tindall, G., 53n2
Tiwari, R., 56n25, 110
Trouillot, M-R., 13
Tsing, A.L., 7, 18n10
Tucker, M.B., 35, 189–90
Turner, B.S., 86

Index

Uberoi, P., 161–2, 191n3, 210

Van der Veer, P., 10
Vatuk, S., 185, 189
Vera-Sanso, P., 36, 182, 185–6, 230

Wadley, S.S., 191n3
Wallace, K.E., 26, 63, 99–100
Warden, J.J., 68, 70, 97
Washbrook, D., 226–7
Werbner, P., 12, 14, 21, 119–20, 231
Werbner, R., 10–11
Weston, C.N., 24, 26, 42, 68, 181, 223–4
Westwood, J.N., 29–30
Wheeler, J.T., 3, 22
White, D.L., 120, 126n37

White, D.S., 43, 99
Wilkinson, A., 31
Wilkinson, T., 2, 60
Williams, P., 10
Williamson, Capt. T., 3
Wilson, W.J., 83, 189–90
Wolpert, S., 126n29
Wright, R.D., 24, 62, 73, 83, 99
Wu, C-T., 134

Young, R.J., 4–5, 7, 10, 13, 88n10
Younger, C., 5, 61, 77, 133, 148, 204, 211, 231
Yule, H. Col., 88n6

Zinn, M.B., 190

Subject Index

Index

commissioners, 7, 66–76 *passim*
class(es), 7, 21, 25–37 *passim*, 40, 42, 52
  and cultural practices, 219, 224
  and food, 206–9
  and dress, 198–204
  and identity, 102–5, 226–7
  and modes of belonging, 102–6, 120,
    226–7
  and race, 25
  see also poverty
colonial
  and postcolonial, 10–15, 223
  as privileged category, 11
  as unitary category, 10
  discourse, 21
  encounter(s), 1, 8–10
    and domestic regimes, 157–8, 188
  identities, 59, 102–5
  language, 12
  past, 1, 11
  period, 13–14
    fluidity of, 91
  rulers, 8, 10, 63
  see also colonialism
colonialism, 5,
  bi-polar approach to, 7
  offspring of, 11, 51, 223
  see also colonial
community, 2, 15, 106, 228
  boundaries of, 59, 119–20
  consciousness of, 92, 95, 106–13,
    119–22, 226
  divisions within, 24
  domiciled, 7, 67
  ethnic heterogeneity of, 24
  'evaporation' out of, 68–76 *passim*
  fluidity of, 85, 87, 228
  'infiltration' into, 69–73
  politics, 92
  see also Anglo-Indian(s)
concubinage, *see* marriage
courtship, 137, 212, 221n13, 222n14
creolization, 9–10, 13
  of cultural field, 15, 231
cultural
  belonging, 14
  boundaries, 9, 195
  continuum, 9, 219, 231
  identity, 15, 209

English as, 193–4
  loss of, 193
  practices, 17, 226–7
  differentially clustered, 195
  distinct from 'Indians', 218
  emblematic, 194, 198
  European, 97–8
  perceptions by outsiders, 195–8
  see also culture(s); dance; dress; food
culture(s), 8–9, 14, 195
  Anglo-Indian- 14, 195–8
  as autonomous, 9
  as hybrid, 19n20, 11
  essentialist perspective on, 14
  loss of, 220
  see also cultural; dance; dress; food

dance(s) 196–7, 211–13, 221n2, 222n19
dress, 17, 65, 194
  as indicator of identity, 198
  changes in, 199–203
  European, 65–6, 199
  female, 65, 201
    frock, 201–2
    sari, 201–3
  in orphanages, 199
  in workplace, 198
  leaders', 200–1
  male, 198–200
  stereotypical 'Indian', 199–200
drink
  alcoholism in India, 182
  and drugs, 182, 229
  and poverty, 192n13
  male penchant for, 180–2, 229

East India Company, 1, 7, 22, 37, 60–1,
  94–5
education, 21, 37–43, 80
  Anglo-Indian schools, 38–43 *passim*,
    56n24, 71, 92, 109
  admission, 124n16
  anti-Indian emphasis, 99–102
  Christian emphasis, 94, 99–100
  curriculum, 93
  Indian languages in, 92–3
  see also orphanages
elites, 12, 42, 52, 102
employment(s), 21, 26–34, 224

Index